PIONEERS OF MODERN ECONOMICS IN BRITAIN

PIONEERS OF MODERN ECONOMICS IN BRITAIN

Edited by
D. P. O'Brien and John R. Presley

795818

Barnes & Noble Books
Totowa, New Jersey

First published 1981 by
THE MACMILLAN PRESS LTD
London and Basingstoke
Companies and representatives
throughout the world

First published in the USA 1981 by
BARNES & NOBLE BOOKS
81, Adams Drive
Totowa, New Jersey, 07512

MACMILLAN ISBN 0 333 23175 9

BARNES & NOBLE ISBN 0 389 20181 2

Typeset in Great Britain by
Preface Ltd, Salisbury, Wilts
and printed in Hong Kong

Contents

List of Figures

Notes on the Contributors

Robert Denis Collison Black was born in 1922 and educated at Trinity College, Dublin (B.A., B.Com., 1941; Ph.D., 1943; M.A., 1945). He was Rockefeller post-doctoral Fellow at Princeton, New Jersey (under Jacob Viner) in 1951, Visiting Professor at Yale from 1964 to 1965, and has been Professor of Economics at Queen's University, Belfast, since 1962. He was made a Fellow of the British Academy in 1974. His research interests include the history of economic thought and income distribution. His publications include *Economic Thought and the Irish Question*, *A Catalogue of (Economic) Pamphlets in Irish Libraries*, *W. S. Jevons: Theory of Political Economy*, *Mountifort Longfield: Economic Writings* and *Papers and Correspondence of William Stanley Jevons*. He has published articles in *Economic Journal, Manchester School, Oxford Economic Papers, Economica* and other journals.

John Creedy was born in 1949 and educated at Bristol University (B.Sc., 1970) and Oxford University (B.Phil., 1972). He was a temporary Lecturer in Economics at the University of Durham (1972–3), Lecturer in Economics at the University of Reading (1973–7), Research Officer with the National Institute of Economic and Social Research (1977–8), and from 1978 he has been Professor of Economics at the University of Durham. His research interests include income distribution, labour economics and economics of social policy. He has published articles in *Economic Journal, Oxford Economic Papers, Oxford Bulletin of Economics and Statistics, Scottish Journal of Political Economy, Review of Income and Wealth, History of Political Economy*, and other journals.

David Collard was born in 1937 and educated at Cambridge (B.A. in economics, 1960). He was formerly Lecturer in Economics at University College, Cardiff, and the University of Bristol. He has been Professor of Economics at the University of Bath since 1978. His research interests include the history of economic thought and welfare economics. His publications include *Altruism and Economy*, and he has published articles in *Economic Journal* and other journals.

Adrian Darnell was born in 1953 and educated at the University of Durham (B.A. in mathematics and economics, 1974) and Warwick University (M.A. in economics, 1975). He has been Lecturer in Economics at the University of Durham since 1976. His research interests include econometrics and the history of economic thought.

Eric G. Davis was born in 1942 and educated at Queen's University, Ontario (B.Sc. in mathematics, 1964) and Brown University, R. I. (Ph.D. in economics, 1968). He was Assistant Professor at Purdue University in 1968–9, researching at the Bell Laboratories from 1969 to 1972, and Assistant Professor at Carleton University from 1972 to 1974. He has been Associate Professor there since 1974. He has published articles in *American Economic Review*, *Econometrica*, *Economic Development and Cultural Change*, *American Statistical Association Proceedings*, *Bell Journal* and *Journal of Finance*.

Denis P. O'Brien was born in 1939 and educated at Douai School, University College, London (B.Sc.Econ., 1960) and Queen's University, Belfast (Ph.D., 1969). He was Assistant Lecturer, Lecturer and Reader at Queen's University, Belfast, from 1963 to 1972, and since 1972 has been Professor of Economics at the University of Durham. His research interests include the history of economic thought and competition policy. His publications include *Information Agreements, Competition and Efficiency* (with D. Swann), *J. R. McCulloch: A Study in Classical Economics*, *The Correspondence of Lord Overstone*, *Competition in British Industry* (with D. Swann *et al.*), *Case Studies: Competition in British Industry* (with D. Swann *et al.*), *J. R. McCulloch: Treatise on Taxation*, *The Classical Economists* and *Competition Policy, Profitability and Growth* (with W. S. Howe, D. M. Wright and R. J. O'Brien). He has published articles in *Economica*, *Scottish Journal of Political Economy*, *History of Political Economy*, *Manchester School*, *Journal of Industrial Economics* and other journals.

John R. Presley was born in 1945 and educated at Woodhouse Grammar School, Sheffield, Lancaster University (B.A., 1968) and Loughborough University (Ph.D., 1978). He was lecturer in Economics at Loughborough University from 1969 to 1976, and since 1976 he has been Senior Lecturer. In 1979 he was Senior Economic Adviser to the Ministry of Planning in Saudi Arabia. His research interests include the history of economic thought and monetary economics. His publications include *European Monetary Integration* (with Peter Coffey), *Currency Areas: Theory and Practice* (with Geoffrey E. J. Dennis), *Robertsonian Economics*, and he contributed to R. Lee and P. E. Ogden (eds), *Perspectives in Spatial Integration in the EEC*, and to *Case Studies in Macroeconomics*.

G. L. S. Shackle was born in 1903 and educated at London University (B.A., 1931; Ph.D. (Econ.), 1937) and Oxford University (D.Phil., 1940). He was made a Fellow of the British Academy in 1967, Hon. D.Sc., New University of Ulster in 1974, and Hon. D. Soc. Sc., Birmingham in 1978. He was a member of Sir Winston Churchill's Statistical Branch in 1939–45 and of the Economic Section of the Cabinet Office from 1945 to 1950. He was Reader in Economic Theory at the University of Leeds in 1950–1, Brunner Professor of Economic Science at the University of Liverpool in 1951–69, Professor F. de Vries Lecturer in Amsterdam in 1957, Visiting Professor at Columbia University, New York, in 1957–8, and Visiting Professor at Pittsburgh in 1967, and at Queen's University, Belfast, in 1970. He became Keynes Lecturer at the British Academy in 1976. He has published fourteen books between 1938 and 1974, including *The Years of High Theory*, *Expectations, Investments and Income*, *A Scheme of Economic Theory* and *Epistemics and Economics*, and over eighty articles in learned journals and in books edited by others.

Introduction

The eight essays in this volume discuss the work of major contributors to the development of economics in this country during a period when the UK was probably still pre-eminent in economic writing (despite the ever increasing importance of American economists) and its economists still, perhaps, rather insular.

The order of the essays in this volume is approximately that of the seniority of their subjects in the profession in this country. We have tried to select economists who have played a key role in the development of economics in Britain. The economists included are undoubtedly important; but obviously there were other candidates. Some of these were excluded because they are still active in the profession – Hicks and Robbins for example. Others were omitted simply because there is a limit to what could be done in one volume – Cannan, Stamp and Nicholson are examples in this category. Keynes was excluded for reasons which must be obvious – with the wealth of material pouring from the presses including (and resulting from) the *Collected Works*, an essay here, even if it had not been otiose (which it might well have been), would have incurred the exclusion of another economist who has received much less attention but whose work does merit further discussion.

Of the eight economists included here, five (Marshall, Pigou, Robertson, Hawtrey and Bowley) are products of Cambridge, though Hawtrey did not receive his economic training there;[1] the first three were of crucial importance in the development of the Cambridge School, and the remaining two occupied important positions in the Treasury and LSE. Of the remaining three, one, Jevons, has, as the essay in the volume makes clear, the premier claim to be considered a pioneer in the sense of our title; one, Edgeworth, was the premier pure theorist in this country for very many years, though the elegance, compactness and allusiveness of his work still lead many to fail to appreciate fully the extent of his achievements; and one, Hayek, was a leading figure in the development of economics in London in the 1930s.

The work of the economists discussed in this volume is

representative of the development of economics at a time when it was in an intermediate stage between the Classicists and modern economics; for example, utility functions figured in the analysis but tastes could change. Pre-occupations like the development of human wants with activities and the quality of the population were evident.[2] The kind of approach which typifies so much of the modern literature – obtaining comparative static results with given utility and production functions, an activity which in its more extreme mathematical forms sometimes shows signs of arteriosclerosis – occupies a relatively subordinate place in the work of the writers discussed in this volume. Their horizons were wider. They shared a common belief in the progressive and evolutionary nature of man, stemming very largely from the late Victorian outlook typified by Herbert Spencer and Darwin. Later in the period covered by this volume there was, however, a certain faltering of confidence – the First World War and its aftermath in the 1930s cleared the way for Keynes and ensured that he had far more impact than he would have done in an earlier period. But the generalisation remains broadly true of much of the work of the majority of the writers included here. They also shared a general utilitarian ethic, stemming partly from Bentham and their classical inheritance, but more directly from Sidgwick.

The period was also transitional in another sense. For these writers were contributing during the period of professionalisation of economics and the closing of its discourse to outsiders[3] – something which Marshall (and to a certain extent Edgeworth) tried to resist but which rolled relentlessly forward and was marked not only by the increasingly frequent appearance of formal modes of analysis but also by the rise of professional economic journals, especially the *Economic Journal* (from 1890) and the *Quarterly Journal of Economics* (from 1886). At the beginning of the period covered by this volume, the economists were contributing to publications like the *Fortnightly Review*, the *Pall Mall Gazette*, the *Contemporary Review* and the *Athenaeum*. But well before the end of our period the important contributions appear in the professional journals.

Because the subject was in a transitional state, and not at the outset professionalised, the education and interests of our subjects in this volume covered a much wider range than those of today's economists. Three of them – Marshall, Bowley and Hawtrey – were trained as mathematicians; Pigou had a predominantly arts background and a wide variety of literary and historical interests; Robertson's background was in classics, before turning to economics, Jevons's in natural science, and Edgeworth's in classics and in (a probably self-taught) mathematics, while Hayek's background was in law and economics. If nothing else this gave their contributions some style and humanity. But the wide range of their education resulted in part from the fact that economics was regarded as a much smaller subject than it is today and its literature was correspondingly less; thus, it was the era in which (at least until 1914) the definitive treatise could still be attempted.

Although there is no one common line of development through the economists discussed in this volume, there are many interconnecting threads resulting from their inheritance, their objectives and their backgrounds. Starting with Jevons we have a grand vision of a new economics based on the 'atomic' principle of marginal utility and utility maximisation, but with these purely theoretical concerns buttressed by path-breaking quantitative applied work. Jevons is followed by Marshall, who, in a grand attempt at synthesis, essayed the blending of the 'magnificent dynamics' of classical economics with comparative statics, and the utility analysis stemming from Jevons. But the formal mathematics of comparative statics were either banished to a mathematical appendix or remained unpublished altogether, while his emphasis on applied and descriptive material increased with the passing of time.

From Marshall we proceed to the Cambridge inheritance – Pigou as the obvious and direct successor, with his welfare economics stemming (somewhat to Marshall's discomfort) from Marshall, while his macroeconomics fought what Keynes believed to be a Marshallian rearguard but which resulted in a body of work which is viewed in this volume as post-Keynesian in its insights. Pigou's work is more directly a product of Cambridge, with the nineteenth century inheritance received through Marshall rather than directly from the work of Jevons, Marshall or Edgeworth. The same is true of Robertson's work which, like Pigou's, suffered unmerited eclipse (and a degree of misrepresentation) as a result of the Keynesian whirlwind with all its subordinate gusts. Yet, as the essay in this volume shows, Robertson's macroeconomics was for long developing along much the same lines as those followed by Keynes, and when the work of these two writers finally parted it was Robertson who stayed with macrodynamics while Keynes started on a path which led ultimately (though not in his hands) to the 'hydraulic'[4] comparative statics of the IS/LM model.

The field in which Keynes and Robertson worked was only a part of (and only partially from) the Marshallian inheritance. There was also Marshall's vision of a great scheme of statistical collection and interpretation. In this Bowley played a critical role – as a pioneer social and economic statistician his enormous achievements have been for long under-rated. Bowley's contribution to statistical procedures, however, was not negligible; Edgeworth's work, which was pioneering in the field of statistical theory, has received discussion elsewhere[5] but Bowley's treatment of sampling has been more neglected and some attempt to remedy this is made in chapter 5. Bowley also published, in 1924, an important work on mathematical economics. Though this disclaimed originality, it helped to push pure theory along the road laid down by Edgeworth and also to anticipate important later work. Edgeworth's own work as a pure theorist has itself been neglected and often unfairly criticised, largely because of its lack of accessibility. Chapter 3 shows, within a short compass, the range and subtlety of this economist, who, though his mathematical and pure theory obsessions irritated Marshall, remained in close personal and professional contact with the leader of the English school of economics and who undoubtedly, if only through his connection with the *Economic Journal*, himself occupied a key role in the profession. Finally there is Hayek. The essay in this volume concentrates on the manifest intricacies of his theory of capital and fluctuations; since this is the part of his work which has been neglected in the recent revival of interest stimulated by his political and constitutional law writings, it may help to give some idea both of the 'London' approach to the analysis of macroeconomic fluctuations[6] and also of the very high level of abstraction on which Hayek was capable of moving – mathematics and abstraction are very far from synonymous.

Taken together the eight essays in this volume should help to provide a picture of important figures in the development of economics in this country at a time when the subject was going through a critical phase of development. Within a limited compass they provide, we believe, material which may enable the reader to gain some appreciation of the importance of the distinguished contributors to the subject during this period.

NOTES

1. Some aspects of the importance of Cambridge during this period are discussed in A. W. Coats, 'Sociological Aspects of British Economic Thought', *Journal of Political Economy*, LXXV (1967) 706–29, at pp. 706–19.
2. See the references cited in chapter 2, notes 74 and 76; and A. C. Pigou, *The Economics of Welfare*, 4th ed. (repr. London: Macmillan, 1962) chs IX and X.
3. See T. S. Kuhn, *The Structure of Scientific Revolutions*, 2nd ed. (Chicago: University of Chicago Press, 1970) pp. 18–20; and C. D. Goodwin, pp. 287–9, 302, and G. J. Stigler, pp. 310–15 in R. D. C. Black, A. W. Coats and C. D. Goodwin (eds),*The Marginal Revolution in Economics* (Durham, NC: Duke University Press, 1973).
4. See G. L. S. Shackle, *The Years of High Theory* (Cambridge: Cambridge University Press, 1968) p. 189.
5. See the reference to S. M. Stigler in chapter 3, note 11.
6. For historical material reflecting this period see G. L. S. Shackle, *Expectations, Investment and Income*, 2nd ed. (Oxford: Clarendon Press, 1968) pp. xviii–xix; and J. R. Hicks, 'Recollections and Documents', *Economica*, n.s., XL (1973) 2–11.

1 W. S. Jevons, 1835–82

R. D. COLLISON BLACK

Introduction – biographia

It is arguable that William Stanley Jevons has a better claim to the title 'pioneer of modern economics' than any of his British contemporaries. Forty-two years ago Keynes described Jevons's *Theory of Political Economy* as 'the first treatise to present in a finished form the theory of value based on subjective valuations, the marginal principle and the now familiar technique of the algebra and diagrams of the subject'.[1] The *Theory of Political Economy* undoubtedly succeeded in doing what Jevons, equally undoubtedly, intended it to do – to mark a sharp break with all previous presentations of the principles of the subject. As a result it gained him a sharply-defined place in the history of economic thought as one of the initiators of what has come to be called the Marginal Revolution. Yet at the same time this very success has tended to overshadow the rest of Jevons's economic writing and to some extent prevented a balanced assessment of his achievements as an economist from becoming generally known.

The full range and extent of those achievements is considerable, and becomes even more remarkable when it is remembered that Jevons lived less than 47 years and was working as an economist for only the last 20 of these. Yet his family background and training were in a number of senses peculiarly appropriate to a pioneer of modern economics. The classical economists had numbered among them Scots philosophers, London stockbrokers and bankers, East India Company men, Oxbridge dons and divines. On the whole it would be true to say that their background was professional, their training for the most part in what was then called 'moral philosophy' rather than in natural philosophy. Jevons by contrast came out of the industrial heart of Victorian England; he was born in Liverpool, into a Unitarian family which made, and lost, its money by dealing in one of the basic commodities of the Industrial Revolution, iron. His early

1

interests and training were in the 'natural sciences', particularly chemistry, and his first ideas about his future career were typical of the northern nonconformist attitudes of his time:

> It is now however settled finally . . . that I am to go into some office at Liverpool. I have had doubts whether it will not be exceedingly difficult for me to acquire ready business habits, but I think that after settling my mind upon it for a year before, I shall have sufficient determination to do it. . . . For several of the first years that I shall be at home, I shall also give most of my leisure time to science, because I know that to do a thing well the mind should be engaged with it as singly as possible. . . . After those years are past, and when I shall be a man at 22 or 23, I shall make a gradual transition to Literary studies, and especially history, though always keeping up my scientific knowledge, a little. I don't know how far I shall be able to learn any mathematics by myself.[2]

Jevons wrote this when he was an undergraduate at University College, London, and not yet 18. But his dreams of becoming a man of business both diligent and cultured, like so many worthies of Liverpool and Manchester and notably his own maternal grandfather William Roscoe, were not to be realised. In the summer of 1853, when Jevons was in his last term at University College, through the good offices of his chemistry professor Thomas Graham,[3] he was offered the potentially lucrative post of Assistant Assayer to the newly established Royal Mint in Sydney, Australia. His father, whose financial position had been undermined by the bankruptcy in 1848 of the firm in which he was a partner, strongly encouraged Stanley to accept. Jevons did so and spent the years from 1854 to 1859 in New South Wales. Once the initial problems of setting up the assay office were overcome, his duties were light and left him ample time both to explore the developing colony in which he found himself and to continue his scientific studies. At first Jevons devoted himself to meteorology and published various articles on the climate of Australia, but gradually his interests began to shift from the study of nature to the study of man. As that shift became more marked, so Jevons became more clear in his own mind that he must return to England and seek to equip himself more thoroughly for what he now saw as his real life-work, even at the cost of abandoning the lucrative position and pleasant way of life which he enjoyed in Australia.

For myself [he wrote to his sister Henrietta at the beginning of 1859] I have long felt the same desire for a useful life but while I was at school and college, it remained comparatively latent. I gave my attention chiefly to physical science feeling much interest in it and being sure that it could not prove useless . . . but within the last few years I have become convinced that more is really to be done in the scientific investigation of *Man*. . . . To attempt to define the foundations of our knowledge of man, is surely a work worth a lifetime, and one not excelled in usefulness or interest by any other.

Why then should anything beyond my necessary moral obligations debar me from it? While I should never consent to sacrifice them, why should I care to sacrifice my own present ease and amusements? Why should I care for money, for fine possessions, for present name and position, or even for the real pleasures of scientific study, while there is such an important and interesting work evident to me?[4]

Thus Jevons enunciated the concept of present sacrifice for future returns which was later to form the foundation of his theory of capital and put it into practice in his own life. In October 1859 he returned to University College, London, to complete his BA degree. He remained a student until 1862, undertaking a formidable programme of work in logic, philosophy and political economy, mathematics, classics and history.

Even while he was thus completing his study of the subjects which he had come to regard as essential foundations for 'the scientific investigation of Man' Jevons was beginning to make his own contribution to social science. In the three main areas in which he was destined to make a mark – logic, applied economics and economic theory – his ideas were developing rapidly and by 1863 he had produced important work in all of them. Nevertheless recognition was slow to come and Jevons went through a period of doubt and disappointment. He had thought of himself as becoming a writer, but soon decided 'that the professorial line is the one for me to take'. It was not an easy line for in the small British academic community of those days posts, particularly for Nonconformists, in such subjects as political economy and logic were few. Jevons went first as a tutor to Owens College, Manchester, 'to aid the students in any of the branches of knowledge then taught at the college'. He remained there for 13 years, becoming Cobden Professor of Political Economy and Professor of Logic, Mental and Moral Philosophy in 1866. These were the years in which Jevons's reputation became firmly established, first nationally by the publication of *The Coal Question* in 1865, then internationally by the *Theory of Political Economy* in 1871 and the *Principles of Science* in 1874. With his career prospects settled he married Harriet Ann Taylor, a daughter of the proprietor of the *Manchester Guardian*, and the intense and solitary young man who had returned from Australia matured into the respected professor, respected not only by his Manchester colleagues and students but by his peers who elected him a Fellow of the Royal Society in 1872, and by two noted Chancellors of the Exchequer, Gladstone and Robert Lowe.

In order to achieve all this within a decade Jevons drove himself relentlessly and before the *Principles of Science* was finished his health broke down. After a year's leave he was able to return to his duties in 1874, but in 1876 he resigned his appointments at Manchester and moved to London. He became Professor of Political Economy at University College, an appointment whose narrower scope and lighter teaching duties gave him more opportunity for his own writing. Yet by 1880 Jevons found it 'quite impossible to go on with trying fixed duties when I have so much literary work on my mind'[5] and he resigned the University College chair in order to devote himself wholly to writing. 'With the doctor's help and freedom from harassing engagements, I hope soon to be more up to par, though I can never again be really strong as I was ten or twelve years ago', he wrote to Foxwell.[6]

He sought to establish a regime of 'steady but moderate work' and continued to publish actively, but his health never was fully restored. On holiday near Hastings in August 1882 he made an ill-fated decision to go swimming, collapsed in the water and was drowned.

Microeconomic theory

But as all the physical sciences have their basis more or less obviously in the general principles of mechanics, so all branches and divisions of economic science must be pervaded by certain

general principles. It is to the investigation of such principles –
to the tracing out of the mechanics of self-interest and utility,
that this essay has been devoted. The establishment of such a
theory is a necessary preliminary to any definite drafting of the
superstructure of the aggregate science.[7]

So wrote Jevons in the preface to the second edition of the
Theory of Political Economy and it must be recognised that this,
'the first modern book on economics', was strictly confined to
'tracing out the mechanics of self-interest and utility' as the basis of
the science. It thus represented a departure both in method and
content not only from the works of Ricardo and J. S. Mill with
which Jevons explicitly contrasted his *Theory*, but even from a
book like Senior's *Outline of the Science of Political Economy*
which he considered 'the best piece of writing on the subject . . . I
believe, ever written'.[8]

All the disciplines which Jevons had studied when he decided
to devote himself to 'the scientific investigation of man' –
mathematics, logic and philosophy – were put to work in the
Theory. It was ultimately the way in which Jevons combined these
which made the book an important contribution to the
development of economic thought, but it could be argued that it
was the philosophy which Jevons used which was at once the most
important and the least original component. That philosophy was
simply Benthamite utilitarianism. During his years in Australia
Jevons had adopted the view of 'man . . . as essentially selfish, that
is as doing everything with a view to gain enjoyment or avoid pain'
although he does not appear to have become acquainted with
Bentham's writings until he returned to University College.[9] From
then onwards Jevons remained a convinced utilitarian and it was
on Bentham's theory of pleasure and pain that the whole analysis
of the *Theory* was squarely founded. Logic and mathematics were
the techniques by which the analysis was built up on that
foundation. The logical method of economics Jevons regarded as
being the same as that of any other science:

Possessing certain facts of observation we frame an hypothesis
as to the laws governing those facts; we reason from the
hypothesis deductively to the results to be expected; and we then
examine those results in connection with the facts in question;
coincidence confirms the whole reasoning; conflict obliges us

either to seek for disturbing causes, or else to abandon our hypothesis. In this procedure there is nothing peculiar; when properly understood it is found to be the method of all the inductive sciences.[10]

Using the pleasure and pain hypothesis to explain the observed facts of economic behaviour, Jevons found the mathematical technique of the calculus which he had learned from De Morgan[11] a natural aid to the process of deductive reasoning in a science which 'must be mathematical, simply because it deals with quantities'.

Taking the theory of pleasure and pain as his starting point led Jevons to the view that 'to satisfy our wants to the utmost with the least effort . . . in other words, to *maximise pleasure*, is the problem of Economics'. The first step in the solution of this problem was the development of a Theory of Utility, explaining how pleasure is derived from the consumption of commodities. Here Jevons set out the famous distinction between total utility and degree of utility on which so much of the theory of consumer behaviour was to be based. But 'utility arises from commodities being brought in suitable quantities and at the proper times into the possession of persons needing them, and it is by exchange, more than any other means, that this is effected'. Hence the Theory of Exchange becomes the focal point of the work; the derivation of the equations in this chapter and the demonstration that for each party to the exchange to maximise satisfaction final degrees of utility must be proportional to prices are deservedly among the best-known parts of his economic writings.[12]

Jevons developed his Theory of Exchange first with reference to the case of two individuals, or 'trading bodies', who began trading with fixed stocks of commodities in their possession. In practice, however, stocks can be altered by production. Production Jevons described first in terms of the expenditure of labour alone, and labour he considered as normally involving 'painful exertion'. Hence if consumption provides utility, production involves disutility and the two are related by the process of exchange, in which values are established. 'Labour affects supply, and supply affects the degree of utility, which governs value, or the ratio of exchange.'[13]

After presenting a theory of labour, Jevons rounded off his book with two further chapters – one on rent and one on capital. There was for long a tendency to regard these as completing, if not very tidily, a theory of distribution of the usual tripartite form – explaining wages as the price of labour, rent as the price of land and interest as the price of capital. In point of fact, as I have argued elsewhere,[14] such a view involves a misunderstanding of Jevons's intentions. There are important pointers towards a marginal productivity theory of distribution in these chapters, but they are incidental to the main purpose.

In his Theory of Labour Jevons had sought to show that 'no increment of labour would be expended unless there was sufficient recompense in the produce, but that labour would be expended up to the point at which the increment of utility exactly equals the increment of pain incurred in acquiring it'. His Theory of Rent is an elegant re-statement of Ricardian theory in calculus terms but its purpose is to show how when labour is combined with land (in the production of commodities to satisfy wants) a surplus over and above this 'necessary recompense' for the pain of labour can emerge.

In the Theory of Capital, according to Jevons, 'we enter a distinct branch of our subject'. 'Both by the use of capital and by exchange we are enabled vastly to increase the sum of utility which we enjoy; but it is conceivable that we might have the advantages of capital without those of exchange. . . . Economics, then, is not solely the science of Exchange or Value; it is also the science of Capitalisation.' Both Exchange and Capitalisation can increase the sum of utility – the latter essentially by affording the means of carrying on what Böhm-Bawerk was later to call 'roundabout methods of production'. 'The single and all-important function of capital', according to Jevons, 'is to enable the labourer to await the result of any long-lasting work – to put an interval between the beginning and the end of an enterprise.'[15]

From this outline of the method and content of the *Theory of Political Economy* it should be evident that it was indeed a major departure from the orthodox classical approach but almost equally far from what has come to be thought of as orthodox neoclassical microeconomics.

The departures from classical orthodoxy – the switch from cost to utility in value theory, the shift of emphasis from growth to allocation and efficiency, the adoption of mathematical methods – are so well known as to need no more than recalling here. On the other hand, the differences between Jevons's *Theory* and what has come to be regarded as neoclassical orthodoxy have received much less notice and so require correspondingly more discussion. There has indeed been a tendency, as one recent commentator has put it, to see Jevons 'through the spectacles of Marshall'[16] and from that point of view some differences are obvious enough – Jevons's use of utility curves as against Marshall's use of demand curves and the 'measuring rod of money', the absence of a theory of the firm in Jevons's work and of a symmetrical treatment of factor prices on the basis of marginal productivity. There is certainly not to be found in the *Theory of Political Economy* the fully rounded explanation of the determination of equilibrium prices in markets for both final products and factors of production which appears in the work of Marshall and Walras and was to become the hallmark of neoclassical economics. In point of fact there is more of it than Jevons is usually given credit for providing: in three pages of his chapter on the Theory of Labour he gives a marvellously economical summary of the relations between price, utility, cost of production and productivity. While it is true that the ensuing chapters seem to apply marginal productivity analysis explicitly only to the determination of the rate of return on capital, it is by implication applied to the returns to land and labour as well.[17]

Nevertheless it is surely wrong to think of neoclassical economics as developing in some sort of straight line fashion from the incomplete beginnings of Jevons to the mature equilibrium analysis of Marshall and Walras. A better analogy, and one perhaps appropriate in the case of Jevons, would be that of a goldfield in which he as a pioneer prospector brought out nuggets from a number of veins which were to be more thoroughly worked by others after him. Some of the veins which Jevons opened were very successfully worked by Marshall – consumer theory is the obvious example; others Marshall did not work at all or developed in a different direction.

In capital theory, for example, Marshall's approach was fundamentally different from that of Jevons. To use the illuminating terminology developed by Sir John Hicks,[18] Marshall was a Materialist – one to whom real capital consists of physical goods – whereas Jevons was a Fundist – one to whom real capital is a sum of values, a fund which may be embodied in physical goods in different ways. Here Jevons, paradoxically enough, was closer to Ricardo than was Marshall and his views on capital and interest have greater affinities with later Austrian rather than Marshallian thought.

It might be suggested that more of the veins which Jevons prospected were worked by Wicksteed and Edgeworth than by Marshall, and there is a great deal of truth in this. Indeed Wicksteed followed up one idea of Jevons which Marshall and his followers completely ignored. This was the concept of the dimensions of economic quantities, only hinted at in the first edition of the *Theory of Political Economy*, but very much emphasised by Jevons in the second as a subject 'which lies at the basis of all clear thought about economic science'.[19]

As often with Jevons, his insights into this question were brilliant but his working out of the details was incomplete and in some respects inaccurate. Wicksteed corrected and extended Jevons's first sketch of the subject and endorsed his view of its importance – a view which is only now coming to be recognised and accepted after many years of neglect.[20]

Similarly, there has lately been a notable revival of interest in the work of Edgeworth and his theory of exchange has been described as 'one of the few great insights into the nature of economic activity'.[21] That theory is based on Jevonian foundations and indeed Edgeworth's *Mathematical Psychics* was avowedly an attempt to develop and extend the utilitarian calculus which Jevons had set forth.

Wicksteed, summing up the position of economic thought as he saw it in 1905, had argued that in the years since Jevons's *Theory* first appeared two schools of thought had grown up – one, mainly in Austria and America, sought to develop the 'universal application of the theory of margins':

Under their analysis the conception of costs of production is being reduced from a position co-ordinate with that of marginal utilities to a secondary manifestation of that principle itself. [The other] the school of economists of which Professor Marshall is the illustrious head, accepts . . . and applauds the Jevonian principles, but declares that, so far from being revolutionary, they merely supplement, clarify, and elucidate the theories they profess to destroy. To scholars of this school the admission into the science of the renovated study of consumption leaves the study of production comparatively unaffected. As a determining factor of normal prices, cost of production is coordinate with the schedule of demands registered on the 'demand curve'.[22]

In the light of this it seems natural to contrast the Cambridge tradition of real cost theory, deriving from classical origins, with a 'London tradition' developed by Wicksteed and others and embracing not only Austrian notions of objective opportunity cost but treating cost in a utility dimension as purely subjective – 'the anticipated utility loss upon sacrifice of a rejected alternative'.[23] It is tempting to see Jevons as forerunner, perhaps founder, of this tradition, and indeed it has recently been contended that 'Jevons, in fact, is the originator of the subjective theory of cost'.[24] Yet it seems doubtful if this claim can be sustained. There are well-known passages in the preface to the second edition of the *Theory* where Jevons approaches an alternative-product theory of cost and other passages in the book itself which can be interpreted as implying a subjective theory of cost in terms of rejected alternatives. Nevertheless the whole cast of the book makes clear that the cost to the individual which Jevons thought of was not utility loss but quite simply pain – 'the painful exertion which we undergo to ward off pains of greater amount, or to procure pleasures which leave a balance in our favour'.[25] In this respect, then, Jevons is perhaps closer to Marshall than to Wicksteed. Again this may seem paradoxical, but only if one is attempting to classify Jevons as a forerunner of one or the other rather than seeing him as a highly original thinker who threw out ideas which could and did have their influence on many economists and whose implications are still generating fresh work even at the present time.

Applied economics

The *Theory of Political Economy* earned for Jevons a lasting reputation as an economic theorist, but to his contemporaries at the time of its appearance he was better known as an applied economist. It is perhaps not surprising that a reputation in this latter field should prove less lasting than one built on theoretical studies, given the transitory nature of many practical problems. Yet for his achievement in applied economics Jevons is just as much, perhaps more, deserving of the title of a pioneer of modern economics as for his work in theoretical analysis. For here again the conception of scientific method and technique which he developed and employed consistently had much closer affinities with the approach of the economist of the present day than with those of Jevons's classical predecessors.

The classical school had included within it advocates both of inductive and deductive approaches, but under the influence of Ricardo, Senior and Cairnes the latter had tended to become dominant and in Jevons's own day the 'vicious abstraction' of the classical economists was frequently attacked by advocates of a more empirical and historical method.

To Jevons the dichotomy between induction and deduction appeared false. One of the main points which he stressed in his treatment of scientific method was that *'induction is really the inverse process of deduction....* Just as the process of division necessitates a prior knowledge of multiplication ... so induction requires a prior knowledge of deduction'.[26] Facts without theory and theory without facts were both equally barren in Jevons's view, and his success in applied research was the result of combining exceptional skill and patience in the handling of large masses of statistical data with an ability to strike out novel and potentially fruitful hypotheses for their interpretation.

'Jevons had decided in Australia that if economics and the social sciences were to develop, an essential factor must be the assembly of exact basic data, suitably analysed'.[27] Not surprisingly this was one of the first tasks to which Jevons devoted himself when he returned to England:

About October 1860 – having recently commenced reading at the Mus[eum] Libr[ary] and met some stat[istics] I began to form some diagrams to exhibit them. .... I hit upon a method of dividing a sheet of paper into 1/10 inch and then pricking off curves through it when in Sydney, and the square was ready at hand. .... I finally undertook to form a Statistical atlas of say 30 plates exhibiting all the chief materials of *historical stat[istics]*. For the last year this atlas has been my chief employment and I fear to look back upon the labour I have spent in searching all likely books for series of stat[istics] then copying, calculating, arranging and drawing the diagrams.[28]

Thus Jevons the young chemist and meteorologist began to apply the methods with which he was already familiar to 'the scientific investigation of Man'. From the outset two ideas were of fundamental importance to him – 'the collection, analysis and presentation of time series data' and 'the systematic and scientific classification of trades and occupations'.[29] Almost all of the considerable body of work in applied economics which Jevons accomplished can be seen as fitting into the framework of these two ideas – ideas which could only have come out of a training in the natural sciences. Prophetically Jevons's cousin, the chemist Henry Enfield Roscoe, had written to him in 1858: 'There is certainly that one comfort about being of a Scientific turn – that one feels that one is ahead of the crowd . . . .'[30] That was precisely what Jevons was to be; as Keynes said of him, 'it is remarkable, looking back, how few followers and imitators he had in the black arts of inductive economics in the fifty years after 1862. But to-day he can claim an unnumbered progeny . . .'.[31]

(i) *Exhaustible resources*

The time series data which was most readily accessible and most amenable to analysis in the early 1860s took the form of statistics of prices. Already Tooke and Newmarch had produced a monumental *History of Prices*[32] and Thorold Rogers was extending the same approach to earlier periods. The interpretation of price movements, both secular and cyclical, was a central feature of Jevons's contributions to economics throughout his whole career, but this work was not what brought him first into the public eye and gave him a national reputation. That was the result of the publication in 1865 of *The Coal Question: An Inquiry Concerning the Progress of the Nation and the Probable Exhaustion of our Coal Mines*. During the debates on the Cobden–Chevalier Treaty of 1860 the question of possible exhaustion of British coal supplies affecting her competitive and strategic position had been raised in the House of Commons and some widely varying and vaguely based statements had been made about the size of British coal reserves. So the issue of depletion of coal reserves was 'in the air' in the early 1860s and Jevons, already interested in the statistical treatment of economic problems, decided to take it up as 'the coming question'. His decision was not unaffected by his own need, as a struggling young tutor at Owens College, Manchester, to make a reputation for himself. 'A good publication on the subject would draw a good deal of attention', he wrote to his brother. 'I am convinced that it is necessary for the present at any rate to write on popular subjects . . . .'[33]

Jevons succeeded in producing very quickly a good publication, which certainly did draw a good deal of attention – *The Coal Question*. Starting from estimates of coal existing in England given in Edward Hull's *Coalfields of Great Britain* published in 1861, Jevons endeavoured to show first 'that there is no reasonable prospect of any relief from a future want of the main agent of industry', whether through economy in the use of coal, the development of substitutes, or importation. After estimating the rate of increase of coal consumption, he then proceeded to demonstrate 'that, should the consumption multiply for rather more than a century at the same rate, the average depth of our coal mines would be 4,000 feet, and the average price of coal much higher than the highest price now paid for the finest kinds of coal'. From this followed the stark and striking conclusion 'that we cannot long continue our present rate of progress'.[34]

Jevons was not predicting an early exhaustion of coal measures as such, but asserting that the rapid growth of population and industry in Britain during the nineteenth century had produced a *rate* of increase of coal consumption (then 3.5 per cent per annum) which could not be maintained without steep increases of cost – so that in so far as Britain's industrial progress and supremacy depended on coal it was bound to suffer a check within the next half-century or so.

As to possible remedies for this situation, Jevons was not optimistic. He discounted the possibility of adequate substitutes being discovered, stressing that even if they were there was no reason to expect that Britain would possess the same advantages in these as she did in coal. Little help was to be expected from efforts to economise in the consumption of coal, and Jevons's belief in the principles of free trade and the benefits derived from their application led him to reject any attempt to restrict exportation of coal, whether by taxes or prohibitions. 'It would seem,' he confessed, 'that we have placed ourselves in a painful dilemma; we must either retract the professions we have made to the world and the principles we have so recently adopted, or else we must submit to see our material resources exhausted in a shorter period than could have been thought possible.'

'The only suggestion I can make towards compensating posterity for our present lavish use of cheap coal', he went on, '. . . is the reduction or paying off of the National Debt' which 'would serve the three purposes of adding to the productive capital of the country, of slightly checking our present too rapid progress, and of lessening the future difficulties of the country.'[35]

At first the book attracted comparatively little attention, but the well-known astronomer Sir John F. W. Herschel expressed himself convinced by its arguments.[36] Early in 1866 Alexander Macmillan, the book's publisher, took the shrewd step of sending a copy to Gladstone who, typically, 'perused it with care' and wrote that 'it makes a deep impression on me, and strengthens the convictions I have long entertained but with an ever growing force as to our duty with regard to the National Debt'.[37]

The same view was expressed soon afterwards in the House of Commons by no less a person than John Stuart Mill, and Gladstone, in his Budget speech of 3 May 1866, made the danger of coal exhaustion one of the grounds for his plans to reduce public debt. 'The Coal Panic' filled the newspapers for some time and led to the appointment of a Royal Commission on Coal, which did not report until 1871. The Commission produced the first detailed estimates of the size of the total stock of coal in Britain; this, as Jevons's son later pointed out, was not the question to which Jevons had addressed himself.[38] However, the results produced by the Commission were reassuring and public interest in the issue was not revived.

Jevons's concern with the coal question gains fresh interest today in the light of our own concern with the oil question and problems of energy reserves generally. Economists have for the most part been content to take the volume of natural resources as a datum; Jevons was one of very few to question this position, and go into the consequences of so doing. But we can perhaps do more than award him a posthumous good mark for being so clever as to take up a question which has interest for us today; we may be able to learn one or two lessons from the way in which he treated it.

First of all, it must be recognised that the question which Jevons posed was not quite the same as that which now concerns us. He was not concerned with the exhaustion of world energy reserves, or even British energy reserves, but merely with the effects on British economic growth and international competitiveness of the rapid rate of consumption of cheap coal.

It is interesting to note that this is the only point in Jevons's economic writings where he developed anything like a theory of growth. What he described as the 'Law of Social Growth' is in fact a fairly simple modification of the Malthusian theory of population and the Ricardian view of diminishing returns. Commencing from the statement 'that living beings of the same nature and in the same circumstances multiply in the same geometrical ratio' Jevons stressed that:

> even if we do not change in inward character, yet the aggregate of our exterior circumstances, our *environment*, as Mr Spencer expresses it, is usually changing. This is what Malthus argued. He said that, though our numbers *tend* to increase in uniform ratio we cannot expect the same to take place with the supply of food. We cannot double the produce of the soil, time after time, *ad infinitum*.
> ... *The whole question turns upon the application of these views to the consumption of coal.* Our subsistence no longer depends upon our produce of corn. The momentous repeal of the Corn Laws throws us from corn upon coal.[39]

Thus for the limitation of fertile soil which Ricardo had seen as the cause of the stationary state was substituted the limitation of supplies of accessible coal, whose consumption Jevons saw as increasing in geometrical progression. Keynes, writing in 1936, characterised this argument as unsound and said that 're-read today it appears over-strained and exaggerated'.[40] Re-read today it may seem less so, if for coal we read energy supplies generally. And as we begin to glimpse the social frictions which a reduction in economic growth, and in expectations from it, bring about we may read with more sympathy Jevons's response to those who:

> say that they never supposed we should long progress as we are doing, nor do they desire it ... have they taken time to think what is involved in bringing a great and growing nation to a stand? It is easy to set a boulder rolling on the mountain-side; it is perilous to try to stop it. It is just such an adverse change in the rate of progress of a nation which is galling and perilous.[41]

Nowadays we can appreciate again the validity of Jevons's warning that industrial development which is founded on the premise of cheap energy may be a passing thing; but why *again*?

The prophecy which Jevons made on the basis of extrapolating the then existing demand for coal was obviously not correct; where did it go astray?

Jevons's estimate of coal consumption in 1961 was 2607 million tons (on the basis of a continuing rate of growth of 3.5 per cent per annum from 1861); the actual figure was 192 million tons.[42] What Jevons did not anticipate was that in the same year the direct use of coal represented only 46 per cent of total UK energy consumption.[43] In other words he underestimated the possibilities of developing coal substitutes. Some of the substitutes which he discussed – not only in *The Coal Question* but in correspondence with scientists like Herschel – appeared visionary at the time, but are now practical on both technical and economic grounds. Hydroelectric power is the most important case in point. Others which Jevons regarded as not visionary but equally not significant have proved to be of far greater importance than he imagined – the most obvious being petroleum and natural gas.[44]

Jevons was not afraid to assert dogmatically '*The progress of science, and the improvement in the arts, will tend to increase the supremacy of steam and coal*'[45] and characterised the optimistic views of Dionysius Lardner about the prospects of invention and technical change as being 'in him, as a scientific man, inexcusable'.[46] A century later Lardner's attempts at prophesy have worn better than those of Jevons, and there may be a lesson here for members of various scientific communities who are providing us with estimates of energy production and consumption in so far as these depend on extrapolating present trends.

On the question of possible remedies Jevons's proposal, which for him 'required some boldness to make', for the reduction of the National Debt, may strike us today as somewhat of an irrelevance, enshrining typically Victorian values on private and public finance. But even if this is accepted there may be another lesson to be learnt from it – that even for a very original mind it is not easy to transcend the paradigms of the age. Some of the economic nostrums offered at the present time for the solution of our 'energy crisis' may well appear as irrelevant to our grandchildren as Jevons's now do to us.

Nowadays we should not see the redemption of the National Debt as a means of 'adding to the productive capital of the country' but budgeting for a surplus as a means of reducing inflationary pressures in the economy would not be deemed an irrelevance. Nor does the modern tendency to dismiss lightly the burden of public debt extend to external liabilities. In this connection it is worth pointing out that Jevons was hoping to relieve posterity from some of the burdens of an increased cost of coal by leaving a smaller tax requirement to be met for debt service and redemption. But while he envisaged a time when Britain might be outstripped by other nations, and specifically the United States, in industrial development, he did not consider the effect this might have on her creditor status and how changes in this might affect policy.

(ii) *Money, prices and the trade cycle*

Although the general public had lost interest in the 'coal question' by the early 1870s, Jevons had not and as late as 1881 he was reporting to his brother Thomas that 'the census reports in England together with the coal statistics, are wonderfully bearing out my *Coal Question*'.[47] Nevertheless in the perspective of history this study, while it establishes Jevons as a pioneer in yet another field, the economics of exhaustible resources, still appears as something set apart from the main body of his work in applied economics.

In order to understand properly the character and development of that work it is necessary to refer back to 1860, the key year in Jevons's intellectual growth as an economist. Already in the spring of 1860 he had 'fortunately struck out . . . the true theory of Economy' and the autumn found him 'compiling quantities of statistics . . . to be exhibited in the form of curves'.[48] It seems clear that it was in the course of the preparation of his projected Statistical Atlas that Jevons was struck by the periodicities which his data exhibited and from that time onwards the concept of periodic variation was as central to his thinking on questions of applied economics as utility was to his thinking on questions of theory.[49]

At first it seemed to Jevons that 'the chief interest of the work will be in the light thrown upon . . . commercial storms . . . the causes of which will be rendered more or less apparent' and he afterwards related how his examination of his diagrams 'produced upon my mind a deep conviction that the events of 1815, 1825, 1836-39, 1847 and 1857 exhibited a true but mysterious periodicity'.[50]

Nevertheless it was not this so much as seasonal and other

fluctuations which were emphasised in the second paper[51] which Jevons presented to the British Association meeting at Cambridge in 1862 – 'On the Study of Periodic Commerical Fluctuations'. In this Jevons suggested

that all commercial fluctuations should be investigated according to the same scientific methods with which we are familiar in other complicated sciences, such especially as meteorology and terrestrial magnetism. Every kind of periodic fluctuation, whether daily, weekly, monthly, quarterly or yearly, must be detected and exhibited, not only as a subject of study in itself, but because we must ascertain and eliminate such periodic variations before we can correctly exhibit those which are irregular or non-periodic, and probably of more interest and importance.[52]

Indeed soon after this paper had been presented Jevons's attention had turned to an important non-periodic variation. 'In the meantime', he wrote to his brother Herbert in January 1863, 'I have been led to observe the great rise in prices of nearly all things since 1851, which is obviously due to a fall in the value of gold. This I am now trying to ascertain and prove in a conclusive manner, which will of course be a very important and startling fact.'[53]

The outcome was the first work which gained Jevons recognition among his professional contemporaries – *A Serious Fall in the Value of Gold Ascertained and its Social Effects Set Forth*.[54] In this Jevons pointed out that some 12 or more years after the great Californian and Australian gold discoveries 'men who give their whole attention to public and monetary matters, or to questions of statistics and economy, remain in a state of doubt as to whether any depreciation of gold is really taking place'.[55] This state of affairs he set out to remedy, with a typical combination of scientific thoroughness and accuracy. The magnitude of the task which the 28-year-old Jevons took on in setting out to measure secular price changes accurately, and the success with which he accomplished it, have been classically stated by Keynes: 'Jevons had to solve the problem of price index-numbers practically from the beginning; and it is scarcely an exaggeration to say that he made as much progress in this brief pamphlet as has been made by all succeeding authors put together'.[56]

The conclusion which Jevons reached was that there had been a depreciation of gold of the order of 9–15 per cent since 1845–50. He examined fully the effects of this on different classes in the community, reaching the conclusion that 'it cannot be proved that positive hardship . . . is inflicted upon any person by the present depreciation of gold'.[57] Comparative hardship for some there might be but for the community as a whole the effects were beneficial, stimulating enterprise and reducing the burden of debt.

In the course of this remarkable pamphlet, which covered with lucid precision almost every aspect of a change in the value of money, Jevons insisted 'that we must discriminate permanent from temporary fluctuations of prices' and his lengthy studies of prices brought home clearly to him and to his contemporaries not only that long-term variations of price levels did take place but that they could be measured with considerable accuracy by index-number techniques.

Yet if the work which Jevons did in *A Serious Fall* and in his 1865 paper 'The Variation of Prices and the Value of the Currency since 1782'[58] was path-breaking in the development and use of index-number techniques, there was nothing revolutionary in its implications for monetary theory. Essentially it served to support the quantity theory, and although Jevons wrote little directly on that topic the implications of all his writings on money and price levels are that he accepted a version of the theory in which the supply of money was ultimately governed by the cost of production of the precious metals and the demand for it was a pure transactions demand.[59]

It has sometimes been suggested that there is an element of paradox in the fact that Jevons who broke so irrevocably from the classical theory of value should have adhered so meekly to the classical theory of money; but any such paradox is more apparent than real. For Jevons saw the problem of changes in the value of money as essentially a long-term one, and in the long run he fully accepted 'that value is proportional to the cost of production'.[60] Perhaps for this very reason, there is a notable absence in all of Jevons's monetary writings of any attempt to analyse the demand for money in terms of 'desired cash balances', along the lines later developed by Walras and Marshall.

In one respect Jevons did depart in some degree from classical monetary orthodoxy. He never had any doubt that the danger of permitting the issue of inconvertible paper money was real and the benefits illusory, and he was a supporter of the gold standard in the sense that he saw no advantage in a bimetallic rather than a monometallic currency system. Yet his studies of the effect of gold discoveries on prices had convinced him of its instability as a monetary standard. Hence when he came in later years to set out his ideas on 'An Ideally Perfect System of Currency' he argued that it was essential to separate the functions of money – functions which were classically set out in his textbook on *Money and the Mechanism of Exchange*. 'Gold must be employed as the common denominator and temporary standard of value, in terms of which all prices will be expressed. It should cease to be the permanent standard of value . . . long-enduring debts and transactions will be regulated by the Tabular Standard of Value, the amounts of debts, although expressed in gold, being varied inversely, as gold varies in terms of other commodities.'[61] Jevons was here, as he himself stated, following up a proposal put forward by Joseph Lowe in 1822 and Poulett Scrope in 1833; thus while he did not originate the idea, his name can be added to the list of those who foreshadowed present day plans for 'indexation'.

Jevons returned to the question of short-run periodic variations in monetary phenomena in his 1866 paper 'On the Frequent Autumnal Pressure in the Money Market, and the Action of the Bank of England',[62] but it was not until 1875 that he sought again to investigate and explain the 'true but mysterious periodicity' of 'commercial storms'. In *A Serious Fall* he had put forward the significant hypothesis that 'the remote cause of these commercial tides . . . seems to lie in *the varying proportion which the capital devoted to permanent and remote investment bears to that which is but temporarily invested soon to reproduce itself'*.[63]

It must be a matter for conjecture why this early insight was never followed up in Jevons's later work; but to have made much progress with it he would have had to develop the idea that plans to save and plans to invest might not coincide. No such idea seems ever to have come into Jevons's thinking; perhaps because of his faith in the quantity theory and his view of the demand for money as purely a transactions demand his acceptance of the validity of Say's Law was complete and he had no patience with underconsumptionist views.[64]

Jevons was thus much more clearly possessed than his classical predecessors of the idea of a periodic overall fluctuation of the economic system, but no more capable than they of explaining it in terms of factors endogenous to the system. Already in 1862 he had suggested that commercial fluctuations would require to be investigated 'according to the same scientific methods with which we are familiar in other complicated sciences, such especially as meteorology and terrestrial magnetism'.

In his *Principles of Science* (1874) Jevons included a section on 'Periodic Variations' in which he referred to 'a most important and general principle which has been demonstrated by Sir John Herschel for some special cases . . . the meaning of the proposition is that the effect of a periodic cause will be periodic, and will recur at intervals equal to those of the cause'. He went on to quote 'the most extensive and beautiful instance of induction concerning periodic changes which can be cited . . . that of the discovery of an eleven-year period in various meteorological and astronomical phenomena' – a reference to the connections which had been suggested between the sunspot cycle and the recurrence of auroras.[65]

For someone with Jevons's training, interests and view of scientific method, it was a natural step to put forward and test the hypothesis that the decennial cycle which he had observed in many economic phenomena might be the periodic effect of a periodic but exogenous cause – the sunspot cycle.

Initially Jevons formulated this hypothesis in terms of a straightforward connection between the sunspot cycle and grain prices. His argument was that 'the success of the harvest in any year certainly depends upon the weather, especially that of the summer and autumn months. Now, if this weather depends in any degree upon the solar period, it follows that the harvest and the price of grain will depend more or less upon the solar period, and will go through periodic fluctuations in periods of time equal to those of the sun-spots.'[66]

In support of this, Jevons endeavoured to relate the average prices of various types of grain in the years between 1259 and 1400, as given in Thorold Rogers's *History of Agriculture and Prices*,[67] with a sunspot period of 11.11 years. He did find that 'remarkably high' prices 'manifest a tendency to periodical recurrence'. He did not 'venture to assert positively that the average fluctuations . . . are solely due to variations of solar power' but concluded that 'they seem to show that the subject deserves further investigation, which I hope to give to it when I have leisure'.[68]

Subsequently Jevons admitted that 'the same data would give

other periods of variation equally well' but nevertheless declared his conviction that 'the inquiry is far from being an absurd one'.[69] During the years 1876 and 1877 he devoted much time and effort to accumulating evidence of periodic commercial crises extending back to the South Sea Bubble of 1720 and he became more and more convinced that the period involved was a decennial one – a view which indeed was coming to be quite widely held at this time.[70]

Two other points seem to have come to Jevons's notice at about this date; one was the publication of a paper by the astronomer J. A. Broun suggesting a correction of Wolf's numbers which would have altered the average period of the sunspot cycle from 11.11 to 10.45 years, the other the evidence of the decennial periodicity of Indian famines adduced by Sir William Wilson Hunter, the government statistician of India, and others.[71]

This led Jevons to formulate another 'working hypothesis as to the production of decennial crises' which he once stated as follows:

A wave of increased solar radiations favourably affects the meteorology of the tropical regions, so as to produce a succession of good crops in India, China and other tropical or semi-tropical countries. After several years of prosperity the six or eight hundred millions of inhabitants of those countries buy our manufactures in unusual quantities; good trade in Lancashire and Yorkshire leads the manufacturers to push their existing means of production to the utmost and then to begin building new mills and factories. While a mania of active industry is thus set going in Western Europe, the solar radiation is slowly waning, so that just about the time when our manufacturers are prepared to turn out a greatly increased supply of goods famines in India and China suddenly cut off the demand.[72]

For the few remaining years of his life Jevons maintained this hypothesis and sought evidence to support it. As he himself put it, 'continued investigation of the subject produces almost perfect conviction that the principal – that is to say, the recurring – decennial crises of the 18th and 19th centuries are due to solar variations; but it is a matter of great difficulty to disentangle the requisite statistics in such a manner as to prove the exact *modus operandi*'.[73]

As Foxwell pointed out in his Introduction to *Investigations in*

Currency and Finance, Jevons did not seek to show any exact correspondence between the solar cycle and the trade cycle, but only that the latter followed the former as a result of climatic effects on tropical harvests, which in turn affected European trade. Nevertheless, even this broad argument involved sequences of events which the time series data did not always support. It is difficult to deny the truth of Keynes's comment that Jevons passed over these difficulties 'with surprising levity' and that 'the details of the inductive argument are decidely flimsy'.[74]

Subsequent research, both into solar activity and economic activity, has not borne out the truth of Jevons's trade cycle theory, as he himself was convinced it ultimately would. Yet it must be remembered that at the time when he began to work on the subject even the existence of trade cycles was not well recognised, much less explained. The hypothesis which he put forward was a characteristically bold one, as well deserving of investigation as many others which were to be put forward in the ensuing half-century. And the immense volume of painstaking work which he did on time series, guided always by the concept of periodicity, entitles him to be ranked with Juglar as one of the ancestors of later business cycle analysis.[75]

(iii) *Economic policy and the role of the State*

It has been suggested above[76] that almost all Jevons's work in applied economics can be seen as fitting into the framework of two main ideas – the analysis of time series and the classification of trades and occupations. With the first of these ideas he succeeded to a remarkable degree in carrying into effect what he had planned at the time when he first began collecting materials for his Statistical Atlas. With the second he made less progress; he always cherished the idea of 'a true natural system of classifying trades' which would parallel in social science what had long existed in natural sciences like botany and geology. This was the basis of the work he began as early as 1856 'on Social Statistics or the Science of Towns, especially as regards London and Sydney' and he returned to it again near the end of his life when he was starting to work on his *Principles of Economics*.[77] His intention was to present a view of the industrial structure of society in terms of a cross-classification by orders and classes, but he confessed that 'after . . . twenty-five years, I have come to the conclusion that it is hopeless to attempt to draw any written or printed scheme of classification which could in the least degree cope with the complexities of industrial relations'.[78]

While Jevons thus did not achieve his aim of presenting a quantitative view of social structure, he did in the course of these years produce a number of qualitative studies in what would now be termed 'social economics'. Taken together these constitute a significant contribution to a line of enquiry for which Jevons himself stressed the need – 'a new branch of political and statistical science which shall carefully investigate the limits to the *laissez-faire* principle, and show where we want greater freedom and where less'.[79] Since Jevons's active years as an economist cover exactly the period which is often thought of as marking the breakdown of the laissez-faire doctrine, his writings on this and related topics have a particular interest, coming as they do between the better-known contributions of John Stuart Mill, on the one hand, and Sidgwick and Marshall, on the other.

If it be true, as Professor John M. Robson has said, that 'Mill is once and for all a utilitarian'[80] then Jevons's position on questions of economic and social policy was closer to Mill's than he probably would have cared to admit, for it was the utilitarian principle which he took as his guide in all such matters. As Wicksteed wrote, 'his determining principle was purely Benthamite. "Will a measure increase the sum of happiness?" was the only question which he would admit as ultimately relevant.'[81] In fact the utilitarian philosophy was in a sense the common factor linking Jevons's economic theory and his work on economic policy – in the one he employed the concepts of pleasure and pain and in the other the 'greatest happiness principle'.

Yet while 'the greatest good of the greatest number' was for Jevons always the deciding principle in matters of social and economic policy, beyond that he had little faith in the use of theory in such questions.

'In social philosophy, or rather in practical legislation', he held 'the first step is to throw aside all supposed absolute rights or inflexible principles. The fact is that legislation is not a science at all. . . . It is a matter of practical work, creating human institutions . . . there may be general sciences of ethics, of economics, of jurisprudence, which may much assist us in the work of legislation. But before we can bring the principles down to practice they run into infinite complications, and break up into all kinds of exceptions and apparent anomalies.'[82]

In the light of this approach, it is scarcely surprising that Jevons was 'not concerned very far with that analysis of economic principles in relation to State action on which Sidgwick was to found modern English "welfare" economics'.[83] He could not commit himself to either individualism or collectivism and reason from such a basic premise. Rather each individual case had to be judged on its merits – 'when followed out, this is the outcome of the Benthamist doctrine'.[84]

The quite considerable number of cases of State intervention which Jevons did examine can conveniently be grouped into two main categories – cases of State regulation of the economic activities of individuals and groups, and cases involving the State itself in undertaking economic activities. Under the first heading Jevons, like most of his contemporaries, started from the position that the State should merely uphold freedom of contract but he was prepared to endorse measures such as the inspection and branding of commodities 'when the individual is not able to exercise proper judgment and supervision on his own behalf'. Similarly he approved the restrictions on hours and conditions of labour contained in the Factory Acts, and was sceptical about the reasons for which they were not applied in his day to shop assistants and agricultural labourers.[85]

On the other hand, Jevons's attitude to trade unions was always critical. He was willing to concede their value in acting as friendly societies, and in making 'efforts to shorten the hours of labour to render factories more wholesome and safe, and generally to improve the conditions of the workman'. But he would not admit the desirability of trade unions making any attempts to regulate wages by collective bargaining, contending, with more logic than realism, that 'the rate of wages and the length of hours are two totally distinct things' and that those who demanded a reduction of hours should be willing to concede a proportionate reduction of wages.[86]

Not unnaturally the expression of views such as these brought upon Jevons some sharp attacks from the trade unionists of his day; his critics sometimes attributed to him a general and uncompromising hostility to trade unions and their purposes but Jevons was at pains to deny this and to assert that he was not 'involved in the prejudices of the capitalists'.[87] Certainly his views, which were always consistent both with his economic theory and his Benthamism, were as likely to disconcert capitalists as trade unionists. For while wage increases secured by union action were, to Jevons's mind, obtained at the expense of the community at large and would not therefore contribute to the greatest good of the greatest number, he saw considerable advantages not only in schemes of 'industrial partnership' between capital and labour but also in workers' co-operatives for production purposes.[88]

On the question of public versus private enterprise, Jevons also took a characteristically eclectic position:

My own strong opinion is that no abstract principle, and no absolute rule, can guide us in determining what kinds of industrial enterprise the State should undertake, and what it should not. State management and monopoly have most indisputable advantages; private commercial enterprise and responsibility have still more unquestionable advantages. The two are directly antagonistic. Nothing but experience and argument from experience can in most cases determine whether the community will be best served by its collective state action, or by trusting to private self-interest.[89]

Despite his reluctance to generalise about the limits to State enterprise, Jevons did lay down certain conditions under which he thought that State management would possess advantages:

(1) where numberless widespread operations can only be efficiently connected, united, and coordinated, in a single, all extensive Government system;
(2) where the operations possess an invariable routine-like character;
(3) where they are performed under the public eye or for the service of individuals, who will immediately detect any failure or laxity;
(4) where there is but little capital expenditure, so that each year's revenue and expense account shall represent, with sufficient accuracy, the real commercial conditions of the department.[90]

These conditions would be most fully realised in the case of the Post Office, and indeed Jevons implied that they were derived from a study of its characteristics. Working from these criteria, he contended that the State should take over the management of telegraphs and the parcel post (neither of which it operated at the time when he first wrote), but declared himself against nationalisation of the railways. 'The moment we consider the vast capital concerned in railways, and the intricacy of the mechanism and arrangements required to conduct the traffic, we must see the danger of management by a department of the English Government.'[91]

Such a form of public management was the only one which Jevons, in common with many of his contemporaries, could envisage and he could produce ample evidence to support his view 'that a Government department cannot compete in economy with an ordinary commercial firm subject to competition'.[92] Jevons would have been much ahead of his times if he had entered on any discussion of alternative forms of organisation for State trading; but his comments here raise the question of how far bodies such as railway companies are 'subject to competition'. This question of monopoly and its consequences was one to which Jevons gave but little attention. His general belief, however, appears to have been that railway companies and similar concerns did not use their powers against the public interest, but 'in whatever points exceptions to this favourable state of things can be shown to exist, Parliament ought to apply strong remedies'.[93]

Apart from the question of public versus private enterprise, Jevons also dealt fairly extensively with various aspects of what would nowadays be called the provision of public and quasi-public goods by the State. Again his position on such matters was eclectic. 'Free public infirmaries, dispensaries and hospitals' he deplored as tending 'to relax the habits of providence, which ought to be most carefully cultivated, and which cannot be better urged than with regard to the contingency of sickness.'[94] On the other hand he favoured generous public expenditure on education, on museums and on 'popular outdoor concerts' – all things which he considered would improve rather than undermine the character of the people.

That there is an element of Victorian complacency, a reminiscence of Samuel Smiles, in all this is undeniable. In his search for the methods of social reform which would accord with the greatest happiness principle, Jevons arrived at a position closely similar to that stated by John Stuart Mill – 'Laissez-faire the general rule – but liable to large exceptions'.[95] The number of exceptions to the rule which he was prepared to admit increased somewhat as he grew older; in 1876 while describing 'the laissez-faire principle' as 'the wholesome and true one' Jevons nevertheless argued that 'while population grows more numerous and dense, while industry becomes more complex and inter-dependent, as we travel faster and make use of more intense forces, we shall necessarily need more legislative supervision'.[96]

Nevertheless it seems undeniable that Jevons never went as far in favouring socialism and collectivism as even Mill did. Yet it does not follow that, as has recently been suggested,[97] Jevons fits the role of a 'vulgar bourgeois economist' who, apprehensive of working class demands for reform, designed his theory of value as an escape from the stark realities of the labour theory and an instrument of quietist propaganda. Perhaps enough has been said above to show that Jevons was an independent-minded individualist rather than a capitalist lackey; if further evidence is needed, consider the following quotations:

> One result which clearly emerges from a calm review is that all classes of society are trades unionists at heart and differ chiefly in the boldness, activity and secrecy with which they push their respective interests. . . . Legislation with regard to labour has almost always been class-legislation. It is the effort of some dominant body to keep down a lower class, which had begun to show inconvenient aspirations.[98]

These are scarcely the words one would expect to come from a vulgar apologist for the bourgeoisie; but they are the words of Jevons.

Conclusion

At the time of his death, Jevons had begun on 'what he regarded as "the work of his life" – the preparation of a book which he intended to call The Principles of Economics: A Treatise on the Industrial Mechanism of Society'.[99] Had he lived to complete it, would it have enlarged his contribution and enhanced his reputation as much as the publication of his Principles in 1890 did in Marshall's case? On this point, divergent views have in the past been expressed. Foxwell, who knew Jevons personally, saw him in the last years before his death as 'concentrating himself with ever-increasing interest and intensity upon his economics' and branching out in new directions in it;[100] Keynes looking back more than half a century later considered that 'his work was done. It was in the decade of his youth from 1857 to 1865 that he had genius and divine intuition and a burning sense of vocation. His flame was paler and less steady at the close.'[101] Between these opposite views it is impossible now to decide finally, but the available evidence gives more support to Keynes than to Foxwell.

Eventually though, what might have been is unimportant by comparison with what was. Considering the fact which has often been remarked,[102] that Jevons lost his life at an age by which other pioneers of modern economics such as Marshall and Edgeworth had not completed more than a small part of the works on which their reputation came to rest, the magnitude of his contribution is difficult to exaggerate. Prophetically, he foresaw the sub-division and specialisation of modern economics and in a number of its branches, both theoretical and applied, he made innovations which have proved of lasting significance.[103]

NOTES

1. J. M. Keynes, 'William Stanley Jevons 1835-1882. A Centenary Allocution on his Life and Work as Economist and Statistician', in *Essays in Biography*, repr. as vol. x of *Collected Writings* (London: Macmillan for the Royal Economic Society, 1972) [hereafter cited as *EB*] p. 131.
2. Journal of William Stanley Jevons, 16 January 1853, R. D. Collison Black and R. Könekamp (eds), *Papers and Correspondence of William Stanley Jevons* (London: Macmillan, 1972-7) [hereafter cited as *P&C*] vol. I. pp. 78-9.
3. Thomas Graham (1805-69), Professor of Chemistry at the Andersonian Institution, Glasgow (1830-7), then University College, London (1837-55) and Master of the Royal Mint (1855-69).
4. W. S. Jevons to Henrietta Jevons, 30 January 1859, *P&C*, vol. II, p. 362.
5. W. S. Jevons to T. E. Jevons, October 1880, *P&C*, vol. v, p. 110.
6. W. S. Jevons to H. S. Foxwell, 30 November 1880, *P&C*, vol. v, p. 117.
7. W. S. Jevons, *Theory of Political Economy* (2nd edn, 1879; repr. London: Pelican. 1970) [hereafter cited as *TPF*] p. 50.

8. *P&C*, vol. VI (*Lectures on Political Economy 1875-1876*) p. 3.
9. Journal of W. S. Jevons, 13 September 1856. *P&C*, vol. I, p. 133.
10. R. D. Collison Black, 'Jevons, Bentham and De Morgan', *Economica*, XXXIX (1972) 119-34.
10. *TPE*, pp. 87-8. This particular passage first appeared in the second edition of the *Theory*, after Jevons had written the *Principles of Science*. For a fuller discussion of Jevons's view of the relation between the method of economics and that of other sciences, see W. Mays, 'Jevons's Conception of Scientific Method', *Manchester School*, XXX (1962) 223-50.
11. Augustus De Morgan (1806-71), Professor of Mathematics at University College, London (1828-66). For some account of Jevons's studies under De Morgan, see Black, 'Jevons, Bentham and De Morgan', op. cit., pp. 131-4.
12. *TPE*, ch. IV, p. 126.
13. Ibid., p. 187.
14. Introduction to *TPE*, pp. 17-19.
15. *TPE*, p. 226.
16. P. R. Brahmananda, 'Jevons's *Theory of Political Economy* – A Centennial Appraisal', *Indian Economic Journal*, XIX (1972) 128.
17. Cf. *TPE*, pp. 203-5 and 222-4.
18. J. R. Hicks, 'Capital Controversies: Ancient and Modern', *American Economic Review*, LXIV (1974) 309.
19. *TPE*, p. 46.
20. Gavin C. Reid, 'Jevons's Treatment of Dimensionality in the *Theory of Political Economy*: An Essay in the History of Mathematical Economics', *Manchester School*, XL (1972) 85-98; R. Shone, 'On Dimensionality in Economics', University of Stirling Discussion Paper 54 (1978).
21. P. Newman, *The Theory of Exchange* (Englewood Cliffs, NJ: Prentice-Hall, 1965) p. 80.
22. P. H. Wicksteed, 'Jevons's Economic Work', *Economic Journal*, XV (1905) 435; rept. in L. Robbins (ed.), *The Common Sense of Political Economy* [hereafter cited as *CSPE*], vol. II (London: Routledge, 1933) p. 812. Recently, some commentators have sought to emphasise the differences between the thought of Jevons and Menger, rather than the similarities which Wicksteed stressed. On this, see H. N. Gram and V. C. Walsh, 'Menger and Jevons in the Setting of post-von Neumann–Sraffa Economics', *Atlantic Economic Journal*, VI (1978) 45-56.
23. J. M. Buchanan, *Cost and Choice* (Chicago: Markham, 1969) p. 43.
24. C. W. Noller, 'Jevons on Cost', *Southern Economic Journal*, XXXIX (1972-3) 113.
25. *TPE*, p. 188.
26. W. S. Jevons, *The Principles of Science* (2nd edn, London, 1877; repr. New York: Dover Press, 1958) [hereafter cited as *PS*] p. 12.
27. R. Könekamp, Biographical Introduction, *P&C*, vol. I, p. 35.
28. Journal of W. S. Jevons, 8 December 1861, *P&C*, vol. I, p. 180.
29. This quotation is taken from Jevons's posthumous *Principles of*

Economics (London: Macmillan, 1905) [hereafter cited as *PE*] p. 104, but the idea dates back to his *Notes and Researches on Social Statistics, or the Science of Towns*, commenced in 1856.

30. H. E. Roscoe to W. S. Jevons, 1 February 1858, *P&C*, vol. II, p. 316.
31. J. M. Keynes, *EB*, p. 119.
32. T. Tooke and W. Newmarch, *A History of Prices from 1792 to the Present Time* (London: Longmans, 1838–57).
33. W. S. Jevons to Herbert Jevons, 18 February 1864, H. A. Jevons (ed.), *Letters and Journal of W. Stanley Jevons* (London: Macmillan, 1886) p. 195.
34. *The Coal Question*, 3rd edn (London: Macmillan, 1906) [hereafter cited as *CQ*] pp. 9–11.
35. *CQ*, pp. 447–8.
36. Sir John Herschel to W. S. Jevons, 23 November 1865, *P&C*, vol. III, p. 77.
37. Gladstone to Macmillan, 24 February 1866, *P&C*, vol. I, p. 203.
38. H. S. Jevons, *The British Coal Trade* (London: Kegan Paul, 1915) pp. 722–3.
39. *CQ*, pp. 194–5.
40. Keynes, *EB*, p. 259.
41. *CQ*, Preface, p. xxxii.
42. *CQ*, p. 272; Michael P. Jackson, *The Price of Coal* (London: Croom Helm, 1974) p. 192.
43. Coke and other solid fuel accounted for another 15 per cent – ibid., p. 193.
44. Of petroleum, Jevons wrote that 'its natural supply is far more limited and uncertain than that of coal' and added that 'to the extent to which this country relies on imported supplies of fuel oils, it ceases to occupy the position of advantage, relative to other industrial countries, conferred by its extensive deposits of excellent and accessible coal' (*CQ*, pp. 184–5).
45. *CQ*, p. 188. (Italics as in original.)
46. *CQ*, p. 158.
47. W. S. Jevons to T. E. Jevons, 8 July 1881, *P&C*, vol. V, p. 143.
48. W. S. Jevons to Herbert Jevons, 1 June 1860 and 7 April 1861, *P&C*, vol. II, pp. 410 and 425.
49. I am glad to acknowledge here my indebtedness to Mrs Barbara Lowe, of Cambridge, who, while compiling the index to *P&C*, drew my attention to the central importance of the idea of periodicity throughout Jevons's writings, both published and unpublished.
50. *P&C*, vol. II, p. 427, and *Investigations in Currency and Finance* (London: Macmillan, 1884) [hereafter cited as *ICF*] p. 224.
51. The first was the now much better known 'Brief Account of a General Mathematical Theory of Political Economy'.
52. 'On the Study of Periodic Commercial Fluctuations', *ICF*, p. 4.
53. W. S. Jevons to Herbert Jevons, 18 January 1863, *P&C*, vol. III, p. 4.
54. The fact that this was first published in April 1863 by Edward

Stanford is a remarkable indication of the rapidity and intensity with which Jevons was working at this period. The work is repr. in full in *ICF*, pp. 13–118.

55. Preface to *A Serious Fall*; repr. in *ICF*, p. 16.
56. J. M. Keynes, *EB*, p. 120. A recent commentator, Professor S. M. Stigler, has perhaps given a better balanced summary view of Jevons's contribution to statistics:

> Jevons was also a great statistician, in the sense the term was used in the 1860s. While he was not the originator of index numbers and graphical displays, at least Jevons realized their potential and pursued them with a perspicacity far beyond his predecessors', and he displayed such keen good sense in the analysis of large quantities of data that we can still today describe him as a statistician without apology or serious qualification. If there was any nineteenth-century empirical social scientist who could have been expected to develop the techniques of the theory of errors into tools for the quantification of uncertainty in social sciences it was W. Stanley Jevons. But he did not.

Stephen M. Stigler, 'Francis Ysidro Edgeworth, Statistician', *Journal of the Royal Statistical Society* [hereafter cited as *JRSS*], series A, CXLI (1978) 287–8.

57. *ICF*, p. 95.
58. *JRSS*, XXVIII (1865) 294–320; repr. in *ICF*, pp. 119–50.
59. Cf. *Money and the Mechanism of Exchange* (London: Kegan Paul, 1875) p. 82; *Primer of Political Economy* (London: Macmillan, 1878) p. 106.
60. *TPE*, p. 200. For comment on the relation between Jevons's approach to the theory of value and the theory of money, see W. E. Mason, *Clarification of the Monetary Standard* (University Park, Pa.: Pennsylvania State University Press, 1963) pp. 58–62. In attempting to explain what he calls 'the Jevonsonian Paradox', Professor Mason has, to my mind, been led to under-rate substantially the originality of Jevons's contributions to the theory of value.
61. 'An Ideally Perfect System of Currency', *ICF* (1875) p. 297. Intended as a concluding section in *Money and the Mechanism of Exchange*, this short paper was not in fact published until after Jevons's death. No doubt this is the reason for Professor F. W. Fetter's statement (*Development of British Monetary Orthodoxy* [Cambridge, Mass.: Harvard University Press, 1965] p. 248) that Jevons 'wrote but did not publish a proposal for a tabular standard of value', but in fact ch. XXV of *Money*, entitled 'A Tabular Standard of Value' contains a discussion in which Jevons's approval of such a standard is made clear.
62. *JRSS*, XXIX (1866) 235–53; repr. in *ICF*, pp. 160–93.
63. *ICF*, p. 28. (Italics as in original.) See also W. S. Jevons to Herbert Jevons, 7 April 1861, *P&C*, vol. II, p. 427.

64. See his comments on R. S. Moffat's *The Economy of Consumption* in a letter to W. Jack, 28 March 1877, *P&C*, vol. IV, p. 193.
65. W. S. Jevons, *PS*, vol. II, pp. 66–7.
66. 'The Solar Period and the Price of Corn', *ICF*, pp. 194–5. This paper was originally read to Section F of the British Association at Bristol in 1875, but Jevons withdrew it from publication when he became dissatisfied with the method he had used.
67. J. E. Thorold Rogers, *A History of Agriculture and Prices in England*, vols I and II (Oxford: Clarendon Press, 1866).
68. *ICF*, p. 203.
69. W. S. Jevons to J. Mills, 3 January 1877, *P&C*, vol. IV, pp. 188–9.
70. Cf. W. S. Jevons to J. Mills, 11 February 1878; *P&C*, vol. IV, p. 228. John Mills (1821–96), a Manchester banker, wrote much on what he called 'the Credit Cycle', stressing its decennial period but attributing it, as Pigou was later to do, to alternations of optimism and pessimism in the business community. Others who had recognised the existence of a decennial cycle, and whose work was known to Jevons, included James Wilson, of *The Economist*, William Langton, another Manchester banker, and the now almost forgotten polymath Hyde Clarke; cf. *ICF*, pp. 222–4.
71. J. A. Broun, 'On the Decennial Period in the Range and Disturbance of the Decennial Oscillations of the Magnetic Needle and in the Sunspot Area', *Transactions of the Royal Society of Edinburgh*, XXVII (1876) 563; W. W. Hunter and N. Lockyer, 'Sunspots and Famines', *Nineteenth Century*, II (1877) 583–602. Although Jevons first presented this version of his sunspot theory fully in the paper entitled 'The Periodicity of Commercial Crises and its Physical Explanation' read to the British Association in August 1878, he had earlier given an indication of it in the chapter on 'Credit Cycles' in his *Primer of Political Economy*, see esp. p. 120.
72. W. S. Jevons, letter to the editor of *The Times*, 17 January 1879; repr. in *P&C*, vol. V, pp. 10–11.
73. *P&C*, vol. V, p. 10.
74. Keynes, *EB*, p. 126.
75. J. A. Schumpeter, *History of Economic Analysis* (London: Allen & Unwin, 1955) p. 1124. The considerable influence which Jevons's theory had on later contributors to trade cycle analysis deserves to be remembered. D. H. Robertson ranked it with the work of Aftalion as 'the most suggestive contribution ever made to a constructive theory of fluctuations' – *Economic Journal*, XXIV (1914) p. 88 – while Keynes in the *General Theory*, described it as 'an extremely plausible approach to the problem'.
   Keynes did not concern himself with the validity or otherwise of the sunspot hypothesis but pointed out that 'even today fluctuation in the stocks of agricultural products as between one year and another is one of the largest individual items amongst the causes of changes in the rate of current investment: whilst at the time when Jevons wrote – and more particularly over the period to which most

of his statistics applied – this factor must have far outweighed all others' (*General Theory of Employment, Interest and Money: Collected Works*, vol. VII, p. 329). I am indebted to Dr J. R. Presley for drawing my attention to Robertson's comment.

76. See p. 12.
77. See pp. vii and viii of Henry Higgs's Introduction to Jevons's *Principles of Economics* (1905) (n 29 above) and ch. XXIII of the text.
78. *PE*, p. 115.
79. 'The Future of Political Economy', Introductory Lecture at the opening of the session 1876–77, University College, London; repr. in *PE*, p. 204.
80. J. M. Robson, *The Improvement of Mankind, the Social and Political Thought of John Stuart Mill* (Toronto: Toronto University Press, 1968) p. 118.
81. P. H. Wicksteed, 'Jevons, William Stanley' in Palgrave's *Dictionary of Political Economy*, vol. II (London: Macmillan, 1910) pp. 474–8; repr. in *CSPE*, vol. II, p. 806.
82. W. S. Jevons, *The State in Relation to Labour* (London: Macmillan, 1882) [hereafter cited as *SRL*] pp. 9–10.
83. T. W. Hutchison, *A Review of Economic Doctrines 1870–1929* (Oxford: Clarendon Press, 1953) p. 47.
84. *SRL*, p. 17.
85. *SRL*, pp. 86–90.
86. W. S. Jevons, 'Trade Societies: Their Objects and Policy' (1868) in *Methods of Social Reform* (London: Macmillan, 1883) [hereafter cited as *MSR*] p. 107.
87. *MSR*, p. 102.
88. *SRL*, pp. 143–51; and cf. W. S. Jevons's letter to the editor of the *Manchester City News*, 3 November 1866, *P&C*, vol. III, p. 138.
89. W. S. Jevons, 'On the Analogy between the Post Office, Telegraphs, and Other Systems of Conveyance of the United Kingdom, as Regards Government Control' (1867) in *MSR*, p. 267.
90. *MSR*, pp. 279–80.
91. *MSR*, p. 289.
92. *MSR*, p. 305.
93. 'The Railways and the State' (from *Essays and Addresses, by Professors and Lecturers of Owens College Manchester* 1874) repr. in *MSR*, p. 382.
94. W. S. Jevons, 'Inaugural Address as President of the Manchester Statistical Society', (1869) *MSR*, p. 189.
95. These are the headings to sections 7 and 8 of Book V, chapter XI of Mill's *Principles* – 'Of the Grounds and Limits of the Laissez-faire or Non-Interference Principle'.
96. 'The Future of Political Economy', *PE*, pp. 203–4. One interesting example of Jevons's changing attitudes can be found in the case of arbitration and conciliation. In 1870 he wrote 'I have never been able to persuade myself that arbitration . . . is a theoretically sound measure' (*MSR*, p. 124). But in 1882, after referring to his own

Theory of Political Economy and to Edgeworth's *Mathematical Psychics* he concluded 'It would appear, then, that, even on the grounds of pure economic theory, there are reasons why a conciliator might be properly called in to resolve an industrial deadlock', *SRL*, p. 159.

97. G. Routh, *The Origin of Economic Ideas* (London: Macmillan, 1975) pp. 203–11.
98. *SRL*, pp. viii and 35.
99. Henry Higgs, editor's Preface to *PE*, p.v.
100. H. S. Foxwell, Introduction to *ICF*, p. xix.
101. Keynes, *EB*, p. 146.
102. Cf. Hutchison, op. cit., p. 49.
103. For a fuller development of this point see R. D. Collison Black, 'W. S. Jevons and the Foundation of Modern Economics', in Black, Coats and Goodwin (eds), *The Marginal Revolution in Economics* (Durham, NC: Duke University Press, 1973) esp. pp. 105–12.

2 A. Marshall, 1842–1924

D. P. O'BRIEN

Introduction – biographia

The main facts of Marshall's life are well-known, and are set out in the very fine account given by Keynes who worked from material supplied by Mrs Marshall.[1] Alfred Marshall was born on 26 July 1842. Rebelling against a parental preference for classics and the Church, he went to St. John's College, Cambridge, read mathematics, and graduated as Second Wrangler in 1865. A period spent as a Fellow of St John's led him to economics and to marriage with Mary Paley, one of the pioneer women undergraduates at Cambridge. The years 1877–82 were spent at Bristol University College, chiefly as its principal. After a short spell at Oxford, Marshall was elected to the Chair of Political Economy at Cambridge, taking up the post in January 1885 and holding it until his retirement in 1908 when he was followed by his chosen successor A. C. Pigou. Greatly revered as the leading economist in the Anglo-Saxon world he died on 13 July 1924.

Marshall pursued a lifetime of literary labour. His first book, written jointly with his wife, appeared in 1879 as the *Economics of Industry*. Although Marshall disliked the book it had sold over 15,000 copies by his death and since then has sold about another 23,000. It was followed in 1890 by his *Principles of Economics* which ran through eight editions up to 1920, had sold 37,000 copies at the time of his death, and has since sold another 95,000. The book was intended to be the first volume of a large work, and Marshall's ambition was partially realised with the publication in 1919 of *Industry and Trade* of which 12,000 had been sold by his death, with a further 4,000 sold subsequently, and by the publication in 1923 of his *Money, Credit and Commerce* of which 7,000 were printed prior to his death, with another 2,000 subsequently.[2] Yet even that was not intended to be the end; in extreme old age he was contemplating a fourth major work.[3]

His marriage, though childless, was happy. The impression which

36

emerges from the accounts of contemporaries is of a shy, rather timid man, devoid of a sense of humour.[4] Yet, with the aid of a legacy of £250, he set off for a trip to the United States in 1875 and was bold enough to visit – and report on – the Wild West.[5] Moreover he engaged in a certain amount of newspaper controversy (a fact which has not been fully appreciated because the Keynes bibliography is incomplete) although he had the bitterest distaste for controversy. He also engaged in controversies within the University of Cambridge, vigorously opposing degrees for women. But he was essentially a thinker and a writer, not an administrator or man of affairs; and it is, for the most part, the extraordinarily diverse tapestry of his writing on economics which makes him chiefly interesting.

Sources and methods

(i) *Sources*

Marshall owed a clear debt to his classical predecessors and it was one which he was anxious to acknowledge. He defended the classical economists vigorously against their latter-day critics especially Jevons and Böhm-Bawerk.[6] His most important debt was undoubtedly to J. S. Mill who influenced not only Marshall's theoretical apparatus, which developed from the application of mathematics to Mill, but also his policy attitudes. His first book is indeed avowedly *an introduction to* J. S. Mill. But a wide range of classical writers influenced Marshall, including Smith, Ricardo, Overstone and McCulloch. Of course Marshall was also influenced by a number of continental writers, especially Cournot, and Von Thünen, and also by Dupuit and the German Historical school.[7] But his attitude to Jevons, to whom he owed his utility analysis, was, for a long time, hostile, and it was only relatively late that Marshall mellowed.[8]

Marshall's general approach, with its emphasis upon continuity, was significantly influenced by the philosopher Hegel and also by Spencer. Of course it is true that Schumpeter has claimed that these influences were so much excess baggage which could be ignored.[9] But it is not easy to sustain this view without taking a narrowly neoclassical view of Marshall's work – which would leave one holding the tautological position that what we choose to ignore is unimportant.

The same point may be made about the influence of Darwin, which led Marshall to look towards biology as providing the way forward in economic methodology and to emphasise the evolving nature of economic phenomena.

(ii) *Methodology*

The influence of Darwin was shown in the first of Marshall's two methodological mottos '*Natura non facit saltum*' (Nature does not make jumps).[10] But perhaps even more important was Marshall's other motto 'The many in the one, and the one in the many'.[11] By this Marshall meant that there are many different forces and causes acting to produce one economic phenomenon which we observe; while these forces and causes are not unique to each case but reappear in different guises throughout the world of economic phenomena. This led him to the conclusion that there must be continuous study of the real world, with the aim of finding a few fundamental principles; but it also led him to lay great emphasis upon the importance of factual material and the particular details of each case, for only in this way could the relative importance of the multiplicity of causes be judged. This was associated with Marshall's emphasis upon the importance of observation; he believed that good methodology followed the eighteenth-century procedure of an inextricable intertwining of induction and deduction. The deduction should only involve short chains of reasoning and there should be a constant return to the facts for verification.[12]

Yet there is something of a puzzle in all this. For Marshall followed his own methodological pronouncements somewhat incompletely. There is an important statement in an article by Marshall of 1885[13] in which he wrote out the following expression:

$$\frac{dU}{dt} = \frac{dU}{dX} \cdot \frac{dX}{dt} + \frac{dU}{dY} \cdot \frac{dY}{dt} + \frac{dU}{dZ} \cdot \frac{dZ}{dt}$$

(where the derivatives on the right-hand side are partial)

and then explained that time series observations supplied

$$\frac{dX}{dt}, \frac{dY}{dt}, \ldots, \quad \text{while theory supplied} \quad \frac{dU}{dX}, \frac{dU}{dY}, \ldots$$

Such a statement would seem to point the way towards development of the eighteenth-century chain of reasoning in conjunction with modern collection of statistics and modern statistical and mathematical methods. Yet Marshall did not follow this road. Despite his view that the nineteenth century had completed the main qualitative tasks in economics, and that the need was now for quantitative analysis, he did not himself do empirical work except through the collection of descriptive material as in *Industry and Trade*. Although he looked forward to such things as the development of empirical studies of demand, and although he collected a great deal of factual information, he did little empirical work of the kind which he said was required, although he used statistical evidence before the Indian Currency Commission and although he constructed a book of time series with a common time axis for his private use.[14]

His methodological ideals led him to adopt a rather deprecatory attitude towards pure theory.[15] He roundly condemned the claims of pure theory to be economics proper; and even his attitude towards mathematics was ambivalent. He was originally trained as a mathematician and was probably, at one time, a good one, although there are differing views on this. He seems to have regarded mathematical training as valuable but to have doubted the usefulness of mathematics in economics. As is well known, he believed that if the results of mathematical economics could not be translated into English they should be burned. The question was not whether it was possible to use mathematics in economics; it was whether it was useful to do so. But there is no doubt that Marshall himself became rather rusty as a mathematician even though his work in the 1870s shows that his early development as an economist owed a great deal to his mathematical training. None the less, the view that he constructed an entire mathematical skeleton for the *Principles*, and then simply clothed it with factual material, is surely no longer tenable.[16]

There were, in any case, characteristics of his whole approach which would have predisposed him against the kind of simple models to which mathematics led. These included the importance of time, his concern with *movements to* equilibrium, and, perhaps most fundamental, his insistence that the whole subject matter of economics involved evolutionary phenomena.

(iii) *Economics as a science*

All this did not prevent Marshall viewing economics as a science – and one for which he was prepared, if necessary, to make very large claims. It should aspire to the same status as the physical sciences even though it was hampered by an inability to experiment.[17] It is arguable that his emphasis on this waned with time; the early *Economics of Industry* is full of 'Laws', some of them very dubious. But though the emphasis may have become less, Marshall did not abandon this position.

To advance the science of economics it was perfectly proper to use such devices as static analysis – though this must not be pushed too far – and partial equilibrium. In the latter connection Marshall was responsible for making explicit the device of *coeteris paribus* which had frequently been implied in classical discussions but not often made explicit. Partial analysis was significantly advanced by Marshall.[18] Nevertheless he was well aware that general equilibrium considerations were sometimes unavoidable, especially in the context of distribution. But he was concerned about the almost total lack of useable content in general equilibrium analysis.[19]

Economic laws would, subject to *coeteris paribus*, produce, 'normal' results. By 'normal' Marshall meant competitive, although the realisation that competition had to be conducted within a framework of some sort seems to have led him to a change of mind which was more apparent than real, in that he came to stress the limitations – of law and custom – on competition under which normality could be achieved.[20]

Marshall drew very wide boundaries for the science of economics, including most things which were subject to the measuring rod of money, and a number that were not.[21] He distinguished, like Senior, between the science of economics and the art of economics, the latter drawing on the results of science but requiring a substantial measure of common sense as well.[22] He also distinguished between normative and positive economics. Yet he systematically ignored these distinctions in his own work, which is full of ethical considerations. These include not only Marshall's pet aversions – alcohol, gambling and lavish personal expenditure – as well as his reverence for motherhood, but also his interests in social reform. He was interested in the limits and benefits of state intervention, of cooperation, and of redistribution, because of the evils resulting from 'excessive' freedom and competition without sufficient regulation, and because of the conflicts which arose between public and private interests.[23] He was, however, in the last resort an individualist; and he was very concerned about the dangers of collectivism and corruption.[24] But all these considerations appear in the broad tapestry of his economic writings.

Demand theory

Perhaps the most important single point about Marshall's demand analysis is that it starts with the prior existence of the negatively-sloped market demand curve. This is initially explained by reference to income distribution. Given the curve, it was natural to explore its properties and this led to Marshall's (subjective) invention, and development, of elasticity, together with an analysis of its determinants. Because the curve was a partial one, and because other things could not be expected to remain equal over time, Marshall concentrated his analysis on the short run.[25]

Marshall's utility analysis, which involved the theory of the maximising consumer, clearly comes after the demand curve and owes a good deal to Jevons. We start from an analysis of wants and the idea that utility is the basis of consumption. We then have a statement of eventually diminishing marginal utility (as the utility of the marginal purchase rather than as the derivative of the utility function) leading to the derivation of the demand curve from diminishing marginal utility. This provided us with the demand curve for the individual.[26] For each individual taken in isolation, price paid is a measure of his marginal utility, though Marshall continually emphasised that a shilling had a different marginal utility for a poor man and for a rich man. The now familiar equilibrium of the consumer is obtained and this is extended to inter-temporal maximisation without discounting of future benefits both for futurity and uncertainty. Intra-temporal and inter-temporal maximisation are then combined.[27] However, for this Marshall used an additive utility function which possesses all the properties and limitations which have been explored at great length in the secondary literature; and, as we shall see, he treated the marginal utility of money as a quasi-constant. Despite awareness of the problems involved, he was, in general, quite prepared to sum the demand curves of individuals to produce a market demand curve and to suggest that, although individual purchases might be discontinuous, in the aggregate they produced a smooth curve.[28]

The utility analysis was linked with his initially high hopes for the development of consumer surplus. As is now well-known, the failure of this concept to prove sufficiently robust for his purposes was one of the great disappointments of his life.[29] So aware was he of the difficulties associated with it that on only one occasion did he throw caution to the wind and estimate consumer surplus.[30] It was defined by Marshall as the now familiar area underneath the demand curve and above the prevailing price.[31] The difficulties with it were formidable. The consumer surplus obtained from one commodity was not independent of the supply of another – Marshall illustrated this with the example of being deprived of both tea and coffee. Secondly, there was the problem of treating this area, which had a money value, as measuring utility – which relied upon a constant marginal utility of money. Thirdly, there was a danger of double counting. Because of these problems it was difficult to aggregate over one individual's consumption of a wide range of commodities while aggregation over the community – moving the apostrophe so that consumer's surplus becomes consumers' – posed even more serious problems. For the integral concerned cannot be a utility (as distinct from a money) measure in the presence of differences in the marginal utility of money income – the existence of which Marshall had recognised publicly since the 1879 *Economics of Industry*. Moreover there are insoluble general equilibrium limitations on using consumer surplus, derived from partial analysis, as a community welfare tool.[32]

The problem which has attracted most attention in the literature however is that of the assumption of constant marginal utility of money. In fact Marshall made this only for convenience; and in other contexts he was prepared to say that it was not justified, or even to make a completely different assumption – Bernoulli's hypothesis that equal percentage increases in income produced equal absolute increases in utility – in order to analyse the particular problem of gambling.[33] Nevertheless, though Marshall's careful and selective use of this particular assumption of constancy was sensible, there are so many different difficulties associated with the concept of consumer surplus, especially in the context of the broad canvas on which Marshall painted, involving, as it did, changing tastes, to make its use as an operational tool highly questionable. In view of these difficulties it is hardly surprising that Marshall lost heart. He had originally hoped that the qualifications applied less strongly to what are now known as the 'Marshallian Triangles' relating to small price and quantity changes, and that the concept might be operationally useful in that kind of context.[34] Yet, although he apparently lost heart, he continued to reproduce, in successive editions of the *Principles*, material, dating from the 1870s, which relied for its validity upon these problems having been solved. Of course he warned his readers against taking the analysis too literally; and he was worried about the implications drawn from it by Pigou.[35] But this was one development over which he ultimately became discouraged.

None the less there is no doubt that Marshall significantly influenced the development of demand analysis. But the main thrust of his contribution to microeconomics concerned problems of supply.

Supply

To Marshall we owe the universal use of the supply curve. This is built up from the supply prices of the services of factors, including gross earnings of management, in a Representative Firm rather than a Marginal Firm.[36] The costs incurred are divided into fixed and variable costs – Marshall led the profession into following accountancy practice – and are money costs, although there is some (imprecise) relation between money and real (i.e. disutility) costs. However there are rents *below* the supply curve, as well as between it and the prevailing price, because of differential efficiencies – Marshall embodied this notion in a concept called the Particular Expenses Curve.[37]

Marshall extensively analysed the supply conditions affecting each of the factors of production, which he classified as land, labour, capital, and organisation.[38] Supply of labour is affected by the growth of population, its health and strength, industrial training and labour mobility which leads, somewhat imperfectly, to equalisation of net advantage.[39] Supply of capital depends on the strength of sources of accumulation and of the motives to save. There is positive time preference in the aggregate and the cost of this 'waiting' has to be covered as part of the normal cost of production.[40]

Marshall's discussion of land is characterised by a wholly classical emphasis on diminishing returns – which might be offset by technical progress – and a tendency to confuse these with decreasing returns to scale and to contrast them with increasing returns. This was despite the fact that he ultimately conceded that they were not the same, and despite the fact also that he generalised the concept of diminishing returns to all factors.[41] It was central to the search for optimal factor combinations by the entrepreneur – dependent upon relative factor prices and productivities – which Marshall called the Principle of Substitution.[42] Two particular points about this are of interest; first, Marshall's discussion did not involve a fixed and unique production function;[43] secondly, he managed to perpetuate the curious classical error that rent did not enter into supply price, despite recognising the existence of transfer earnings.[44]

The fourth factor of production was entrepreneurship or organisation. Marshall attached very great importance to the role of the specialised entrepreneur who was a man with organisational ability in command of capital and who was also the risk bearer. Risk was part of supply price.[45]

It is however important to understand that, for Marshall, supply price is *not* governed by marginal cost as ordinarily understood – though the idea that it is, is commonplace in the secondary literature. For marginal cost is of a different nature from the mathematical concept now familiar. It is the marginal cost of a process and not of a product. Price is determined with respect to large discrete changes in output not (in Marshall's phrase) 'each separate small parcel'. Moreover there are *no* unique costs associated with particular products in a multi product firm.[46]

Central to Marshall's treatment of the firm itself was his concept of the Representative Firm. Marshall envisaged that there was a range of firms from the very powerful to the marginal, and used the Representative Firm, one in the middle of the spectrum, as a device for analysing the response of the industry to a change in conditions facing it. Firms experience a life cycle, and during the course of this they pass through the stage at which they are representative of the industry – the trees of the forest simile.[47] Increase in demand facing the industry will then increase the growth of the rising firms and slow the decay of the falling firms, resulting in an increase in total production.

Competition is important; but it is *not* perfect. Each firm was envisaged as selling in the general market and also to particular customers with whom it had a special relationship.[48] Marshall provided the elements for the construction of the theory of imperfect competition.[49] He examined many of the factors which have become prominent in later discussions of market power such as product-differentiation, advertising, barriers to entry, limit pricing, loss leaders and tying clauses.[50] He envisaged significant oligopolistic inter-dependence between firms, especially where there was a high ratio of fixed to variable costs.[51] He also analysed monopoly at length, and provided a theoretical treatment from which it is only a small, and mathematically trivial, step to reach the analysis of the 1930s. However he also emphasised the conditional nature of monopoly and the limits to maximising behaviour by monopolists, as well as price discrimination and the allocation of overheads according to elasticity and the possibilities of regulation – though not nationalisation.[52] His attitude to cartels was somewhat ambivalent, because he saw a conflict between the advantages of cooperation and the dangers of market power.[53] He was also concerned about the dangers of bureaucracy in large firms, especially joint stock companies, and exercised about the threat to small companies whom he regarded as important in relation to innovation.[54]

The large capitals of joint stock companies afforded them access to economies of scale which gave them particular advantages. Marshall's discussion of these, and their division into internal and external economies is well known, and constitutes a major contribution. External economies, available to all firms, did not represent a threat to competition; but internal economies did so and Marshall eventually relied upon marketing difficulties, managerial diseconomies, the life cycle of the firm, and the mortality of entrepreneurship, as explanations for what he *observed* to be the case – that monopoly had not become the main industrial form.[55]

An important aspect of Marshall's analysis relates to time. Although it is well known that Marshall regarded the length of time in which supply had to adjust to a change in demand as critical, it has not often been recognised that the long run supply curve, as envisaged by Marshall, had a time dimension as well as a quantity one, and that progress along it involved both these variables. Such a device permitted Marshall to include technical change in a downward sloping curve; but it involved the cost that he had to view the supply curve as irreversible, which may partly explain his reluctance to use elasticity of supply as a concept parallel with that of elasticity of demand.[56]

Value theory

In the preceding two sections the elements which Marshall used to construct the blades of his famous scissors were discussed. It should be clear however that these blades were complex constructions; Marshall would not have countenanced the idea that they could be fitted simply together and used to cut, without difficulty, through any value problem:

> changes in the volume of production, in its methods, and in its cost are ever mutually modifying one another; they are always affecting and being affected by the character and the extent of demand. Further all these mutual influences take time to work themselves out, and, as a rule, no two influences move at equal pace. In this world therefore every plain and simple doctrine as to the relations between cost of production, demand and value is necessarily false.[57]

Nevertheless Marshall devoted some attention to the interaction of demand and supply. His treatment starts, as so often with Marshall, from J. S. Mill. Value is defined as relative price at a particular time and place, and it depends upon both demand and supply – hence the scissors. The emphasis is upon mutual determination – following Cournot – and Marshall made clear that he believed the demand-oriented approach of Jevons to be even more faulty than the supply-oriented approach of Ricardo. A market is defined as an area of price uniformity; and the extent of the market depends upon such matters as uniformity and portability of the commodity, information, and the existence of an extensive demand.[58]

Adjustment to equilibrium within the market takes time. This was an early obsession of Marshall – although it really only required the further development of the distinction between the market and the long period in classical economics – and it ultimately led to a treatment which has found its way into all the textbooks. However, Marshall's detailed exploration of market clearing in the case of a commodity, such as corn, with a fixed supply has received a good deal less attention than it really deserves. Closely linked to his discussion of this is the question of stability. As is well known, Marshall relied upon quantity adjustment to achieve equilibrium of normal demand and supply. Marshall's industrial wanderings were perhaps responsible for his possessing a much greater awareness than some of his contemporaries, especially Walras, of the problems associated with equilibrium and, in particular, of the possibilities of multiple equilibria and the difficulties introduced by the recognition that neither long run demand nor supply were truly reversible. At the same time, as D. G. Davis has pointed out, it is not true that Marshall relied solely upon a quantity adjustment model; in his analysis of the corn market he used a price adjustment model. But Marshall's use of quantity adjustment surely makes better sense in terms of the maximising producer than Walras' rather simple *tâtonnement* based, as it probably was, on a country market at Evreux.[59]

The achievement of equilibrium in the market would result in 'normal' value. There were two kinds of normal value; a short run normal value and a long run normal value – a concept derived from Adam Smith – which would only be achieved in the unlikely circumstances of stationary conditions existing over a long period. 'Normal' values for Marshall meant values achieved by competitive forces within the constraints of law and custom – though he came to believe that his increased emphasis on the latter constituted a change of mind.[60]

Marshall also dealt with other problems affecting value. He noted the influence of expectations on value; and he dealt at great length with problems of joint demand and joint supply. His concern with this problem, and much of his treatment of it, stemmed from J. S. Mill; and it would probably be true to say that Marshall left the matter in a somewhat unsatisfactory state. His analysis has been strongly criticised by Stigler; but it would be fair to say that he did not make strong claims for it and that he was aware that there were serious problems with the exposition as it stood.[61]

The main thrust of Marshall's value theory was, then, an attempt to explore the achievement of equilibrium in different time periods through the integration of the supply analysis which he had developed with the demand theory which owed much to the influence of Jevons and, to a lesser extent, Menger. This was a substantial achievement; it significantly affected the development of mainstream value theory and all subsequent expositions owe something to Marshall, though they have tended increasingly to side-step the really interesting problems concerning adjustment which he raised. His own use of the tools in a practical context was limited[62] – at least outside his advanced lectures – but he had achieved, to a considerable extent, his main aim of forging the tools for his successors.

Distribution

Marshall's distribution theory started from the work of J. S. Mill but was worked out fully only in the 1880s and owed a good deal to Von Thünen and F. A. Walker. It took him some time to free himself of the wage fund analysis, but his basic approach came to be to treat the demand for factors as determined by their marginal products in all the different possible employments. Marshall actually used *discounted* marginal *revenue* product although the mathematical basis of the approach remained largely concealed. He did not however regard marginal productivity analysis as more than a part of the theory of distribution; this was partly due to the problem of estimating net marginal product, but mainly because the supply side was of equal (or more than equal) interest. Moreover, he never formally endorsed Euler's theorem and showed considerable reluctance to accept the idea of product exhaustion according to marginal productivity – the latter is in a marginal note to the *Principles* but not in the text.[63]

(i) *Factor supply*

Labour was defined by Marshall as 'any exertion of mind or body undergone partly or wholly with a view to some good other than the pleasure derived directly from the work'. The discussion of labour supply conditions was a curious blend of classical and marginalist considerations. On the one hand, Marshall reproduced the disutility analysis of Jevons (though without always mentioning Jevons), insisting that free human beings have a choice about the supply of factor services and that thus a cost of production approach is inappropriate to the analysis of factor supply. On the other, a great deal of the discussion is of a predominantly classical nature and is concerned with the long run supply conditions of labour including such matters as the growth of population, the health and strength of the population and the costs of investment in education. There is also a discussion of labour mobility, which operated through the ability of each grade of labour to move into the next grade, though it was limited by the existence of non-competing groups. The discussion of the supply of skilled labour was dominated by the question of investment in education and the speed with which supply could adjust to changing demand patterns for different kinds of skills. The supply of unskilled labour was determined primarily by the population mechanism and the conventional level of subsistence. Those fit only for unskilled labour were diminishing relatively in number but their wages had not risen much because the demand for them had been reduced through mechanisation.[64]

Marshall's discussion of labour income is notable for the emphasis on the interaction between poverty and low wages, the one affecting the supply of labour and perpetuating the other, and on the disadvantage of labour in bargaining compared with the employer: 'a man who employs a thousand others, is in himself an absolutely rigid combination'. Marshall was a firm believer in the economies of high wages.[65] However he was cautious about advocating remedies for low wages. He looked rather to technical advance and the rapid growth of capital, together with family limitation amongst the unskilled; his attitude towards minimum wage legislation was uncertain, and his attitude towards trade unions, despite a sometimes naive view of such activities as picketing, was extremely ambiguous. He was sceptical about their role, and opposed to their seeking sectional gains at the expense of other workers; and he ultimately came to view them as destructive of economic growth and even (privately) to be prepared to consider their complete destruction. But his instinctive reaction towards them was warm and friendly – on a par with his romantic attitude towards the cooperative movement. He was also concerned about working hours and the problem of working women.[66]

Capital was viewed by Marshall as a store of things, the result of human efforts and sacrifices, devoted mainly to securing benefits in the future rather than in the present. Profit itself derived partly from interest, which was the supply price of this capital, partly from earnings of management (which could include rent of ability), and partly from compensation for risk and the reward of innovation. Risks were of two kinds; trade risks and the risk of default on the part of an entrepreneur working with borrowed capital.[67]

Marshall regarded the entrepreneur as a vital figure in economic development and believed that total entrepreneurial remuneration was less than government would have 'wasted without good to anybody' under state enterprise. Entrepreneurial earnings were, like other factor rewards, subject to the marginal productivity analysis and the equalisation of task earnings, though they were affected by barriers to entry, and they were higher, the greater the ratio of circulating to fixed capital in an enterprise.[68]

Net interest, after deduction of risk allowance, depended on the demand for and supply of liquid capital – the return to fixed capital was in the nature of a rent ('quasi-rent'). The demand for capital depended upon its expected marginal productivity together with borrowing for consumption purposes. The supply of capital was controlled by the need for 'waiting' – a term which Marshall borrowed from McVane to replace 'abstinence' because of the existence *in the aggregate* of positive time preference, despite exceptions such as the Sargent effect. The sources of accummulation were profits, rent and labour incomes, the latter being directly invested in education and the health of children.[69]

Capital was supplied to the production process in combination with entrepreneurship even though many entrepreneurs worked with borrowed capital. The mobility of entrepreneurs ensured that profits were equalised, in the classical manner, between different employments of capital. In the short run they were, however, subject to wide variations because the first brunt of industrial fluctuations fell upon them.[70]

Marshall's analysis of the income accruing to land formally corresponded with that of the return to other factors. Rents depended upon demand and supply. The demand for land depended upon its marginal productivity (with a small additional demand because of the social distinction of land ownership) while the supply of land was taken to be fixed as in the classical analysis. Rent was then net produce, or the area under the marginal product curve less the return to cooperating factors.[71]

Marshall's discussion of land is surprisingly full of the main classical preconceptions. Rent is due to the existence of diminishing returns, and Marshall has a Ricardo-like emphasis upon variable fertility. Nevertheless he did not accept Ricardo's argument about the conflict of interest between landlords and the community over agricultural improvements. Despite his classical preconceptions – which extended to blurring the role of transfer earnings and avoiding distinguishing rent from an individual and social point of view – he managed to advance the discussion by showing the key role of elasticity of supply in the earning of rent, and was thus able to generalise the rent concept and introduce the important notion of rent of ability.[72]

(ii) *Redistribution*

Marshall viewed the long run trend of distribution as being away from rent and profit and towards wages. Capital accumulation lowered profits and transport lowered the value of agricultural land, while rising labour efficiency raised wages.

Wages had risen over time and middle incomes were increasing faster than those of the rich, because of education, prudence and opportunities for the investment of small capitals. Nevertheless Marshall was very concerned with the poverty which he observed, and with its degrading and self-perpetuating effect in particular. While he believed that many schemes of income redistribution were reckless he did not believe that redistribution would reduce growth. It would merely divert investment to the health of children. He was concerned not only at the skewed nature of the existing distribution of wealth – leading to ostentatious forms of expenditure which offended his puritanism – but, more particularly, with the existence of a 'residuum' of low paid and unskilled people, and the problem of the unemployable. As we shall see later he looked mainly to progressive taxation as a remedy.[73]

Economic growth

Marshall's treatment of economics is permeated by a concern over growth. The post-Walrasian view of Marshall is totally misleading because it fails to appreciate that, for Marshall, economic phenomena were observed not at rest but in the course of growth. Marshall's simile of the man packing parcels on the rack of a moving train 'for although all the things are moving they are relatively at rest' is instructive here. He was impressed by England's industrial leadership, and, after more than a century of growth, was concerned for the maintenance of both that growth and of England's premier position; and in this he was wholly classical. He saw both material and non-material wealth increasing with economic growth which followed three stages and produced rising living standards with expanding wants. This last was itself an important part of Marshall's view of the process of economic growth, for he saw wants expanding with activities and the development of the human character.[74]

Marshall approached the analysis of economic growth in two different, but complementary, ways. One the one hand there was a pioneering (and until recently unpublished) system of growth equations for the size of the working population, the standard of living, the efficiency of the worker, the capital stock, total output, net annual product, the task wage, the time wage and the rate of interest. There is, unfortunately, not space to reproduce that here; but modern readers are much in the debt of Professor Whitaker for disentangling all this from Marshall's unpublished manuscripts.[75] At the same time it is arguable that Marshall showed good sense in suppressing what was simply a mathematical translation of J. S. Mill because, like all mathematical growth models, it really said nothing about the genuinely interesting questions affecting economic growth, and the conscientious Marshall would have been acutely aware of this.

(i) *Factor supply in growth*

Marshall's published treatment of growth, however, was a broad classical discussion, firmly grounded in economic history, with detailed consideration (as distinct from the facile assumption of suitably signed partial derivatives) of the conditions for a process of growth. He paid particular attention to factor supply.

Marshall discussed the growth of population – the chief means of production – and coupled consideration of its size and increase, advancing a sort of weak Malthusian mechanism, with eugenic and natural selection preoccupations (under Darwin's influence). This was a recurrent concern of Marshall and one which should never be left out of account in evaluating his work. It naturally related to the health and strength of the population, which affected the efficiency of the labour force.[76] In this connection he devoted considerable attention to human capital and investment in education. He was particularly concerned about industrial training and scientific education, and he had a very forward-looking concern with the development of business education.[77]

Capital was vital to growth because it provided the essential means without which increasing division of labour could not proceed. It was necessary for the realisation of internal economies made possible by technical progress and assisted by standardisation. External economies were also important in growth, particularly in relation to the labour force and transport and their origin lay largely in localisation of industry.[78] Accummulation of capital depended upon the size of the net product and the motives to saving including foresight, security, family affection and the rate of interest. Marshall ultimately looked forward, in the standard classical manner, to a 'secular' decline in the rate of profit – although if he took the idea of a stationary state seriously this was probably due more to Jevons's prediction of the exhaustion of coal reserves.[79]

Associated with capital was Marshall's fourth factor of production, organisation, which also had a vital role to play in economic growth because it brought capital and labour together and achieved the division of labour and the use of specialised machinery.[80]

Marshall regarded the English system of cultivation as harsh but effective in using land in economic growth. It produced an excellent technology and diffused this. Despite a lingering affection for smallholdings and peasant proprietorship Marshall clearly considered that the English pattern of farming was the suitable one for growth purposes.[81]

(ii) *The framework for growth*

The analysis of the process of economic growth was combined with a discussion of the institutional framework in which it could take place, and it was strongly influenced by the classical literature, from Smith onwards, in its emphasis on security of property and property rights, climate, natural resources, human character and human freedom – which Marshall associated with free enterprise though not in an unbridled form.[82]

The growth of financial institutions was also important, as was the rise of joint stock companies (despite the continuingly important role of the entrepreneur) and the development of communications.[83] However Marshall was not, on balance, enthusiastic about the direct involvement of government in the process of production, through government enterprise. He was convinced that the involvement of government was inimical to efficient management and, above all, to the innovation which was vital to growth. His pet hate in the sphere of government enterprise was the postal monopoly. Government certainly had a vital role to play in the sort of areas – health, welfare, defence and, perhaps above all, education – which had found favour with the classical economists; and Marshall was also a strong advocate of steeply progressive taxation. This was partly because of his concern about the National Debt – Marshall subscribed to the classical view that it was a burden rather than to the comfortable Mercantilist and Keynesian view that it was what the right hand owed to the left – but mainly because he believed that increased activities which the State would have to undertake should be financed more than proportionately by the rich.[84]

(iii) *Growth, welfare and poverty*

The desirability of growth was very much linked in Marshall's mind with the question of welfare. In particular he was genuinely and intensely anxious to find remedies for poverty. As already noted, he was very concerned about the vicious circle of poverty leading to poor health and education, leading in turn to low productivity and thus perpetuating low wages; and he was also very anxious about the problem of urban deprivation which was a recurrent theme in his writings. He was very exercised about overcrowding and the lack of fresh air in towns, and he advocated such remedies as a Fresh Air Rate and the removal of large parts of the population and industry of the cities to the country.[85] One fancies that Marshall approved of the Garden Cities and would even have welcomed the New Towns.

For the relief of those in need Marshall favoured a combination of public and private provision. His attitude towards the 1834 Act was not unfavourable and he was, like his predecessors, very hostile to the Speenhamland system and indeed to outdoor relief in general – though he was not prepared to argue for its total abolition. He offered only limited approval of public works as a supplement to poor relief and believed that the latter should be confined to deserving cases – he took a strong interest in the work of the Charity Organisations Society.[86] Although he was genuinely concerned with the alleviation of poverty, Marshall did not believe that socialism had much to offer in this connection. He respected the hearts of socialists; but not their heads. Indeed he came to believe that socialism represented a considerable threat to economic progress and to liberty; 'I think it more important to dwell on the truths in Mill's *Liberty* than on those in his *Essays on Socialism*'.[87]

Ultimately he looked towards economic growth, and the softening of economic conditions through the development of economic chivalry, to alleviate poverty.[88]

International trade

Marshall's trade theory was one of the earliest parts of his work to be developed. A manuscript which Professor Whitaker dates at 1872–4 includes offer curves, multiple equilibria, exploration of the effects of tariffs and a variety of other material. Moreover Marshall wrote, and never published, a book on international trade which was largely completed by 1877. It is in his international trade theory that Marshall's development as an economist through the mathematisation of J. S. Mill is most strikingly apparent.[89]

(i) *Theoretical apparatus*

The most famous part of Marshall's apparatus is the aggregate demand curve which he related to the downward sloping demand curves in the home market. He used these curves to explore the implications of the elasticity concept and the question of stability of equilibrium in international trade, developing – though only fleetingly – the well-known 'Marshall–Lerner condition'.[90] The main use to which he put the apparatus was to analyse the effects on the terms of trade of shifts in the curves, particularly in relation to the imposition of duties. The discussion is very classical with its emphasis upon specie flows; and it is unfortunate that Marshall does not appear to have taken much account of the work of Torrens. He was quite clear that elasticity was in part dependent upon the range of *potential* exportables within a country; and that, outside a two-country model, the scope for turning the terms of trade in a country's favour was extremely limited.[91] He also used his apparatus to show the gains from trade in the form of a surplus.[92] His treatment gave rise to two celebrated controversies in both of which he was ultimately vindicated. The first was the claim by F. D. Graham that there was no link between the offer curves and the underlying production conditions. The second arose from criticism by Graham of Marshall's results concerning the effect on the net barter terms of trade of an increase in demand. The first criticism was unfair even in terms of what Marshall himself had published, although Professor Meade has shown the full implications of the analysis; the second criticism hinges upon an ambiguity in the term 'increase in demand'.[93]

(ii) *The development and effects of trade*

Much of what Marshall had to say under this heading is available in writings which were, until recently, unpublished. Foreign trade developed, in Marshall's view, from supplying the luxuries of the rich, to supplying basic foodstuffs. It was of benefit to all countries, including backward ones, despite the scale economies enjoyed by the developed ones. It limited the freedom of an individual industry with regard to prices, including the prices paid to inputs; but its effect on capital and labour was discussed primarily in the context of migration opportunities which produced a tendency towards factor price equalisation. It facilitated technical advance and increased division of labour, but it also led to increased use of fixed capital, a separation of the employers and the employed, and the development of money and capital markets which increased fluctuations. However the widening of markets and improvement of communications steadied demand and Marshall concluded that, on balance, trade had steadied employment in England – though there was always a risk of over-specialisation.[94]

The most immediate benefit of trade lay in the principle of comparative advantage which Marshall, stressing the usual classical distinction between intra-country factor mobility and inter-country factor immobility, expressed in opportunity cost form. Even if capital and labour were mobile, trade would still take place on the basis of comparative advantage because land was immobile and there would also be trade arising from technological superiority and important natural resources. Marshall provided a 'range of comparative advantage' table leading to the kind now common in international trade textbooks, indicating how the selection of exports from the possible range would be affected under various assumptions. His publication postdated Edgeworth's more sophisticated treatment; but it is quite possible that Marshall had subjective priority.[95]

(iii) *Free trade and protection*

Marshall was not only a free-trader by conviction, but a unilateral free-trader. Free trade was essential for England, though not for America, in the interests of the stimulation to economic progress which was required. A broad system of protective duties would deprive Britain of financial strength, confer sectional benefits at the cost of much greater injury to the public at large, make it harder to reduce the National Debt, and reduce total trade, depriving the country of scale benefits while yielding little revenue and causing much friction. There were more urgent tasks for government than the imposition of protection. Taxes on imported raw materials were particularly harmful; and the only justification for protection to agriculture was strategic.[96]

There is no doubt of the strength of Marshall's condemnation of protection. Taxes on foreign trade would help to turn the terms of trade in favour of the dutying country but only to a very limited extent and at the cost of a dead-weight loss, a distortion of consumer choice, the substitution of high cost for low cost sources of supply, and regressive effects.[97]

It is clear, then, that Marshall believed that duties fell in part on the consumer. He analysed their incidence with the aid of his aggregate demand apparatus and concluded that the burden would fall largely on the foreign exporter where home demand was elastic and foreign demand was inelastic. The price of imports *appeared* to rise by the full amount of the tariff but this failed to take account of the redistribution of the precious metals following the imposition of the tariff. But the scope for this was very limited because exports would be diverted to non-tariffed markets outside a two country model. After the tariff controversy of 1903 Marshall seems to have come to the conclusion that the incidence of import duties was largely on the consumer in the home country, whatever the theoretical niceties. Apart from the effects on the exchange rate and on the consumer, import duties also had collection effects which hampered production and trade.[98]

Marshall's analysis really amounted to working out, on the basis of what had been supplied by J. S. Mill, results which had already been obtained by Torrens, Senior and G. W. Norman. Nevertheless it is only with Marshall's apparatus that we can see clearly what the earlier authors meant.

Marshall was also opposed to the levying of import duties because of the danger of political corruption – and on this ground he believed in free trade for the United States. Marshall believed that tariff lobbyists had strategic political advantages compared with the vast inarticulate mass of consumers. He was quite unmoved by the protagonists of an Imperial Zollverein which would, in his view, be largely trade-diverting, in contrast to the original German model.[99]

He was no more enthusiastic about export duties. They required a lack of competitive alternatives to be successful and their importance was largely a short-run one. With the possible exception of coal we were not in a position to levy export duties.[100]

Nor would duties help the British export performance which should be assisted by more direct intervention. This was even true of the case of infant industries which Marshall did regard as one of the legitimate grounds for protection, although he believed that such protection was likely to be retained long after it was necessary and that in any case the argument was not applicable to Britain. The only other duties which he regarded as defensible were non-differential (revenue) duties on luxuries, and special export duties if some export indispensable to foreigners were found – a prospect which he regarded as unlikely.[101]

Money

(i) The quantity theory

Marshall's monetary theory was undoubtedly derived almost entirely from classical writings, especially those of J. S. Mill; though he drew upon the work of Giffen, the latter possessed no insights not available to the classical writers.[102] But Marshall was an important bridge between the classical writers and twentieth-century theorists like Keynes.

Money was defined in a classical way so as to exclude deposits; and Marshall identified the usual classical functions of money as a medium of exchange, store of value, and standard for deferred payments, with particular emphasis on its role in transactions. He used the quantity theory as his main theoretical framework though he was aware that it was reconcilable with the cost of production theory of the value of money,[103] and although he was aware also of the danger of tautology. This latter point led him to spell out what other things were assumed to be equal for the relationship between money and the price level to be straightforward. They included population, transactions per person, the percentage of business effected directly by money, and the velocity of circulation of both goods and money. He was clear that the latter was variable; and Marshall followed the Bullion Report in stressing fluctuations in commerical confidence and activity as well as the growth of credit and changes in transport and production. Like Thornton he recognised that the velocity of circulation of paper money was intimately linked to the confidence which people felt in it, which was likely to vary inversely with quantity. Because he did not regard bank deposits as money he treated banks as institutions which affected velocity, though he advanced the concept of a deposit multiplier. His source for this was Giffen rather than the classical writers who had worked it out, notably Torrens.[104]

His treatment of the quantity theory was, however, distinctive in that a primary place was given to the demand for cash balances. This was determined by equating the marginal utility of cash holdings with alternative uses for funds. Such an approach came relatively late in his writings after he had come under the influence of Jevons and the latter's work on marginal utility; but it provided an important bridge between the classical analysis, especially that of Thornton, and the Keynesian analysis of liquidity preference.[105]

As the inheritor of the classical analysis, Marshall clearly understood the mechanism of specie flows and the achievement of equilibrium in the balance of payments and in the distribution of the precious metals. He has been credited by Keynes with anticipation of Cassel's 'restatement' of Purchasing Power Parity. This is perhaps a little unfortunate; the classical economists showed good sense in not advancing Purchasing Power Parity as a theory, for it is only very roughly true, due to the importance of non-traded goods and of capital movements. But it is true that Marshall did advance a position very close to Cassel's, only occasionally referring to the problem of non-traded goods, though he may have been relying upon factor mobility to produce the relationship between the prices of traded and non-traded goods. But he recognised the power of interest rates to affect exchange rates; and it is noticeable that he does not mention Cassel in his 1923 *Money, Credit and Commerce*.[106]

Although Marshall inherited the classical analysis there were different strands in this and he, like J. S. Mill, exhibited certain Banking School influences. In particular he advocated the plan, which Tooke had put forward, of a large gold reserve which could be allowed to fall some way before contraction of the note issue was initiated, an increased fiduciary issue, a formal power to suspend the 1844 Act at times of crisis, and an issue of £1 notes to reduce the sensitivity of the money supply to metal flows. Serious objections had been advanced by participants in the Currency and Banking controversy to these suggestions, and it is rather surprising that Marshall did not feel it necessary to take much account of the problems.[107]

He did however attempt to clarify the nature of the transmission mechanism. He argued that changes in the supply of precious metals affected the money supply partly through the effect on 'hoards' of changes in expectations generated by the discoveries, but mainly through the inflation of credit. The main effect of an inflow of metal was to increase banking reserves and bring about a lowering of the rate of interest. This in turn caused an increased demand for loans and an upward speculative movement which was itself fuelled by expectations of rising prices consequent upon the arrival of the gold. As prices rose the demand for loans increased because of the higher price level, and some of the extra money was absorbed into cash balances in order to retain their real value. The extra demand for loans following the lowering of the rate of interest was brought about through a discrepancy between the money and the real rate, the latter being determined by investment and consumption demand on the one hand and the supply of free capital (income minus consumption plus non-specialised circulating capital) on the other. Marshall tended to identify it with the average profitability of business. A money rate below this would cause a demand for loans and a speculative upward movement, with equilibrium occurring only when the rates were equated. The analysis was borrowed from Thornton; and Marshall deserves credit, together with Wicksell, for reintroducing it. It explained the positive correlation observed between rising prices and the rate of interest; as Fisher had pointed out, once prices started rising there was greater eagerness to borrow and interest rates had to rise again in order to check the demand for loans.[108]

Marshall was well aware of the theory of the inflationary mechanism which had been present in classical economics since David Hume; but he was not an enthusiast for price inflation. The effect on wages and prices was regressive, rising prices were not of much assistance to employment, and falling prices caused beneficial caution in consumption and managerial behaviour. He was also unhappy about the benefit to debtors in inflation.[109]

(ii) *The analysis of fluctuations*

Marshall accepted the validity of 'Say's Law', as expressed by J. S. Mill, regarding the idea of general overproduction as a 'monstrous fallacy' but qualified this view by insisting on the possibility of a *short-run* failure of aggregate demand, for 'though men have the power to purchase they may not choose to use it'. A failure of economic confidence could, as indeed Mill had envisaged, bring about a short-run failure of effective demand, resulting in disorganisation of credit, production and (especially) consumption.[110]

Fashion also caused a problem for it induced demand fluctuations resulting, where elasticity of supply was low, in considerable price fluctuations. There was also a short-run cycle of commercial confidence – Marshall derived this from Overstone. Associated with this was a theory of regular shocks to the economic system produced by wars and harvest failure, and a credit cycle. Credit expansion followed a good harvest which would also encourage demand for other commodities because food prices were low. This strengthened entrepreneurial optimism and encouraged speculation. The banks would have difficulty in contracting their loans, but once they refused to renew them a cumulative failure of speculators would follow. In all this the capital goods industries were hardest hit. The cycle was intensified by the problem of moral hazard – entrepreneurs continued trading when they should have closed down because, having lost all their own capital, they had only that of lenders to lost thereafter, and it was intensified also by stock exchange and other forms of speculation which Marshall was anxious to discourage, as well as by changes in expectations.[111]

Price fluctuations in the cycle produced uncertainty, altered the distribution of income in favour of fixed income receivers, and produced changes in profit margins which magnified both the upswing and the downswing, while wages, being rigid, helped to intensify these profit fluctuations.[112] Despite the occasional assumption, for theoretical convenience, of full employment, and a belief that the inconstancy of employment in modern industry had been exaggerated, Marshall was concerned about unemployment and discussed a number of possible remedies of a rather cautious kind. These included an improvement in market knowledge, avoidance of fashion changes, discouragement of fraud, gambling and speculation, the use of a tabular standard of value, an increased fiduciary issue, and a reduction in trade secrecy. He also believed that the interest rate was a suitable policy variable to check expansion, and that stocks, which otherwise moved cyclically, were interest-elastic. But it is quite clear that he did not see government expenditure as a desirable remedy for unemployment because it would harm incentives and induce corruption.[113]

Marshall also envisaged a variety of real-balance effects, some of them counter-cyclical (the desire to maintain the real value of cash balances) but others of a pro-cyclical nature, particularly the inducement to substitute commodities for cash in a period of rising prices. It would be misleading to give the impression that Marshall neglected these matters altogether, though it would be equally misleading to suggest that he was aware of all the considerations to which Patinkin has drawn attention.[114]

(iii) *The debate over the standard*

During the period when Marshall's monetary views were largely formed bimetallism was a subject of frequent and vigorous public debate. Marshall did not believe that bimetallism would reduce price fluctuations because it was not necessarily true that gold and silver output fluctuations would offset each other. The comparative steadiness of silver prices in recent years had been caused by an increase in silver output paralleling an increase in commodity output. But in any case Gresham's Law would be bound to operate and bimetallism would degenerate into monometallism.[115]

Marshall was particularly concerned to counter the argument that bimetallism would encourage Indian exports. He was correct to oppose the argument in that bimetallism was irrelevant to it – a fall in the price of Indian exports expressed in silver would still encourage Indian exports even if Britain were on a gold standard – but he did so in a way which was wrong because, by telescoping the long- and short-run together, he denied that there could be any significant effect of this sort.[116] His own preference was for a plan, stemming from Ricardo, for symetallism, involving two bars of different metal, in exchange for a fixed amount of paper. Anyone who wanted silver or gold alone could obtain it through the market. The attractiveness of the scheme was that it could not degenerate into monometallism. The gain from selling one of the metals which had risen in price would be mirrored by the loss from selling the other metal which could not be used as currency because we would be on a paper standard. But Marshall did not press this case very strongly; rather his aim was to show what was required for true bimetallism, with the subsidiary possibility of paving the way for an international currency.[117]

He was much more enthusiastic about a plan which he put forward for a tabular standard of value which would become the standard for deferred payments, especially contracts, and which would, because it was not subject to the hazards of mining, help to reduce price instability. It would discourage speculation by those hoping to benefit as debtors in inflation; indeed he believed that the lack of a proper standard of this sort explained the persistence of the fallacy of the possibility of over-production. Marshall acknowledged that the plan was not his but derived from Lowe, Scrope, and above all Jevons. He put forward the plan seriously, and it was attacked; but he failed to recognise that, over a long period, the precious metals might very well adjust to changing weights in the commodity basket better than a price index.[118]

Conclusion

Most of the literature on Marshall's economic writings concentrates upon minutiae. This is perfectly understandable for two reasons. First, Marshall was an extremely powerful theorist, especially in his youth, and it is worth taking the trouble to try to tease out the meaning from some of his apparently obscure theoretical positions. Secondly, much of the literature has been written by people who were more or less weaned on Marshall and for whom it constituted the major source book in their economic education. But this is certainly not true for the bulk of the present generation of economists and it seems necessary to try to get some overall view of an economist who, whatever his theoretical powers, was very concerned to produce a balanced overall picture of the economic system with due weight given to historical and institutional factors and with due acknowledgement of the insights of earlier writers to whom he, and his contemporaries, were deeply indebted. In many ways what Marshall wrote, in a private letter to L. L. Price, about Adam Smith could apply very well to him.

It was his balance, his sense of proportion, his power of seeing the many in the one and the one in the many, his skill in using analysis to interpret history and history to correct analysis (especially as regards the causes that govern human nature, but also in other matters), that seemed to mark him out as unique.[119]

NOTES

1. J. M. Keynes, 'Alfred Marshall, 1842–1924', in A. C. Pigou (ed.), *Memorials of Alfred Marshall* (London: Macmillan, 1925) [hereafter cited as *Mems.*] pp. 1–65. Reprinted with minor alterations in J. M. Keynes, *Essays in Biography* (London: Macmillan, 1933), repr. as vol. x of *The Collected Writings of John Maynard Keynes* (London: Macmillan for the Royal Economic Society, 1972). Further biographical material is to be found in J. K. Whitaker (ed.), *The Early Economic Writings of Alfred Marshall, 1867–1890*, vol. i (New York: Free Press, 1975) [hereafter the two volumes of this work will be cited as *Wh.*i and *Wh.*ii], and in journal articles by Professor Whitaker cited therein.
2. I am grateful to Macmillan Press for these sales figures.
3. A. Marshall, *Money, Credit and Commerce* (London: Macmillan, 1923) [hereafter cited as *MC&C*] pp. 210, 245.
4. *Mems.*, pp. 74–80; C. W. Guillebaud, 'Some Personal Reminiscences of Alfred Marshall', *History of Political Economy* [hereafter cited as *HOPE*], iii (1971) 1–8; B. Webb, *My Apprenticeship* (London: Longmans, 1926) p. 314.
5. *Wh.* i, pp. 53–5.
6. See, in particular, his unusually caustic comment about Böhm-Bawerk in a letter to Wicksell, reproduced in T. Garlund, *The Life of Knut Wicksell*, trans. N. Adler (Stockholm: Almqvist & Wiksell, 1958) pp. 342–3, and his defence of J. S. Mill in *Mems.*, pp. 119–33.
7. A. Marshall, *Principles of Economics*, 1890, 9th (variorum) edn, ed. C. W. Guillebaud (London: Macmillan, 1961) vol. i, pp. ix–x, 522–3, 723–34; vol. ii, pp. 617, 764, 782 [hereafter the two volumes will be cited as *G.*i and *G.*ii]; *Wh.*i, pp. 39–40, 48, 69 and *passim*; *Wh.*ii, pp. 178–204, 240–52, 302–5 and *passim* (the two Whitaker volumes contain much excellent material on Marshall's sources); *Mems.*, p. 165.
8. *Mems.*, pp. 93–100, 163, 371.
9. J. A. Schumpeter, *History of Economic Analysis* (London: Allen & Unwin, 1955) p. 780.
10. *G.*i, title page and pp. xiii, 249.
11. A. Marshall, *Industry and Trade* (London: Macmillan, 1919; repr. New York: A. M. Kelley, 1970) [hereafter cited as *I&T*] pp. v, 5, 6; *Mems.*, p. 423; *Wh.*i, p. 110.
12. *G.*i, pp. v–vi, 29–31, 771–4, 781–2; *Mems.*, p. 153.
13. *Mems.*, p. 181.
14. *Mems.*, pp. 175–87, 301, 324, 358–9, 422, 429, 438–9, 474–5; J. M. Keynes (ed.), *Alfred Marshall Official Papers* (London: Macmillan for the Royal Economic Society, 1926) [hereafter cited as *OP*] pp. 284–8.
15. *G.*ii, pp. 72, 534–6; *Mems.*, p. 437; *I&T*, pp. 449–50n; see also *Wh.*ii, pp. 118, 129; R. H. Coase, 'Marshall on Method', *Journal of Law and Economics*, xviii (1975) 25–32; A. W. Coats, 'Alfred

Marshall and the Early Development of the London School of Economics: Some Unpublished Letters', *Economica*, n.s., 34 (1967) 408–417, at pp. 410, 413.

16. *Mems.*, pp. 313, 382, 422, 427–8; *Wh*.I, p. 38; *Wh*.II, pp. 265–8. On the question of Marshall's mathematical competence contrast Keynes in *Mems.*, at pp. 24–5 and Whitaker in *Wh*.I, pp. 4–5.

17. *G*.I, pp. 26, 30–1, 43–4; *G*.II, pp. 161–81.

18. *G*.I, pp. 366, 379–80, 460–1; *G*.II, p. 49; *Mems.*, pp. 312, 314–15.

19. *Mems.*, p. 417. Those who have quoted this passage have usually failed to note that Marshall was concerned to give note XXI of his Mathematical Appendix *'realistic form'* (italics supplied). On Marshall's relations with Walras, see *Wh*.I, pp. 103–7.

20. *G*.I, pp. 32–6; *G*.II, pp. 155–6.

21. *G*.I, pp. 1–3, 14–17, 22–3, 40–3, 770–1, 780; *G*.II, pp. 762–70; *Mems.*, pp. 158–64 *passim*.

22. *Mems.*, pp. 164–5; A. Marshall and M. P. Marshall, *The Economics of Industry* (London: Macmillan, 1879; 2nd edn, 1881) [hereafter cited as *EI*] pp. 3–4; R. Harrsion, 'Two Early Articles by Alfred Marshall', *Economic Journal* [hereafter cited as *EJ*], LXXIII (1963) 422–30.

23. *G*.I, pp. 2–4, 35–6, 41–3, 750–2; *Mems.*, pp. 172, 174, 326.

24. *G*.I, pp. 5–10, 46–8, 712–14, 721–2; *Mems.*, pp. 282–3, 333–7; *I&T*, pp. 43–4.

25. *G*.I, pp. 99, 100, 103, 106n, 108, 109–10, 839–40; *EI*, pp. 69, 71; *I&T*, pp. 403–4; *Wh*.I, p. 42; for Marshall's (subjective) invention of elasticity (Whewell can objectively claim priority) see Keynes' *Essays* (n 1 above) p. 240.

26. *G*.I, pp. 64, 86–91, 93–4, 95–6.

27. *G*.I, pp. 92–3, 94–5, 100, 117–23, 230–4, 838–9, 841, 845–6; *G*.II, pp. 236–8, 245; *EI*, pp. 69–70, 71.

28. *G*.I, pp. 98–9, 104–5; *G*.II, p. 244.

29. *HOPE*, p. 6.

30. *The Times*, 12 April 1891, p. 13 (b–c).

31. *G*.I, pp. 124–5, 841–2.

32. *G*.I, pp. 96, 128–9, 130–1, 131–2n, 133n, 134, 842; *G*.II, p. 241; *EI*, p. 70; *Mems.*, p. 162.

33. *G*.I, pp. 717, 842, 843.

34. *G*.I, p. 133. Marshall was aware that it was unlikely, in any case, that the entire demand curve could be estimated with any accuracy.

35. *G*.I, pp. 467–75, 489–93, 811; see also *Wh*.II, pp. 72, 285–302; K. Bharadwaj, 'Marshall on Pigou's *Wealth and Welfare*', *Economica*, XXXIX (1972) 32–46.

36. *G*.I, pp. 317, 338–9, 342–3, 344 (and Fig. 18), 459–61, 808–9n; *EI*, pp. 72–3, 74, 76, 77.

37. *G*.I, pp. 140–1, 339, 359–60, 419–20, 811; *EI*, pp. 74, 96–7.

38. *G*.I, pp. 138–9.

39. *G*.I, pp. 173–219, 312, 661; *G*.II, pp. 303–4.

40. *G*.I, pp. 229–36, 353, 618–20.

41. *G*.I, pp. 150–2, 153, 157, 163, 166, 169–72, 319n, 355, 407–9;

G.II, p. 358. See also C. J. Bullock, 'The Variation of Productive Forces', *Quarterly Journal of Economics* [hereafter cited as *QJE*], XVI (1901–2) 473–513.

42. *G*.I, pp. xvi, 169–72, 341, 351–4, 404–6, 418–21, 434–37, 662–3, 665–6. Strangely, G. J. Stigler asserts that Marshall does not use the concept of opportunity cost explicitly – *Production and Distribution Theories* (New York: Macmillan, 1941) [hereafter cited as *P&D*] p. 66. However it is to be found in *G*.I, p. 626.

43. *G*.I, p. 355.

44. For example, *G*.I, pp. 427–8. See also *G*.II, p. 439. For implicit recognition of the existence of transfer earnings, see *G*.I, pp. 499–500; see also *EI*, p. 74.

45. *G*.I, pp. 138–40, 291–313, 357–9, 398–400, 612–13; *EI*, pp. 114–18; *I&T*, pp. 350–94, 645–6; *Mems.*, pp. 281–4; *MC&C*, pp. 290–4.

46. *G*.I, pp. xvi, 361–2, 376 (the quoted phrase is from here), 394–402, 501–2, 850; *G*.II, p. 529; *I&T*, pp. 181–96, 269–71, 424; *EI*, pp. 79–80.

47. *G*.I, pp. 285–6, 315–17, 323, 342–3, 378, 457–9; *G*.II, pp. 69–70. See also R. Frisch, 'Alfred Marshall's Theory of Value', *QJE*, LXIV (1950) 495–524 at pp. 512–13.

48. *G*.I, pp. 5–12, 374, 458, 500–1, 540–1, 849–50; *G*.II, pp. 75, 411–12, 569, 573–4; *I&T*, p. 182. See also G. J. Stigler, 'Perfect Competition, Historically Contemplated', *Journal of Political Economy* [hereafter cited as *JPE*], LXV (1957) 1–17 at pp. 9–10; ibid., 'Marshall's *Principles* after Guillebaud', *JPE*, LXX (1962) 282–6 at p. 282.

49. *G*.I, pp. 341–2, 412, 425–6; *I&T*, p. 397. See also S. Stykolt, 'A Curious Case of Neglect: Marshall on the Tangency Solution', *Canadian Journal of Economics* [hereafter cited as *CJE*], XXII (1956) who cites *G*.I, p. 616 n. 3; G. Gerbier, *Alfred Marshall. Théoricien de l'action efficace et critique radical de l'économie pure* (Doctoral thesis, Grenoble, 1976) p. 409. (I am indebted to Professor A. W. Coats who kindly lent me this excellent thesis.) S. Peterson, 'Anti-trust and the Classic Model', *American Economic Review*, XLVII (1957) 60–87; E. H. Chamberlin, 'Origin and Early Development of Monopolistic Competition Theory', *QJE*, LXXV (1961) 515–43.

50. *I&T*, pp. 270–1, 300–2, 304, 396–7, 398, 458n, 524, 597.

51. *G*.I, pp. 360, 373–5, 458–9, 497–8; *EI*, p. 18; see also R. Frisch, op. cit. (n 47 above).

52. *G*.I, pp. 478–9, 486–9, 493–5, 663, 856–8; *G*.II, pp. 534–6; *EI*, p. 181; *I&T*, pp. 395–672, esp. 397–8, 403–6, 414–22, 440–4, 449–50n, 467–71, 481–2, 492–7, 520–2, 596–7; *Mems.*, pp. 274–7.

53. *G*.I, pp. 375n, 686n; see also *G*.I, pp. xiv, 282–3, 304–5, 417n, 477; *G*.II, pp. 47, 57, 390–1, 504n; *I&T*, pp. 179, 507–26, 533, 544–65, 576, 600, 604, 620–35; *EI*, pp. 182–4; *Mems.*, pp. 272–4, 277–81; 'How far do Remediable Causes Influence Prejudicially (a) the

Continuity of Employment, (b) the Rates of Wages?', *Industrial Remuneration Conference: The Report of the Proceedings and Papers ... under ... Sir Charles W. Dilke* (London: Cassell, 1885) [hereafter cited as *Ind. Rem.*] pp. 173–99 at p. 179.

54. *G*.I, pp. 298–304; *G*.II, pp. 659–60; *EI*, pp. 139–42; *I&T*, pp. 171–4, 308–28, 667; *Mems.*, pp. 279–81, 307, 332–3; see however *Mems.*, p. 308.

55. *G*.I, pp. 250–66, 278–90, 457–9, 471–8, 500–1; *G*.II, pp. 69n, 333, 334, 521, 523–9; *I&T*, pp. 214–34, 424–5; *Mems.*, p. 407; *Wh*.II, pp. 194–8; Stigler, *JPE*, loc. cit., 1962.

56. *G*.I, pp. 455–7, 807–10; *I&T*, pp. 107–8n; *Mems.*, pp. 439–41; *Wh*.II, pp. 184–5, 190, 193; see also P. Newman, 'The Erosion of Marshall's Theory of Value', *QJE*, LXXIV (1960) 587–601 at pp. 589–90.

57. *G*.I, p. 368.

58. *G*.I, pp. 61, 84, 85, 90, 324–30, 348–9, 813–21; *EI*, pp. 67, 68, 91–3, 147, 148, 165.

59. *G*.I, pp. 330–6, 345, 348, 369–72, 378–80, 805–9; *G*.II, pp. 361–3; *EI*, pp. vii, 158; *Wh*.I, pp. 119–64, esp. pp. 132, 143–4; P. Newman op. cit.; D. G. Davies, 'A Note on Marshallian versus Walrasian Stability Conditions', *CJE*, XXIX (1963) 535–40.

60. *G*.I, pp. 32–6, 337–50, 363, 366–9, 372; *G*.II, pp. 155–6, 380; *EI*, pp. vi–vii, 65–6, 77–8, 146–9; see also *Mems.*, pp. 285–9, 342–6; C. W. Guillebaud, 'Marshall's Principles of Economics in the Light of Contemporary Economic Thought', *Economica*, n.s., XIX (1952) 111–30 at p. 122.

61. *G*.I, pp. 337, 381–93, 852–6; *G*.II, p. 400; *Wh*.I, pp. 160–4; J. S. Mill, *Principles of Political Economy, with Some of their Applications to Social Philosophy*, (ed.) J. M. Robson (Toronto: University of Toronto Press, 1965) [hereafter cited as JSM] Book III, ch. XVI, pp. 582–6; Stigler, *P&D*, pp. 83–7.

62. He applied the tools he had created to urban rents and to taxation – *G*.I, pp. 440–54.

63. The marginal note is at *G*.I, p. 536. For material relating to the rest of the paragraph see *G*.I, pp. 138, 140–1n, 357, 385, 387, 406, 407, 409n, 410–11, 447–9, 514–18, 521–3, 525–9, 532, 580–3, 598–600, 660–1, 670–1n, 678–9, 704–6, 822–9, 846–54; *G*.II, pp. 39–41, 232–3, 580–1, 598–614, 818–19, 822–7; *EI*, pp. 13–20, 22–3, 72–3, 95–6, 119–27, 131, 133–4, 142–3, 146–9, 199–213; *Ind. Rem.*, pp. 186, 194; *Mems.*, pp. 161, 405, 412–14; *Wh*.I, pp. 43, 70, 73–6, 81, 96, 120, 129, 178–204; *Wh*.II, pp. 322–33; Lecture 2 (pp. 191–200) of 'Three Lectures on Progress and Poverty by Alfred Marshall' (ed. G. J. Stigler and R. Coase), *JPE*, LVIII (1950) 181–226 [hereafter cited as *P&P*]; Stigler, *P&D*, pp. 344–56 *passim*; J. K. Whitaker, 'The Marshallian System in 1881: Distribution and Growth', *EJ*, LXXXIV (1974) 1–17 at pp. 3–4, 5, 15–16.

64. The quotation in the paragraph is from *G*.I, p. 65. For other references relating to this paragraph see *G*.I, pp. 67–70, 80, 138–43,

173–203, 217–19, 331, 504–5, 525–30, 556–8, 567–74, 660–2, 716–19, 721–2, 843; *G*.II, pp. 670–5; *EI*, pp. 101–13, 128–34, 147, 173–5; *Wh*.II, pp. 385–93; Whitaker, *EJ* (1974) op. cit., p. 7; Stigler, *P&D*, pp. 63–6.

65. The quotation is from *G*.I, p. 568. See also *G*.I, pp. 509–10, 529–33, 546–50, 559–63; *EI*, p. 173; *Wh*.I, pp. 79–80.

66. *G*.I, pp. 5–10, 684–5, 693–700, 702–8, 714–15; *I&T*, pp. 289–307, 577–98, 854–6; *EI*, pp. 102, 128–9, 175–7, 187, 228; *Wh*.II, pp. 112, 126–7, 345–52; *Mems*., pp. 113–14, 227–53, 384–6, 396–9, 402–3; *Ind. Rem.*, p. 182; Lecture 3 of *P&P*, pp. 200–10; Preface to L. L. F. R. Price, *Industrial Peace: Its Advantages, Methods, and Difficulties: A Report of an Inquiry made for the Toynbee Trustees* (London: Macmillan, 1887) pp. xi–xiii, xviii, xxii, xxv; Whitaker, *EJ*, op. cit.; ibid., 'Alfred Marshall: The Years 1877 to 1885', *HOPE*, IV (1972) 1–61, App. D, pp. 49–61; A. Petridis, 'Alfred Marshall's Attitudes to the Economic Analysis of Trade Unions: A Case of Anomalies in the Competitive System', *HOPE*, V (1973) 165–98.

67. *G*.I, pp. 71–82, 138–43, 313, 505–10, 589–92, 598, 612–15, 618–20, 635–6, 719, 785–90; *G*.II, pp. 670–5; *EI*, pp. 13–20, 75, 78–9, 135; *MC&C*, pp. 285–90; *Wh*.I, pp. 204–24.

68. *G*.I, pp. 605–15, 622–4, 657–75; *G*.II, pp. 661–2; *EI*, pp. 74–5, 135–45, 177–8; *Ind. Rem.*, p. 174 (the quotation is from here); *Wh*.I pp. 211–12.

69. *G*.I, pp. 21, 73, 74, 81–2, 122, 220–36, 362n, 377, 411–12, 419–20, 518–21, 533–5; *G*.II, pp. 358, 374, 461–83, 495; *EI*, pp. 41–2, 119–27, 146–9; *MC&C*, pp. 289–90; *Wh*.II, pp. 181–236.

70. *G*.I, pp. 596–8, 602–8, 620–4; *G*.II, pp. 648–9, 670–5; *EI*, pp. 135–45, 147.

71. *G*.I, pp. 155, 422–4, 534–6; *EI*, pp. 81–7, 169; *Wh*.I, p. 231; *Wh*.II, pp. 319–22.

72. *G*.I, pp. 149–70, 418–31, 436–9, 450, 499–500, 577–9, 622–4, 629–36; *G*.II, pp. 431, 439, 441–61, 492–512, 516–17, 540–1, 670–5; *EI*, pp. 21–6, 82, 84–6, 88–90, 110, 179; *Wh*.I, pp. 244–60.

73. *G*.I, pp. 229–30, 248, 625–8, 678–88, 712–15, 717–18, 843–4; *EI*, pp. 48, 113, 132, 145; *Mems*., pp. 162, 228–9, 324–5, 347–50, 366, 443, 462–3; preface to Price (n 66 above) p. ix; *The Times*, 18 January 1887; *OP*, pp. 249–50; A. Marshall, 'National Taxation after the War' in W. H. Dawson (ed.), *After-war Problems* (London: Allen & Unwin, 1917) pp. 313–45 [hereafter cited as *NT*] at pp. 317–29.

74. The quotation is from *Mems*., p. 312. For references relating to the rest of the paragraph, see *G*.I, pp. 49, 56–7, 59, 80–1, 220–39, 587, 675–8, 689–93, 749–52; *EI*, pp. 6, 13; *I&T*, p. 697; *P&P*, Lecture I, pp. 184–91; *OP*, pp. 402–12; *Wh*.II, p. 112; T. Parsons, 'Wants and Activities in Marshall', *QJE*, XLVI (1932) 101–40; T. Parsons, 'Economics and Sociology: Marshall in relation to the Thought of his Time', *QJE*, XLVI (1932) 316–47; J. K. Whitaker, 'Some Neglected Aspects of Alfred Marshall's Economic and Social Thought', *HOPE*, IX (1977) 161–97.

75. *Wh.*I, p. 97; *Wh.*II, pp. 305–16; Whitaker, *EJ* (1974) op. cit., at pp. 11–15.

76. *G.*I, pp. 173–203, 219, 243–8, 739–42; *G.*II, pp. 303–4; *Ind. Rem.*, p. 198; *EI*, pp. 9, 27–37; J. J. Spengler, 'Marshall on the Population Question', *Population Studies*, VIII, IX (1955) 264–87, 56–66.

77. *G.*I, pp. 204–19, 229–30, 236, 560–6, 571, 619, 622, 660–1, 670–5, 681–4, 858; *EI*, p. 39 (see also pp. 10–11, 32); *I&T*, pp. 121–39, 356–7; *Mems.*, pp. 117–18, 173; *The Times*, 3 March 1905 (15a–b), 29 November 1905 (4c), 18 December 1905 (13d), 29 December 1905 (5d). See also R. Blandy, 'Marshall on Human Capital: A Note', *JPE*, LXXV (1967) 874–5.

78. *G.*I, pp. 221, 240–1, 250–90; *EI*, pp. 43, 46–7, 49–59; *I&T*, pp. 106, 140–62, 214–34, 281–2, 698–9; *MC&C*, pp. 77–80, 244–5.

79. *G.*I, pp. 223–30, 236, 680–1; *EI*, pp. 25–6, 36–9, 41–2, 48, 127, 146.

80. *G.*I, pp. 240–77, 291–313; *I&T*, pp. 350–94.

81. *G.*I, pp. 645–51, 653–6, 744–7, 833–7; *EI*, pp. 23–4, 57–61; JSM; Book II, ch. vi–vii, pp. 252–96.

82. *G.*I, pp. 528, 691, 726–33, 740–2, 750–2, 798–800; *EI*, pp. 10, 36–8, 64; *I&T*, p. 106.

83. *G.*I, pp. 222, 273–4, 301–4, 678–9, 744–7; *EI*, p. 55; *I&T*, pp. 106, 171–4; *MC&C*, pp. 68–97.

84. *G.*I, p. 304; *EI*, p. 113; *I&T*, pp. 486, 494–7, 666–72; *Ind.Rem.*, p. 174; *Mems.*, p. 118; *NT*, pp. 313–14, 317–22, 325–9, 345; *The Times*, 24 March 1891 (11e), 6 April 1891 (13b–c), 16 November 1909 (10c); *The Economist*, 30 December 1916, p. 1228.

85. *G.*I, pp. 199–200, 202–3, 320–1, 350, 718, 803–4; *OP*, pp. 197–262. 361–3; *Ind. Rem.*. pp. 183–4; *Mems.*. pp. 142–51; *EI*. p. 26; A. Marshall, 'Where to House the London Poor', *Contemporary Review*, March 1884; and 'Is London Healthy?', *Pall Mall Gazette*, 13 April 1887; *The Times*, 25 June 1885 (3e); 16 November 1909 (10c).

86. *OP*, pp. 199, 201, 211–25; *EI*, pp. 32–4; *Ind. Rem.*, pp. 187–8; *Mems.*, pp. 345, 373, 403; *The Times*, 2 February 1885 (3e), 15 February 1886 (13b).

87. The quotation is from *Mems.*, p. 444. See also *Ind. Rem.*, p. 173; *Mems.*, pp. 155–6, 173, 283–4, 291, 327–9, 462; *G.*I, pp. 712–14, 722; *The Times*, 24 March 1891 (11e), 16 November 1909 (10c).

88. *Mems.*, pp. 323–46.

89. *Wh.*I, pp. 260–89; *Wh.*II, pp. 3–181; *Mems.*, p. 451.

90. *MC&C*, pp. 158–65, 167–76, 330–60; *Wh.*II, pp. 117–81; J. Bhagwati and H. G. Johnson, 'Notes on Some Controversies in the Theory of International Trade', *EJ*, LXX (1960) 74–93; A. Amano, 'Stability Conditions in the Pure Theory of International Trade: A Rehabilitation of the Marshallian Approach', *QJE*, LXXXII (1968) 326–39.

91. *MC&C*, pp. 177–89. On Torrens, see D. P. O'Brien, *The Classical Economists* (Oxford: Clarendon Press. 1975) [hereafter cited as O'Brien] pp. 189–97 and references therein.

92. *MC&C*, pp. 338–40; *Wh*.I, pp. 279–81; see also Bhagwati and Johnson, op. cit., and J. Viner, *Studies in the Theory of International Trade* (London: Allen & Unwin, 1964) [hereafter cited as *Studies*] pp. 570–5.

93. A. Marshall, *The Pure Theory of Foreign Trade* (repr., London: London School of Economics, 1930) [hereafter cited as *PT*] pp. 5–6, 13, 26–7 164–5; *MC&C*, pp. 338–40; *Wh*.II pp. 140, 164–5; to abbreviate secondary references, see the following and references therein: Viner, *Studies*, pp. 536–46 and 548–55; Bhagwati and Johnson, op. cit.; J. E. Meade, *A Geometry of International Trade* (London: Allen & Unwin, 1952) chs i–iv.

94. *G*.I, pp. 672–7; *Wh*.II, pp. 14–23, 33–61; *EI*, pp. 18–19.

95. *MC&C*, pp. 1–11, 102–6, 109–12, 156–7, 321–9; *I&T*, pp. 16, 22; *Wh*.II, pp. 31–3; Viner, *Studies*, pp. 458–62 (and Edgeworth references therein). Mangoldt really has priority over both Marshall and Edgeworth.

96. *MC&C*, pp. 213–17; *OP*, pp. 395–9, 408–12; *Wh*.II, pp. 89–91, 106–8; *Mems.*, pp. 258–65, 471–4; *I&T*, pp. 760–2; *NT*, pp. 330–41, 345; 'Discussion on Mr Schuster's Paper', *Journal of the Institute of Bankers*, XXV (1904) 94–8 [hereafter cited as *DS*] at p. 95; *The Times*, 23 November 1903 (10e); H. W. McCready, 'Alfred Marshall and the Tariff Reform, 1903: Some Unpublished Letters', *JPE*, LXIII (1955) 259–67.

97. *Wh*.II, pp. 62–89.

98. *MC&C*, pp. 193–8; *OP*, pp. 365–420; *Wh*.II, pp. 80–88; *Mems.*, pp. 449–50.

99. *MC&C*, pp. 219, 265; *OP*, pp. 389–90, 394, 399, 415–20; *NT*, pp. 329–30, 341–5; *DS*, p. 97.

100. *MC&C*, p. 204; *Mems.*, pp. 320–2; *The Times*, 10 November 1898 (10c), 2 December 1898 (8a); *NT*, pp. 330–2, 336–8; *Wh*.II, pp. 88–9.

101. *G*.I, pp. 464–5; *I&T*, p. 762; *Wh*.II, pp. 56–61, 100–102; *MC&C*, pp. 218–24; *OP*, pp. 387–92; *DS*, p. 97; *NT*, pp. 329–33; *Mems.*, pp. 258–65, 320–2; *The Times*, 22 April 1901.

102. *OP*, p. 37; *Wh*.I, p. 164; E. Eshag, *From Marshall to Keynes: An Essay on the Monetary Theory of the Cambridge School* (Oxford: Blackwell, 1963) [hereafter cited as Eshag] pp. xiii, 16–18.

103. *OP*, pp. 35–8, 139–40, 323; *Wh*.I, pp. 164, 171–2; *MC&C*, pp. 12–20, 38, 49; *The Times*, 25 January 1889 (13f).

104. *OP*, pp. 5–6, 22, 24–7, 34–5, 37, 40, 115ff., 267–8; *MC&C*, pp. 42–3, 46–8, 282–4; H. Thornton in F. A. Hayek (ed.), *An Enquiry into the Nature and Effects of the Paper Credit of Great Britain (1802)* (London: Allen & Unwin, 1939) [hereafter cited as Thornton] pp. 96–100, 197n; Lord Robbins, *Robert Torrens and the Evolution of Classical Economics* (London: Macmillan, 1958) pp. 109–11.

105. *MC&C*, pp. 38–9, 43–5; *OP*, pp. 177, 267–8 (see also pp. 36, 44); *Wh*.I, p. 164–77; Thornton, pp. 232–3.

106. *OP*, pp. 66, 144–7, 150, 170–4, 177–80, 188, 191, 293, 296–7 (see also pp. 189, 193–5, 312); *Mems.*, pp. 30–1; *MC&C*, pp. 147–9, 152–4, 179, 225–33, 315–20.

107. *OP*, pp. 25, 26, 29, 30, 54, 110–12, 124, 162–4, 282–4; *MC&C*, p. 66; *Ind. Rem.*, p. 179; O'Brien, pp. 153–9.

108. *OP*, pp. 10, 22–3, 38, 40–1, 51–2, 124, 126–8, 130–1, 158, 272, 274; *MC&C*, pp. 45, 73–6, 131, 255–8, 270, 272; *Mems.*, p. 190; see also Eshag, p. 13 n 55 and p. 57 n 51.

109. *OP*, pp. 19–20, 58, 75, 91–3, 168–9, 193, 285 (see also ibid., pp. 7, 9, 97–8, 100, 270–2, 284–7, 300–3, 317, 322–3); *G.*I, pp. 593–5; *Mems.*, p. 191; *MC&C*, pp. 18–19, 74; *EI*, pp. 155–7, 165–6.

110. The first quotation is from *Mems.*, p. 192; the second is from *G.*I, p. 710. For references relating to this paragraph see *G.*I, pp. 709–11; *OP*, p. 91; *PT*, p. 34; *EI*, pp. 154, 161, 191–2; *Mems.*, pp. 130, 463; *JSM*, pp. 557–61.

111. *EI*, pp. 150–3, 161–4; *G.*I, pp. 709–11; *MC&C*, pp. 18–19, 75, 89–97, 238ff, 246, 249, 257, 287; *Ind. Rem.*, p. 178; *Mems.*, pp. 190–4; *OP*, pp. 6, 9–10, 209, 451; Marshall had a marked personal copy of Overstone's *Tracts* – Eshag, p. 95.

112. *G.*II, pp. 709–11; *OP*, pp. 9–10; *MC&C*, pp. 18, 261; *Mems.*, p. 191; *EI*, pp. 155–6.

113. *G.*I, pp. 594–5, 687–8; *OP*, pp. 9–11, 92, 94–7, 168; *Mems.*, pp. 191, 205 n 2, 365 (see also p. 206 n 2); *MC&C*, pp. 18, 176–81, 246–8, 251–3, 258–9, 260–3; *Ind. Rem.*, pp. 174–9; see also *EI*, p. 155n.

114. D. Patinkin, *Money, Interest and Prices* (New York: Harper & Row, 1965) pp. 186–8, 603–10; *MC&C*, pp. 18, 43, 256; *OP*, pp. 5–6, 22, 52; see, however, *EI*, pp. 155–6 for neglect of the real balance effect.

115. *MC&C*, pp. 60–4, 67; *OP*, pp. 24–7, 30–1, 55, 292 (see also pp. 13, 26); *Mems.*, pp. 188, 193, 195–6, 199–203, 206, 207 n (see also p. 477); *The Times*, 25 January 1889 (13f), 6 October 1897 (9c).

116. *OP*, pp. 21, 65–7, 75, 82, 115, 173, 192–3, 275–7, 288, 317; *MC&C*, pp. 315–20; *The Times*, 25 January 1889 (13f), 30 January 1889 (13c).

117. *OP*, pp. 14, 28–31, 101–4, 135; *Mems.*, pp. 204–6, 476–7; *MC&C*, p. 65.

118. *Mems.*, pp. 191–9, 207–11, 476–7; *Ind. Rem.*, pp. 178–9, 185–6; *OP*, pp. 10, 31; *MC&C*, pp. 36–7, 52–4, 64–7; *The Economist*, 5 March 1887, pp. 303–4; 12 March 1887, p. 339.

119. *Mems.*, p. 379.

3 F. Y. Edgeworth, 1845–1926

JOHN CREEDY

Introduction – biographia

Francis Ysidro Edgeworth[1] was born on 8 February 1845 in Edgeworthstown in County Longford, Ireland. The family name had in fact been taken from Edgeworth (now Edgeware) in England, where the family settled in the reign of Elizabeth I. Since that time, however, the family has declined in size and the male line has become almost extinct. Richard Lovell Edgeworth, the head of the family in the eighteenth century, had 4 wives and 22 children.[2] One of these children was the novelist Maria Edgeworth (1767–1847), who was friendly with Ricardo and Bentham,[3] and who was described by Edgeworth as 'a very plain old lady with a delightful face'.[4]

The sixth son of Richard was Francis Beaufort Edgeworth (1809–1846); who met his wife Rosa Florentine Eroles, the daughter of a Spanish refugee from Catalonia, in a romantic episode while on the way to Germany to study philosophy, and married within 3 weeks.[5] Edgeworth was the fifth son of this marriage.

Very little is known of Edgeworth's early life. He was educated by tutors in Edgeworthstown until the age of 17, when in 1862 he entered Trinity College, Dublin to study languages. In 1867 Edgeworth entered Exeter College, Oxford, but after one term transferred to Magdalen Hall. He later (1868) transferred to Balliol where he remained for the next two terms, was absent for the next five terms (there were four per year), but returned in Michaelmas 1869 to take a first in *Literae Humaniares*.[6] During the *viva* Edgeworth apparently replied, 'shall I answer briefly or at length?' – whereupon he spoke for half an hour to convert what was to be a second into a first. More important, however, is the acknowledged influence of the master of Balliol, Jowett, in

72

stimulating Edgeworth's interest in economics. Jowett later provided encouragement and possibly financial support for Marshall during the latter's years away from Cambridge.[7]

(i) *Early career*

Even less is known about Edgeworth during the seven years following his graduation. His first paper had been published in *Mind* in 1876, and in 1877 (the year he was called to the bar) his first book *New and Old Methods of Ethics* appeared. Edgeworth was then 32 years old.

The main personal influence was undoubtedly Jevons, who was a neighbour in Hampstead.[8] Jevons recommended Marshall's *Pure Theory of Foreign Trade and Domestic Values*, in which Edgeworth, ' . . . discerned a new power of mathematical reasoning not only in the papers bristling with curves and symbols, but also in certain portions of the seemingly simple textbook'.[9] In 1881, one year after he became Lecturer in Logic (evening classes) at King's College, London,[10] Edgeworth published his highly original *Mathematical Psychics: An Essay on the Application of Mathematics to the Moral Sciences*. In his second and last review Marshall says quite bluntly 'This book shows clear signs of genius, and is a promise of great things to come'.

Edgeworth then turned towards mathematical probability and the problems of statistical inference. The first of many papers on his 'Law of Error' was published in 1883. The same year also saw the first paper on another lifelong interest, 'On a Method of Ascertaining a Change in the Value of Gold', which was the first of many papers subsequently published in the *Journal of the Royal Statistical Society*.[11] Another important early paper was for the Jubilee volume of the *Journal of the Royal Statistical Society* on 'Methods of Statistics'. These papers mark the beginning of many contributions by Edgeworth to mathematical statistics during his lifetime. This chapter concentrates on the contribution to economics made by Edgeworth – though for his economics to be fully appreciated his statistical work cannot be ignored.[12] The importance which Edgeworth attached to the subject is illustrated by a charming anecdote told by Bowley to show how difficult it was, 'to turn the conversation' from the subject of probabilities and the 'Law of Error'. As a party of economists was cycling out of Cambridge in 1904 and Edgeworth began to talk statistics, Cannan drew alongside Bowley and said, 'Put on the pace, Bowley, he can't talk mathematics at more than 12 miles an hour.' Fortunately Bowley, the person best qualified for the task, has preserved Edgeworth's main results in a superb monograph.[13]

A major contribution to the subject of index-numbers was made by Edgeworth in his role as Secretary to the British Association Report on Index-Numbers.[14] The three volumes (1887, 8, 9) have been referred to by Pigou as 'of a kind to which the term "classical" may properly be applied'.[15]

In 1889 Edgeworth became president of section F of the British Association, a position he held again in 1922. Then in 1890 he succeeded Thorold Rogers to the Tooke chair of Economic Science and Statistics.[16] In the next year he again succeeded Rogers, this time to become Drummond Professor and Fellow of All Souls, Oxford, a position which he held until his retirement in 1922.[17] As a teacher Edgeworth seems to have been far from successful,[18] but in 1891 he became the first editor of the *Economic Journal*.[19] Although Edgeworth had not been the first choice as editor, he was well suited for this role. He is acknowledged to have been the most widely known among British and foreign economists, and certainly the most widely read.[20]

(ii) *Editorship of the* Economic Journal

Contrary to what may be expected from his reputation as an unworldly figure, Edgeworth seems to have been an efficient administrator. Keynes, who was co-editor for 15 years, reports that 'He was punctual, business like, and dependable in the conduct of all routine matters'.[21] Edgeworth was later supported by Higgs from 1892 to 1905, with further assistance provided at a later stage by Alfred Hoare.[22] Apart from an early dispute between Edgeworth and John Rae, when the council acquitted Edgeworth of discourtesy, the *Journal* seems to have been run 'with due impartiality'.[23] Indeed many early papers were published by 'outsiders', to whom Marshall strongly objected.

Edgeworth's position as editor of the *Journal* did place him in an important position which greatly affected his future work. First, he reviewed a considerable number of books, and even articles, in the *Journal*,[24] some of his reviews being collected in volume III of his *Papers* (1925). While these now provide interesting reading and show the wide range of his learning, it could be argued that they dissipated his energy to some extent. Secondly, even where his papers were not ostensibly review articles, such as the major papers on distribution, taxation and international trade, they usually consisted of commentaries on all the contemporary work of any value. Thus Edgeworth's own original suggestions are often rather obscurely buried in footnotes.[25] If Edgeworth had been in the position of having to respond to editorial and referees' reports he might have produced much more systematic presentations of his own ideas. Thirdly, Edgeworth used his position to publish many essays on the benefits – and limitations – of the use of mathematics in economics. These are little more than amplification of his more terse 'apology' in *Mathematical Psychics*, although it should be said that mathematical economists and econometricians owe a large part of their present position to Edgeworth.

Fourthly, Edgeworth argued that one of the advantages of mathematical economics is its ability to check the conclusions reached by other methods. Thus

> He that will not verify his conclusions as far as possible by mathematics, as it were bringing the ingots of common sense to be assayed and coined at the mint of the sovereign science, will hardly realise the full value of what he holds, will want a measure of what it will be worth in however slightly altered circumstances, a means of conveying and making it current.[26]

Edgeworth therefore regarded it his duty to point to any fallacies which may have been perpetrated by other economists. The desire to get things right is of course laudable and, in the period of rapid progress in which Edgeworth lived, there was much work to do.[27] But Edgeworth's regular flow of criticism, aided by his easy access to publication, has led many later commentators to suggest that he was only interested in producing *curoisa* and 'illuminating the obscure with the more obscure'.[28]

This criticism carries with it the implication that Edgeworth was interested in paradoxes for their own sake. But when explaining the omissions from his *Papers*, he says quite clearly 'A third class of passages are omitted on the ground of what may be called excessive elaboration. It is not intended thereby to attribute excess to the original publication. What is worth saying once may not be worth repeating',[29] and again 'if such questions are posed, it is better not to answer them carelessly'.[30]

(iii) *Methodology*

There is a further aspect of Edgeworth's work which does not seem to have been fully appreciated, and that concerns his methodology. Edgeworth's approach was strongly *a priori*, and he always tried to show how other leading economists used the same method. His interest in the problems of method led him to make comparisons with scientific 'laws' and in particular to show that the physical sciences also relied on abstraction and approximation. Thus, 'it cannot be considered as paradoxical that a less exact science should rest in part upon similarly inexact axioms'.[31] In particular, Edgeworth was careful to argue that the assumptions are often untestable,[32] though unlike many later theorists he cannot be accused of 'plucking assumptions from the air'. Indeed, he was careful to show that the difficulty is in making the *crucial* abstractions which make the particular problem under consideration tractable, but which are not question begging. Edgeworth's view, stated as early as 1881,[33] was that in general the appropriate *a priori* assumption is that all feasible values (of, say, elasticities) are equi-probable. But, 'this kind of *a priori* presumption is liable to be superseded by specific evidence. . . . There is required, I think . . . in order to override the *a priori* probability, either very definite specific evidence, or the concensus of high authorities.'[34] This statement illustrates the basis of Edgeworth's interest in the problems of statistical inference, to which he devoted considerable energy,[35] and especially his many allusions to other leading economists. Edgeworth always took pains to show that his abstractions were sensible for the problem at hand, and one way of doing this was to show that others had made similar assumptions. Keynes's comment that 'his ostensible reverence for authority and disinclination to say anything definite on his own responsibility led him to waste an abundance of time',[36] unfortunately fails to recognise this important aspect of Edgeworth's approach.

Exchange

Edgeworth's major contributions to economics are contained in *Mathematical Psychics*, which has been described by Stigler as 'probably the most elusively written book of importance in the history of economics'.[37] His object was to apply mathematics to a utilitarian approach to economics, and he expressed the hope that '"Méchanique Sociale" may one day take her place along with "Méchanique Celeste", throned each upon the double-sided height of one maximum principle'.[38] Although utility is 'at first sight as hopelessly incalculable as whatever is in life capricious and irregular – as the smiles of beauty and the waves of passion',[39] Edgeworth thought that *the conception of man as a pleasure machine* may justify and facilitate the employment of ... mathematical terms in social science'.[40]

The theory of exchange presented by Jevons (1871) was without doubt the main inspiration for the first part of *Mathematical Psychics*. Total utility was expressed as the sum of separate utilities of each good available after exchange, with positive but decreasing marginal utility. The conditions guaranteed that demand curves sloped downwards, that an increase in income produced an increase in the consumption of *all* goods and obviously ruled out any complementarity.

Although Jevons and Walras had shown how the quantities demanded could be obtained as the solution to a set of simultaneous equations with prices *taken as given*, it is important to stress that no theory of price formation existed. 'Price taking' was axiomatic, so that no 'higgling' between buyers and sellers was necessary and 'there can only be one ratio of exchange of one uniform commodity at any moment'.[41]

Edgeworth, however, was particularly concerned to examine the precise circumstances in which a determinate and uniform price would result from a stylised process of barter. He explicitly introduced the role of the number of traders into the analysis of competitive markets, and showed the conditions under which competition between buyers and sellers (through his recontracting process) would lead to a *final settlement* which is in fact equivalent to one in which all individuals act independently as price takers.

In *Mathematical Psychics* Edgeworth's concentration on barter was so great that his new analytical contributions to utility theory were given a very terse treatment indeed, and much of the discussion is in an appendix. These aspects will be discussed first, after which his work on contract and competition is examined.

Like Edgeworth, 'we can only practice temperance, not abstinence, in the matter of symbols'.[42]

(i) The utility function

After summarising Jevons's additive utility function, Edgeworth immediately introduced his general form where 'Utility is regarded as a function of the two variables, not the sum of functions of each.'[43] Following Jevons, he considered individuals A and B trading in two goods X and Y. Person A starts with amount a of good X, but no Y; while B begins with no X but with an amount b of good Y. The person A exchanges an amount x of good X for an amount y of good Y, and Edgeworth writes his total utility after exchange as $U_A = U_A(x, y)$. The total utility of B is written $U_B = U_B(x, y)$. Thus, 'the two coordinates . . . represent the quantities of the two commodities exchanged, the *quid* and the *pro quo*'.[44]

Although this may now seem 'an obvious improvement'[45] it is remarkable how slow was the acceptance of the general form. Many leading economists continued to use the additive function and, combined with the considerable extra complexity, this may have been related to Marshall's statement in the *Principles* of his reluctance to follow Edgeworth.[46] It is worth noting that much modern theory, especially in inter-temporal allocation problems, uses the additive form for reasons of tractability; and much empirical work still assumes additivity.[47]

Edgeworth later said 'the whole rigid system bursts up in a universal *débâcle*, as we relax the assumption that the (marginal) utility of one commodity is independent of that of others'.[48] One immediate implication is that it allows for complementarity. Edgeworth did not explicitly define the terms in 1881, although after writing the cross derivative $\partial^2 U_A / \partial x\, \partial y$, he notes in parentheses 'Attention is solicited to [its] interpretation.'[49] The first formal definition is attributed to Auspitz and Lieben (1889), and was used by Edgeworth in his paper on 'The Pure Theory of Monopoly' (1897). With $U = U(q_1, \ldots, q_n)$, goods i and j are complements (substitutes) if $\partial^2 U / \partial q_i \partial q_j > 0 (<0)$. This definition was criticised on the grounds that it is not invariant with respect to monotonic transformations of the utility function, so that the modern definition involves *compensated* price changes.[50] Thus q_i is defined as a *net* substitute (complement) for q_j if $\delta q_i / \delta p_j > 0\ (<0)$, where the use of δ indicates that the price change is compensated, i.e. constant utility.

(ii) *Indifference curves*

Edgeworth then immediately raised the question of the equilibrium which may be reached with 'one or both refusing to move further'. He answered that 'contract' only supplies part of the answer so that 'supplementary conditions ... supplied by competition or ethical motives' will be required, and then wrote the equation of his famous contract curve. All this was in one sentence![51] The problem of obtaining the equilibrium values of x and y which 'cannot be varied with the consent of the parties to it' was clearly stated as follows:

> It is required to find a point (xy) such that, in whatever direction we take an infinitely small step, $[U_A]$ and $[U_B]$ do not increase together, but that, while one increases, the other decreases.[52]

The locus of such points (now referred to as Pareto optimal points) 'it is here proposed to call the *contract curve*'. To consider a movement for person A, the total derivative of U_A is given by

$$dU_A = \frac{\partial U_A}{\partial x}\,dx + \frac{\partial U_A}{\partial y}\,dy \qquad (1)$$

and because A will only consider positive values of dU_A 'it is evident that $[A]$ will step only on one side of a certain line, the *line of indifference*, as it may be called'.[53] The equation of an indifference curve is therefore

$$\frac{\partial U_A}{\partial x}\,dx + \frac{\partial U_A}{\partial y}\,dy = 0 \qquad (2)$$

and the *marginal rate of substitution* of x for y, dx/dy, is

$$- \frac{\partial U_A}{\partial y}\bigg/\frac{\partial U_A}{\partial x},$$

or the ratio of marginal utilities. Modern discussion is predominately in terms of this latter concept, although Edgeworth did not consider it explicitly in 1881. This perhaps also explains why he continued unnecessarily to assume diminishing marginal utility. To obtain the contract curve Edgeworth then asked

> If we enquire in what directions $[A]$ and $[B]$ will consent to move *together*, the answer is, in any direction between their respective lines of indifference, in a direction *positive* as it may be called *for both*. At what point then will they refuse to move at all? When their *lines* of indifference are coincident.[54]

Thus the marginal rate of substitution between the two goods must be the same for each individual, otherwise an opportunity for at least one individual to move to an indifference curve of greater total utility exists. Then

$$\frac{dx}{dy} = \frac{\partial U_A}{\partial y} \bigg/ \frac{\partial U_A}{\partial x} = \frac{\partial U_B}{\partial y} \bigg/ \frac{\partial U_B}{\partial x} \tag{3}$$

and the equation of the contract curve is

$$\frac{\partial U_A}{\partial x} \frac{\partial U_B}{\partial y} - \frac{\partial U_A}{\partial y} \frac{\partial U_B}{\partial x} = 0. \tag{4}$$

Edgeworth's famous box diagram is too well known to require discussion here.[55] The initial endowments of each individual determine the highest indifference curve which may be reached by each individual acting in isolation, and therefore the dimensions of the box. These curves are then placed in the box where the amount of y and x *exchanged* are measured northwards and eastwards respectively. The contract curve, 'the class of contracts to the variation of which consent of *both* parties cannot be obtained',[56] is then given as in equation (3).

The individual demand curve, showing the amount x which person A is willing to exchange for y at a given price was also defined by Edgeworth. This is of course the reciprocal demand curve used by Marshall (1879), although Edgeworth was the first to provide the 'analytics' of the curve in terms of utility theory. He succinctly states 'The problem under consideration may be expressed: find the locus of the point where lines from the origin *touch* curves of indifference.'[57]

(iii) *The recontracting process*

The above discussion has concentrated on the *optimality conditions* for 'efficient' exchange between two individuals. Whether two isolated traders will actually reach a settlement on the contract curve has not been considered, although it is important analytically to differentiate between the two questions. To answer the second question Edgeworth considered a highly stylised process of competition where individuals may form collusive groups.

In defining the market Edgeworth assumed divisibility, but instead of assuming initial perfect information he supposed that free communication took place throughout the 'competitive field'. Knowledge of other traders' dispositions and resources could then be obtained by the formation of tentative contracts which are not assumed to involve actual transfers, and can be broken when further information is obtained.[58] Edgeworth introduces this in typical style

> "Is it peace or war?" asks the lover of "Maud", of economic *competition*, and answers hastily: it is both, *pax* or *pact* between contractors during contract, *war*, when some of the contractors *without the consent of others recontract.*[59]

Thus the role of the recontracting process is essentially to disseminate information between traders. It allows individuals who initially agree to a contract which is not on the contract curve, to discover that an opportunity exists for improvement for at least one person, without another suffering. The purpose of Edgeworth's stylised process is therefore not to direct attention to the role of information, or other market 'imperfections', but to concentrate on the role of the *number of individuals* in a market.

Along the contract curve for two isolated traders 'the settlements are represented by an *indefinite number of points*',[60] so that the recontracting process would not be expected to result in a unique rate of exchange. There is therefore nothing to ensure that individuals will trade on their demand (offer) curves, and this led Edgeworth to make his often quoted remark that[61] 'An accessory evil of indeterminate contract is the tendency, greater than in a full market, towards dissimulation and objectionable arts of higgling.'[62]

Edgeworth then introduced additional traders into the market. His analysis of this problem is characteristically subtle, elusive and terse, and was completed in just ten pages.[63] He began by introducing 'a second *A* and a second *B*', where the new traders are assumed to be exact replicas of the initial pair. This device enables the same box diagram to be used. The first point to note is that in the final settlement which results from recontracting, both the *A*s (and of course the *B*s) must be treated equally. Since they are identical, no individual *A* can have any advantage over his counterpart, and (with convex indifference curves) they would not settle for different allocations on the same indifference curve. Furthermore the settlement must be on the contract curve.

> It is evident that there cannot be equilibrium unless (1) all the field is collected at one point; (2) that point is on the *contract curve*. For (1) if possible let one couple be at one point, and another couple at another point. It will generally be the interest of the [*A*] of one couple and the [*B*] of the other to rush together leaving their partners in the lurch. And (2) if the common point is not on the contract curve, it will be the interest of *all parties* to descend to the contract curve.[64]

The next important question is whether the range of indeterminacy is reduced by the additional competitors. Edgeworth answered this by considering whether the limit of the old contract curve, say point *C* in Fig. 3.1(i) still qualifies as a *final settlement* (that is, to the variation of which the consent of all parties cannot be obtained). Because of the convexity of indifference curves, it is clear that any point along the ray 0*C* represents an improvement over *C* for the two *A*s. With an additional *B* it is now possible for the *A*s to reach a tentative contract which makes B_1 as well off as possible, but leaves B_2 in isolation. Consider the point *P* [Fig. 3.1(i)] which is half-way along 0*C*; remembering that both *A*s

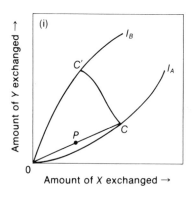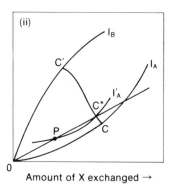

FIG. 3.1   The introduction of additional competitors

begin with endowments of $(a, 0)$, where the first element is the amount of good X and the second element is the amount of good Y. Similarly both Bs begin with $(0, b)$. If point C has coordinates (x, y), a contract which places the two As at P, giving each of them $(a - x/2, y/2)$, B_1 at C [giving him $(x, b - y)$] and B_2 at 0 [with $(0, b)$] is feasible. This is the contract which is most advantageous to B_1. It is important to notice that points between P and C cannot be achieved by this kind of coalition, since the two As and one B do not have sufficient resources to move further than half-way towards C.

This contract would not, however, be permanent because there remains an opportunity for B_2, who has been left at the origin, to form an agreement with at least one of the As. This was clearly noted by Edgeworth:

> the system of three might remain in the position reached; but for $[B_2]$ who has been left out in the cold. He will now strike in, with the result that the system will be worked down to the contract-curve again; to a point at least as favourable for the $[A$s] as $[P]$. Thus the $[A$s] will have lost some of their original advantage by competition.[65]

The point along CC' which is 'at least as favourable' as P is shown in Fig. 3.1(ii) as C^*. Here P is still half-way along the new ray from 0 to C^* and the indifference curve, I'_A of the two As passes through P and C^*. Since no point between P and C^* can be attained by the As, C^* must be the new limit to the contract curve. The same argument can be applied to the point C'. In modern terminology it would then be said that the 'core' of the economy shrinks as a result of the introduction of additional traders.

If a third pair of As and Bs are introduced, there is clearly a possibility for the three As to improve on C^* by forming a coalition with two of the Bs. Here it is possible to reach two-thirds of the way from the origin to any point on the contract curve, so that C^* will move inwards although a certain amount of indeterminacy will remain. In the general case of a number N of each of the As and Bs; then the 'attainable' ratio of $0P$ to $0C$ is $(N - 1)/N$, which has a limiting value of unity.[66] The result of 'working in' from both extremes of the contract curve would be a unique point on the contract curve where the common indifference curve of the As is tangential to that of the Bs. This is shown in Fig. 3.2. Edgeworth

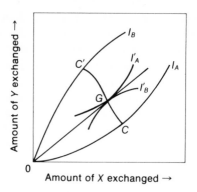

FIG. 3.2   The competitive solution

then states 'If this reasoning does not seem satisfactory, it would be possible to give a more formal proof; bringing out the important result that the common tangent to both indifference curves at the point (G) is the vector from the origin.'[67]

The significance of this result is that the vector from the origin is precisely the price vector which, if imposed, would achieve equilibrium in a market where all individuals were price 'takers'. The equilibrium solution with parametric pricing is therefore the same as that achieved by the cooperative recontracting game.

He then briefly considers different numbers of As and Bs, concluding that 'The theorem admits of being extended to the general case of unequal numbers and natures.'[68] A considerable number of articles have been written since the late 1950s which have examined the recontracting model under these different assumptions, but they cannot be considered here.[69]

Although Edgeworth never attempted to 'refine' the recontracting model further, it provided the basis of much of his later work. A selection of this work is considered in the remaining sections of this chapter.

Monopoly

It has been noted that for a number of years after 1881 Edgeworth's main work was in probability and statistics, resulting in many papers in *Mind*, *Philosophical Magazine* and *Journal of the Royal Statistical Society*, the volumes on Index-numbers, and his last book *Metretike: Or the Method of Measuring Probability and*

Utility (1887). The 1890s are, however, notable for three remarkable, and closely related, contributions to economic theory. These are his huge survey of 'The Pure Theory of International Values' (1894), and the two papers on 'The Pure Theory of Monopoly' and 'The Pure Theory of Taxation' in 1897. Although the monopoly paper contains many original contributions, it was first published in Italian and only available in English for the first time in 1925. Furthermore, since Cournot's long neglected contribution there had been very little interest in monopoly until the 1930s.[70] Referring to the theory of monopoly Marshall notes 'Cournot led the way, and among those who have made chief advances in it Professors Edgeworth and Pigou are prominent. Readers are referred to their masterly work . . . .'[71]

(i) *Indeterminacy*

After a brief discussion of tax incidence the second part of the 1897 paper was devoted to showing that 'when two or more monopolists are dealing with competitive groups, economic equilibrium is indeterminate'.[72] As is often the case with Edgeworth, his contributions revolve around criticism of other major work, in this case Cournot. The criticism relies heavily on his discussion of indeterminacy in *Mathematical Psychics*, but contains many new suggestions. He begins with the case where there are two monopolists, each owning a spring of mineral water (Cournot's 'source minérale') from which the daily output is limited to identical fixed amounts. There are no delivery costs and the demand curve is the same for all consumers; whence demand, x, is given by $N(1 - p)$ with N being the number of consumers and p the unit price. (In fact Edgeworth implicitly assumes that each consumer purchases one unit of the good, so that sales are increased by attracting more customers.)

If each monopolist deals separately with N customers (there are $2N$ in all), then the price which achieves maximum revenue is $p = \frac{1}{2}$, and half of the maximum possible output is sold. If, however, the goods are not independent (and in this case they are perfect substitutes), there is an incentive for one of the monopolists to lower his price, and deprive his rival of part of his initial custom. The rival will of course follow suit and 'by successive steps . . . the price may be lowered to $\frac{1}{4}$, which is just sufficient to take off the whole supply of one monopolist offered to half the market'.[73] This is the 'Cournot solution', but Edgeworth then argues that although no one has an incentive to lower the price further, one of the monopolists may *increase* his price back to $\frac{1}{2}$ (his revenue maximising price) since his rival 'has already done his worst by putting the whole of his supply on the market. The best that the rival can do ... is to follow the example set him and raise his price to $\frac{1}{2}$'.[74] Thus, instead of a determinate stable solution 'There will be an indeterminate tract through which the index of value will oscillate.'[75]

This is the rather extreme statement of the result, which has not surprisingly been criticised as unrealistic; but it is best to interpret the indeterminacy here in the same way as in the theory of exchange – namely in showing that other conditions are required in addition to the profit maximising assumption. Furthermore Edgeworth immediately qualified his statement by suggesting that

> at every stage ... it is competent to each monopolist to deliberate whether it will pay him better to lower his price against his rival as already described, or rather to raise it to a higher ... for that remainder of customers of which he cannot be deprived by his rival. Long before the lowest point has been reached that alternative will have become more advantageous than the course first described.[76]

It is characteristic of Edgeworth that he immediately states 'the matter may be put in a clearer light' – but in the next sentence he defines what is now called the *reaction curve* and *isoprofit lines* (in that order!)[77] for variations in prices. His diagram is also difficult to follow since it represents an extreme case because of the fact that prices must be identical (for perfect substitutes).[78]

Consider, however, Fig. 3.3 which shows for a general case the two sets of isoprofit and reaction curves for two monopolists A and B. These are drawn here as linear for convenience only. Where, 'ξ and η are the coordinates representing the prices of the articles' then the reaction curve was defined by Edgeworth as

> The locus of maximum profit for the monopolist owning the commodity x, of which the price is ξ – the *watershed*, so to speak, of the utility surface for that monopolist (or more exactly the locus of that price of x which for any assigned price of η affords maximum profit to the owner of x).[79]

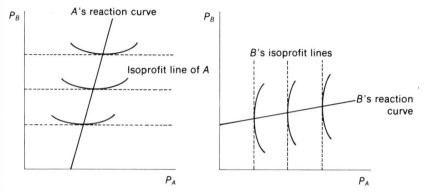

FIG. 3.3   Isoprofit and reaction curves

The isoprofit lines are obviously comparable with indifference curves. Placing the two parts of Fig. 3.3 together in Fig. 3.4 gives the Cournot equilibrium at the intersection of the reaction curves and the 'Edgeworth limits' between which prices are indeterminate as CC'. The line CC' is then comparable with the contract curve of exchange theory.

Edgeworth then considered the case of complementary demand within the context of 'bilateral monopoly', where the two goods are demanded in fixed proportions for use in the production of a further article.[80] The interesting point about this section is that he writes the equations of the reaction curves and explicitly deals with what are now called *Conjectural Variations* – reflecting the extent

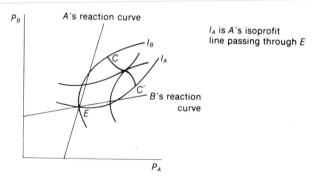

FIG. 3.4   Alternative duopoly solutions

to which one monopolist is expected to change his price in response to changes made by the second monopolist. If V is the revenue of the second monopolist and P_i the prices ('abstracting cost of production'), Edgeworth criticised Cournot for assuming that the monopolist will set $\partial V/\partial P_2 = 0$. 'He will go on varying the price P_2 until . . . $\partial V/\partial P_2 + (\partial V/\partial P_1)\partial P_1/\partial P_2 = 0$.'[81] It is the term $\partial P_1/\partial P_2$ which is the conjectural variation.

In discussing this problem Edgeworth then introduced a further important concept, one which is fundamental to the modern theory of games. This is the 'saddle point', which he called the 'Hog's Back', indicating its importance for stability. However, he admittedly used 'a somewhat fanciful illustration' of two Arctic explorers moving at right angles to each other on the ice.[82] Thus, it is not surprising, but unfortunate, that a long time had to elapse before Edgeworth's contribution was fully appreciated.

(ii) *The taxation paradox*

The third section of Edgeworth's monopoly paper contains the famous tax 'paradox' which states that

> When the supply of two or more correlated commodities – such as the carriage of passengers by rail first class or third class – is in the hands of a single monopolist a tax on one of the articles, e.g. a percentage of first class fares – may prove advantageous to the consumers as a whole. . . . The fares for *all* the classes might be reduced.[83]

Edgeworth regarded this as an example of where 'the abstract reasoning serves as a corrective to what has been called the "metaphysical incubus" of dogmatic *laisser faire*'.[84] The reaction to the paradox is also of interest; Seligman referred to it as 'a slip of Mr Edgeworth', although in 1901 Wicksell provided a simplified exposition using only a diagram.[85]

Again it was not until the 1930s that the paradox attracted serious attention, with the papers by Hotelling.[86] His outstanding 1932 paper showed that the result can occur in *competitive* markets where the related goods are substitutes in both consumption and production, and that in monopoly they must be substitutes in consumption. Hotelling's analysis also led him to show for the first time how restrictions derived from utility theory could be used in the estimation of systems of demand equations, and applied appropriate tests to some results of Schultz.[87]

Taxation

When mentioning Edgeworth's paper on taxation, Schumpeter said 'his exposition proceeds by . . . picking out currants . . . so that we have difficulty in visualising the spacious whole that is in fact the peak performance of its field and age'.[88] The breadth and depth of learning displayed in this paper are indeed staggering, and in order to be as exhaustive as possible Edgeworth used a 'new classification formed by four dichotomous cross divisions', so that the approach is also heavily taxonomic.[89]

He begins, 'the science of taxation comprises two subjects . . . the laws of incidence and the principle of equal sacrifice'.[90] The first part of the paper then proceeds to cover incidence in such contexts as international trade,[91] house rents in a circular city, and various cases of monopoly (which 'presents a bifurcation peculiar to itself'). He characteristically provides two further long discussions of the tax paradox but clearly says that a tax on one of two complementary goods may lower the price of either, but not of both.[92]

The section of the paper which attracted most attention is, however, the discussion of the various 'sacrifice' theories of the distribution of the tax burden, and Edgeworth's qualified support for progressive taxation. This subject is of course a further application of *Mathematical Psychics* – and just as Edgeworth considered the utilitarian principle of maximum utility a suitable arbitrator in cases of indeterminate contract, he applied it to the distribution of the burden of taxation (rejecting the *quid pro quo* principle because taxation is not an economic bargain governed by competition).[93]

The problem is one of determining, 'the distribution of those taxes which are applied to common purposes, the benefits whereof cannot be allocated to particular classes of citizens'.[94] The argument is then succinctly stated

> The condition that the total net utility procured by taxation should be a maximum then reduces to the condition that the total disutility should be a minimum . . . it follows in general that

the marginal disutility incurred by each taxpayer should be the same.[95]

The implication is that if all individuals have the same cardinal utility function, after-tax incomes would be equalised. Edgeworth also clearly recognised that if there is considerable dispersion of pre-tax incomes relative to the total amount of tax to be raised (where there is 'not enough tax to go around'),[96] the equi-marginal condition cannot be fully satisfied unless there is a 'negative income tax' which raises the incomes of the poorest individuals to a common level. Thus, 'The *acme* of socialism is for a moment sighted',[97] but Edgeworth immediately considers the practical limitations to such high progressive taxation. The following quotation illustrates one of Edgeworth's favourite metaphors (and past-times), his respect for Sidgwick, his attitude to authority, his views on utilitarianism and the applicability of pure theory, and of course his unmistakeable style

> In this misty and precipitous region let us take Professor Sidgwick as our chief guide. He best has contemplated the crowning height of the utilitarian first principle, from which the steps of a sublime deduction lead to the high tableland of equality; but he also discerns the enormous interposing chasms which deter practical wisdom from moving directly towards that ideal.[98]

Among the various limitations, Edgeworth notes differences in individual utility functions,[99] population effècts, the disincentives to work, growth of 'culture' and knowledge, savings and of course the problem of evasion. He later provides a long list of questions which should be asked when considering the limits to taxable capacity in any 'concrete case'.[100]

Thus, while minimum, or equi-marginal, sacrifice is 'the sovereign principle of taxation', it should be limited in practice. Edgeworth then considered whether 'equal sacrifice, or any of the cognate subsidiary forms of the hedonic principle' would offer a guide. He had no hesitation, however, in dismissing either of the alternatives – equal absolute sacrifice or equal proportional sacrifice. Both were rejected on the grounds that whereas minimum sacrifice indicates progression on the assumption of diminishing marginal utility, much more information about individuals' utility functions is required before the alternatives give any definite prescription. For equal absolute sacrifice, taxes are progressive, proportional or regressive according to whether or not the elasticity of the marginal utility of income is greater, equal to, or less than unity. For equal proportional sacrifice taxes are progressive if the marginal utility of income schedule is steeper than a rectangular hyperbola.[101] Edgeworth rejected the logarithmic (Bernouilli), or other explicit forms and, for the case of equal proportional sacrifice, later argued that 'In order to obtain a ratio between two "lots" of satisfaction . . . there is required a precision of hedonic units which few utilitarians would venture to postulate.'[102]

Edgeworth later became engaged in yet another controversy with Seligman over the meaning of the various sacrifice principles[103] – employing his usual curious mixture of acrimonious excessive politeness – but it is true to say that his argument is now widely accepted.[104] It may also be noted that Edgeworth did suggest a general formula giving 'effectual continual progression',[105] which related pre- and post-tax incomes (x and y respectively) by $y = \alpha x^\beta$. Nevertheless to the practical question of 'exactly where you should tighten or no' he replied, 'that is beyond my science'.[106]

In the early 1970s the subject of 'optimal taxation' again suddenly became very fashionable, when a number of attempts were made to allow explicitly for possible effects on labour supply.[107]

International trade

Edgeworth's survey of the 'Pure Theory of International Values' was in many ways responsible for a change of emphasis in the approach to international trade, although ironically there are few original analytical contributions.[108] The three papers were later rearranged for the *Papers* into the more convenient divisions of 'on classical lines' and 'mathematical theory', when Edgeworth again retracted his criticisms of Bastable and Pigou concerning the symmetry of import and export taxes.[109]

He began, 'International trade meaning in plain English trade between nations, it is not surprising that the term should mean something else in political economy.'[110] The defining characteristic was of course the immobility of factors of production,[111] but for Edgeworth

> The fundamental principle of international trade is that general theory ... the Theory of Exchange ... which ... constitutes the 'kernel' of most of the chief problems in economics. It is a corollary of the general theory that all the parties to a bargain look to gain by it. ... This is the generalised statement of the theory of comparative cost.[112]

Thus, the gains from trade are analogous to the gains from exchange in simple barter and 'It is useful ... to contemplate the theory of distribution as analogous to that of international trade proper.'[113]

Trade theory is to Edgeworth one more application of *Mathematical Psychics*, and one of his criticisms of Mill was in fact that the latter took as the measure of gain the change in the ratio of exchange of exports against imports. Mill, in this case, 'thus confounds "final" with integral utility', though Edgeworth, while preferring total utility, admits that the measure is adequate for Mill's purposes.[114]

Edgeworth's survey is, as always, extremely wide ranging, though for later developments the most interesting parts are concerned with his elucidation of Mill's 'recognition of the case in which an impediment may be beneficial – or an improvement prejudicial – to one of the countries',[115] using the supply-and-demand (offer) curves of Marshall. These two cases would now be discussed under the headings of the 'optimal tariff' and 'immiserising growth'.[116]

There are, however, two points worth noting about Edgeworth's use of such offer curves. First, he was quite content to use community indifference curves without specifying how aggregation might be carried out.[117] Secondly, he fully anticipated Graham's later criticism by stating

> A movement along a supply-and-demand curve of international trade should be considered as attended with rearrangements of internal trade; as the movements of the hands of a clock correspond to considerable unseen movements of the machinery.[118]

Edgeworth's analysis of the optimum tariff was similar to that of

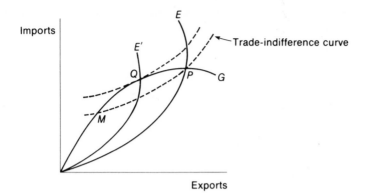

FIG. 3.5   The optimum tariff

'Auspitz and Lieben's beautiful and original reasoning'.[119] From Fig. 3.5 the optimum tariff is one which shifts the home offer curve to $0E'$, thereby cutting $0G$ at the 'highest' point Q.

He also extended his treatment to more than two countries. Although Edgeworth showed that the elasticity of the offer curve of the home country exceeds unity above the point where the tangent is vertical and considered the elasticities of native and foreign demand,[120] the precise specification of the optimum tariff had to wait until Bickerdike and Pigou[121] and the later revivals of interest in the 1940s. Edgeworth's judgement of Bickerdike is not exactly modest, however; 'Mr Bickerdike has accomplished a wonderful feat. He has said something new about protection'.[122] Edgeworth could not, of course, be expected to support such tariffs. In addition to accepting the possibility of retaliation,[123] he noted

> For one nation to benefit itself at the expense of . . . others is contrary to the highest morality. . . . But in an abstract study upon the motion of projectiles *in vacuo*, I do not think it necessary to enlarge upon the horrors of war.[124]

Conclusion

For the last 30 years of his life Edgeworth's major work was in mathematical statistics, in which 'He would give place . . . to no economist.'[125] Indeed, of over 170 published papers, only one-quarter are in economics; but this should be set against his 132 reviews in the *Economic Journal*, 17 reviews in the *Academy* and 131 articles in Palgrave's *Dictionary*!

His economics in this later period became more critical than original, with, for example, the survey of the theory of distribution which was published in 1904. Edgeworth's criticisms of Wicksteed, linear homogenous production functions, and his view of the entrepreneur have been reviewed in detail by Stigler.[126] However, in the later paper on the 'Laws of Returns',[127] he clarifies the (then) common confusion between average and marginal product and develops an almost complete set of the modern textbook cost curves. Stigler also provides a reminder that a general equilibrium model is presented in a footnote to a review.[128]

There is insufficient space here to consider also his interesting discussions of wages of men and women, railway economics, war economics, demography, statistics of examinations and of bees, and especially his original paper on 'The Mathematical Theory of Banking'.[129]

From this brief survey it is nevertheless hoped that, however diverse and 'minute' some of Edgeworth's work seems to be, the theme running through it is sufficiently clear.[130] From his 1879 paper in *Mind* containing a mathematical treatment of the utilitarian optimal distribution, combined with his realisation of the importance of indeterminacy and the increasing need for 'arbitration', the twin subjects of 'exchange and distribution' were of primary importance. Thus, 'The whole creation groans and yearns, desiderating a principle of arbitration, an end to strife.'[131] That the utilitarian principle could provide such a guiding 'star' was fundamental to all his work.

> Now it is a circumstance of momentous interest – that one of the in general indefinitely numerous *settlements* between contractors is the utilitarian arrangement ... the contract tending to the greatest possible total utility of the contractors.[132]

On the unity in his work, Keynes suggested that 'If he had been the kind that produces treatises, he would doubtless have published ... a large volume in five books entitled *Mathematical Psychics*.'[133] His three volumes of *Papers* which he selected and edited, and which were published by the Royal Economic Society when Edgeworth was 80 years old, fortunately serve as a partial substitute for such a treatise. The success of this publication seems to have given him 'as much pleasure as surprise'.[134]

It has already been noted that Edgeworth always stressed the limitations of purely abstract results, and argued that any particular policy question always required detailed analysis of the relevant 'data'. Edgeworth has sometimes been accused of building on 'shifting sands', because of the problems associated with the measurement and comparability of utility. Edgeworth, however, was much too cautious and diffident to suggest *positive* results; indeed the following quotation from his discussion of minimum sacrifice and tax formulae nicely illustrates his view

Yet the premises, however inadequate to the deduction of a definite formula, may suffice for a certain negative conclusion. The ground which will not serve as the foundation of the elaborate edifice designed may yet be solid enough to support a battering-ram capable of being directed against simpler edifices in the neighbourhood.[135]

There is no doubt that Edgeworth's contribution to the pure theory of economics was enormous, whatever the ultimate limitations to the applicability of that theory. It is well to conclude with the advice given by Edgeworth in his inaugral lecture at Oxford in 1891

The margin of profit and loss in the intellectual . . . world will differ with the personality of individuals. No general rule is available except that, like the cultivated Athenian, we should eschew the invidious disparagement of each others' pursuits.[136]

NOTES

1. Keynes quotes Marshall as saying, with reference to Edgeworth's mixed ancestry, 'Francis is a charming fellow, but you must be careful with Ysidro': J. M. Keynes, *Essays in Biography* (London: Macmillan for the Royal Economic Society, 1972) [hereafter cited as *EB*] p. 265.
2. For a fascinating account of the Edgeworth family, see J. H. Butler and H. E. Butler, *The Black Book of Edgeworthstown and other Edgeworth Memories 1585–1817* (London: Faber and Gwyer, 1927).

3. This was a nice combination for Edgeworth, of the first major abstract theorist and the pioneering utilitarian. See also M. Edgeworth, *Memories of Richard Lovell Edgeworth, Esq., Begun by Himself and Concluded by His Daughter, Maria Edgeworth*, 2 vols (London: R. Hunter, 1820).

4. It should be rememberd that Edgeworth was only two when she died! But on his memory, see Keynes, *EB*, p. 254; A. L. Bowley, 'F. Y. Edgeworth', *Econometrica*, II (1934) 113–124, at p. 123, and L. L. Price, 'Obituary of Edgeworth', *Journal of the Royal Statistical Society* [hereafter cited as *JRSS*], LXXXIX (1926) 371–7, at p. 28.

5. He was going with a nephew T. L. Beddoes. The story told by Kendall in E. S. Pearson and M. G. Kendall (eds), *Studies in the History of Statistics and Probability* (London: Griffen, 1970) is incorrect, but see Butler and Butler, op. cit., p. 248.

6. He actually received his degree in 1873 and his MA in 1877. He was later awarded an Honorary DCL by Durham University. See Bowley, op. cit., p. 113.

7. See J. K. Whitaker (ed.), *The Early Economic Writings of Alfred Marshall, 1867–1890*, vol. I (London: Macmillan, 1975). [Hereafter cited as *Wh.*I.] But see also the comments on Marshall, Jowett and the use of mathematics by Edgeworth in A. C. Pigou (ed.), *Memorials of Alfred Marshall 1842–1924* (London: Macmillan, 1925) [hereafter cited as *Mems.*] p. 66.

8. Jevons resigned from Owens College and moved to University College, London, in 1875. Edgeworth had lodgings at 5, Mount Vernon. In a letter to Mrs Jevons after Jevons's death, Edgeworth wrote, 'I shall always remember with gratitude the kind encouragement and a peculiar intellectual sympathy which he extended to one whose studies were in the same direction, however immeasurably behind his': R. D. C. Black, 'W. S. Jevons and the Economists of his Time', *Manchester School*, XXX (1962) 203–22. Keynes wrote, 'I have no evidence that his interest in economics antedated his contact with Jevons' (*EB*, p. 148, n 4). Edgeworth says that his paper on 'The Hedonical Calculus', *Mind*, IV (1879) 394–408, was written in ignorance of Jevons's work. See *Mathematical Psychics* (London: Kegan Paul, 1881) [hereafter cited as *MP*] p. 34.

9. See *Mems.*, p. 66.

10. He earlier lectured on English Language and Literature at Bedford College, London. See T. W. Hutchison, *A Review of Economic Doctrines 1870–1929* (Oxford: Clarendon Press, 1953) p. 109.

11. A list has been compiled under the direction of H. G. Johnson. I am grateful to Klaus Hennings for showing me a copy of this list. See also Kendall, op. cit., and S. M. Stigler, 'Francis Ysidro Edgeworth, Statistician', *JRSS*, CXLI (1978) 287–322.

12. Edgeworth was a Guy Medalist (Gold) in 1907 and President of the Royal Statistical Society (1912–14). Edgeworth's main contributions in statistics concern work on the 'law of error', the correlation coefficient, transformations ('methods of translation') and the

'Edgeworth Expansion'. See the interesting paper by S. Stigler, op. cit.

13. Op. cit., p. 119. See A. L. Bowley, *Edgeworth's Contribution to Mathematical Statistics* (London: Royal Statistical Society, 1928). The only paper of which Edgeworth was co-author was written with Bowley, 'Methods of Representing Statistics of Wages and Other Groups not Fulfilling the Normal Law of Error', *JRSS*, LXV (1902) 325–54.

14. It is interesting to note that the major contributions to the subject of index numbers have been made by economists. See, for example, J. A. Schumpeter, *History of Economic Analysis* (London: Allen & Unwin, 1955). [Hereafter cited as *History*.]

15. See A. C. Pigou, 'Professor Edgeworth's Collected Papers', *Economic Journal* [hereafter cited as *EJ*], XXV (1925) 177–185, at p. 179.

16. Edgeworth had previously applied for chairs in Philosophy at King's in 1880, and in Philosophy and Political Economy at Liverpool in 1881. See Jevons's testimonials in R. D. C. Black (ed.), *Papers and Correspondence of William Stanley Jevons*, vol. III (London: Macmillan for the Royal Economic Society, 1978) p. 98. He also applied for a chair in Greek at Bedford College in 1875; see S. Stigler, op. cit., p. 289.

17. Edgeworth gave up his post at King's and was succeeded by Cunningham. Thorold Rogers actually held the Drummond Chair from 1862 to 1868 and from 1888 to 1890, and was Tooke Professor (1859–1890), holding both chairs simultaneously.

18. One wonders how students would react to the now familiar distinctions, '. . . the two meanings of increased demand . . . are most easily and with least liability to logomachy distinguished as the variation of an ordinate (1) due to displacement of the curve, the abscissa not varying, or (2) corresponding to an increment of the abscissa, the curve being undisturbed'. See F. Y. Edgeworth, *Papers Relating to Political Economy*, 3 vols (London: Macmillan for the Royal Economic Society, 1925) vol. II [hereafter cited as *Papers*, II], p. 275 n 2. On Edgeworth's influence in Oxford, see Bowley, *Econometrica*, loc. cit., p. 123.

19. The formation of the Royal Economic Society in 1890 is described by A. W. Coats, 'The Origins and Early Development of the Royal Economic Society'. *EJ*. LXXVIII (1968) 349–71.

20. Bowley, *Econometrica* (loc. cit., p. 122) notes, 'Edgeworth was thus the most accessible of the English economists', and Keynes (*EB*, p. 264) says. 'I am sure that there was no economist in England better read than he in foreign literature. He added to this what must have been the widest personal acquaintance in the world with economists of all nations.'

21. *EB*, p. 264. Edgeworth had difficulty in spotting misprints in his own papers and also in detecting that his own criticism could be quite sarcastic. It is amusing to read, 'We of the British Association do not lay ourselves out for controversy. The method of rebuttal and

rejoinder does not seem particularly suited to our subject.' Quoted by Kendall, op. cit., p. 261.

22. Higgs was secretary in 1892, then assistant editor from 1896 until he became the Prime Minister's Private Secretary in 1905. Keynes says characteristically: 'I was supported by Edgeworth on the one side and by Alfred Hoare on the other. With the passing of both of them an old and beloved civilisation has departed, and we hear the barbarians at the gate' (*EB*, p. 313).

23. An incident concerning Cunningham and a rejoinder to Marshall (which Edgeworth refused to publish) is discussed in A. W. Coats, 'Sociological Aspects of British Economic Thought 1880–1930', *Journal of Political Economy* [hereafter cited as *JPE*], LXXV (1967) 715–29, at p. 712 n 10.

24. Bowley, *Econometrica* (loc. cit., p. 123) says, 'he appears to have looked critically at every book that reached the Journal's office. A request for a review would be accompanied by some apposite remarks on particular points in the text.'

25. He often had his papers privately printed with additional sections containing further work.

26. *MP*, p. 3

27. Edgeworth referred to the 'age of luxuriant speculation when novel theories teem in so many new economic journals'; quoted by A. W. Coats in 'The Historicist Reaction in English Political Economy', *Economica*, XXI (1954) 143–53.

28. Keynes, *EB*, p. 264.

29. In *Papers*, II, vii.

30. *Papers*, II, p. 143. Edgeworth also said 'much of our reasoning is directed to the refutation of fallacies, and a great part of our science only raises us to the zero point of nescience from the negative position of error ... it is not to be supposed ... that ... we are occupied only in mangling each other's theories' (*Papers*, II, p. 285).

31. *Papers*, II, p. 390. He had earlier been discussing the fact that an engineer making a tunnel may assume that the gravel is a 'continuous substance', but in considering the progress of a worm through the same ground the assumption cannot be used (see *Papers*, II, p. 389).

32. While discussing barter he later asked: 'what is the most appropriate conception of the process by which value is determined through the higgling of the market? Any simple conception must involve a considerable element of hypothesis, not admitting of decisive proof' (*Papers*, I, p. 39). See also *Mems.*, p. 67. Nevertheless, he noted: 'It is difficult to formulate the presumptions of common sense so unequivocally as not to admit of being misrepresented and misapplied by captious critics and stupid practitioners' (*Papers*, II, p. 479).

33. In *MP*, p. 99 he referred to 'the first principle of probabilities, according to which cases about which we are equally undecided ... count as equal'.

34. *Papers*, II, p. 391.

35. But Edgeworth rarely did genuine empirical work. A rare test is presented, rather tongue in cheek, in *Papers*, II, p. 323 n 4 concerning the relationship between wine consumption per head and size of party in 'a certain Oxford college'. The data were given in per cent form, lest he 'should excite the envy of some and the contempt of others'. In fact, he was pessimistic of estimating economic schedules. See *Papers*, I, p. 8, and R. H. Inglis Palgrave (ed.), *Dictionary of Political Economy*, 3 vols (London: Macmillan, 1894) vol. I, p. 473: 'Jevons' hope of obtaining demand curves by statistical observation . . . may appear chimerical'. Contrast this with Marshall's view that 'as time goes on, the statistics of consumption will be so organised as to afford demand schedules sufficiently trustworthy': quoted by A. C. Pigou, *Alfred Marshall and Current Thought* (London: Macmillan, 1953) p. 25.

36. *EB*, p. 265.

37. G. J. Stigler, *Essays in the History of Economics* (Chicago: University of Chicago Press, 1965) p. 246.

38. *MP*, p. 12.

39. *MP*, p. 14.

40. *MP*, p. 15.

41. W. S. Jevons, *The Theory of Political Economy*, ed. by R. D. C. Black (Harmondsworth: Penguin, 1970). [Hereafter cited as *TPE*.]

42. *Papers*, II, p. 458.

43. The utility function is introduced in *MP*, p. 20. The quotation is from *MP*, p. 104.

44. *Papers*, II, p. 291. Unfortunately this method of writing the function led to some confusion: see J. Creedy, 'Some Recent Interpretations of Mathematical Psychics', *History of Political Economy* [hereafter cited as *HOPE*], 12 (1980) 267–76.

45. J. A. Schumpeter, *Ten Great Economists* (London: Allen & Unwin, 1952) p. 127.

46. A. Marshall, *Principles of Economics* (London: Macmillan, 1890) 9th (Variorum) edn, ed. C. W. Guillebaud (London: Macmillan, 1961) vol. II [hereafter cited as *G*.II] p. 844.

47. For a recent examination of the implications of additivity, see A. S. Deaton, 'A Reconsideration of the Empirical Implications of Additive Preferences', *EJ*, LXXXIV (1974) 338–48.

48. *Papers*, III, p. 38.

49. *MP*, p. 34.

50. The first criticism came from W. E. Johnson, 'The Pure Theory of Utility Curves', *EJ*, XXIII (1913) 483–513, followed by H. L. Schultz, 'Interrelations of Demand', *JPE*, XLI (1933) 468–512, and R. G. D. Allen, 'A Comparison of Different Definitions of Complementary and Competitive Goods', *Econometrica*, II (1934) 168–75. For further discussion, see P. A. Samuelson, 'Complementarity: an Essay on the 40th Anniversary of the Hicks–Allen Revolution in Demand Theory', *Journal of Economic Literature*, XII (1974) 1255–89, and J. Chipman, 'An Empirical Implication of Auspitz–Lieben–Edgeworth–Pareto Complementarity', *Journal of Economic Theory*, XIV (1977) 228–31.

51. In *MP*, pp. 20–1. Marshall (*Wh*.II, p. 267) characteristically wrote 'His readers may sometimes wish that he had kept his work by him a little longer till he had worked it out more fully, and obtained that simplicity which comes only through long labour.' Edgeworth said that the theory, 'could be presented by a professed mathematician more elegantly and scientifically' (*MP*, p. 24).

52. *MP*, p. 21.

53. *MP*, p. 21. It is sometimes wrongly suggested that indifference curves were suggested by Marshall, but they are more likely to have been suggested by Jevons (see *TPE*, p. 140). See also *MP*, p. 26 n 1, and Schumpeter, *History*, p. 1065 n 10.

54. *MP*, p. 22.

55. The conventional interpretation has recently been questioned by, for example, W. Jaffé, 'Edgeworth's Contract Curve: A Propadeutic Essay in Clarification', *HOPE*, 6 (1974) 343–59. The box diagram in *MP* (p. 28) has the origin in the south-west corner because Edgeworth was concerned mainly with *exchange*. The modern emphasis on allocation of fixed amounts has led to the box being rotated by 90°. See also Creedy, op. cit.

56. *MP*, p. 28.

57. Edgeworth transforms $U_A(x, y)$ to polar coordinates, where ρ measures the length from the origin along a ray inclined at an angle of θ to the x axis. Then $\tan\theta$ is the rate of exchange and the demand curve of A is $dU_A/d\rho = 0$. See also *MP*, p. 105. This was called the 'offer curve' by A. L. Bowley in *The Mathematical Groundwork of Economics* (Oxford: Oxford University Press, 1924), although Edgeworth disliked the term. The use of offer curves in international trade theory has been extended to include the production function, endowments of factors of production, and tastes all in the same diagram.

58. This has recently been questioned by D. A. Walker, 'Edgeworth's Theory of Recontract', *EJ*, LXXXIII (1973) 138–49, but see Creedy, op. cit.

59. *MP*, p. 17.

60. *MP*, p. 29.

61. The 'indeterminacy' was the source of a disagreement between Marshall and Edgeworth. See *G*.II, pp. 791–8, and Edgeworth's *Papers*, II, p. 317 n 1.

62. *MP*, p. 30.

63. *MP*, pp. 34–43.

64. *MP*., p. 35.

65. *MP*, p. 37.

66. The consumption 'bundle' of each of the N As would be $\{a - x(N - 1)/N, y(N - 1)/N\}$. The B who is 'left in the cold' would get $(0, b)$, while the remaining Bs would each get $(x, b - y)$. Thus, the provisional contract is feasible.

67. *MP*, p. 38.

68. *MP*, p. 43.

69. For further details see M. Bacharach, *Economics and the Theory of*

Games (London: Macmillan, 1976), and W. Hildebrand and A. Kirman, *General Equilibrium Analysis* (Amsterdam: North Holland, 1976). The seminal work is M. Schubik, 'Edgeworth Market Games', in R. D. Luce and A. W. Tucker (eds), *Contributions to the Theory of Games*, vol. IV (Princeton, N.J.: Princeton University Press, 1959).

70. See Edgeworth's introduction in *Papers*, I, p. 111. Subsequent discussions have been divided into those concerned with wage bargaining, and those dealing with monopolised industries. The literature is too large to list here, but see A. J. Nichol, 'Edgeworth's Theory of Duopoly Price', *EJ*, XLV (1935) 51–66, and M. J. Farrell, 'Edgeworth's Bounds for Oligopoly Prices', *Economica*, n.s., XLIX (1970) 341–61.

71. A. Marshall, *Industry and Trade* (London: Macmillan, 1919) p. 399.

72. *Papers*, I, p. 116.

73. *Papers*, I, p. 119.

74. *Papers*, I, p. 120.

75. *Papers*, I, p. 118. In *Papers*, II, p. 101 n 1, Edgeworth states that 'of course I do not suppose such a prolonged series of steps . . . to occur in the concrete. But I think it is a legitimate fiction in order to bring out the contrast' with competition which 'tends to a definite . . . equilibrium'. He also used the analogy of stalemate with chess players, and similar games of strategy where anticipation of a rival's play is important.

76. *Papers*, I, p. 120.

77. These concepts were subsequently clarified by Bowley in the *Groundwork*.

78. *Papers*, I, p. 120.

79. *Papers*, I, p. 121.

80. The general treatment of this case is rather complex, and depends also on the state of the market in which the good is sold.

81. *Papers*, I, p. 123.

82. *Papers*, I, p. 124.

83. *Papers*, I, p. 139.

84. *Papers*, I, p. 139.

85. From E. R. A. Seligman, *Shifting and the Incidence of Taxation* (New York: Macmillan, 1921) p. 214. For a later judgement by Edgeworth of Seligman, see *Papers*, I, p. 93. For Wicksell's treatment, see K. Wicksell, *Selected Papers in Economic Theory*, ed. by E. Lindahl (London: Allen & Unwin, 1958) p. 108 and *Lectures on Political Economy*, vol. I (London: Routledge, 1934) pp. 93–5. See also W. Baumol and S. M. Goldfeld (eds), *Precursors in Mathematical Economics: An Anthology* (London: London School of Economics, 1968) p. 190.

86. These are 'Edgeworth's taxation Paradox and the Nature of Demand and Supply Functions', *JPE*, XL (1932) 577–616, repr. in Baumol and Goldfeld, op. cit., pp. 358–86, and 'Note on Edgeworth's Taxation Phenomenon and Professor Carver's Additional Condition on Demand Functions'. *Econometrica*. I (1933) 408–9.

87. This is the paper by Schultz mentioned in note 50.
88. *History*, p. 946.
89. *Papers*, II, p. 63. Much of Edgeworth's other work on taxation, especially on urban rates, is in *Papers*, II.
90. *Papers*, II, p. 64.
91. Here (*Papers*, II, p. 72) he retracts his criticism of Bastable and Pigou on the symmetry of import and export taxes.
92. See *Papers*, II, pp. 81, 92–95 and *Papers*, II, p. 72. Edgeworth was clearly aware of the result later given by Hotelling with more clarity – that the tax 'paradox' occurs in competition, 'if the commodities are rivals both in production and consumption' (*Papers*, II, p. 63).
93. *Papers*, II, p. 102. The treatment clearly requires cardinality: see *Papers*, II, p. 475, and A. C. Pigou, *A Study in Public Finance*, 3rd rev. edn (London: Macmillan, 1947) p. 41. Schumpeter's statement (*History*, p. 831) that 'we can leave out the utilitarian from any of his economic writings without affecting their scientific content' is either tautological or inaccurate.
94. *Papers*, II, p. 103.
95. *Papers*, II, p. 103.
96. *Papers*, II, p. 103.
97. *Papers*, II, p. 104.
98. *Papers*, II, p. 104.
99. See *Papers*, II, p. 105, which also includes his views of authority as 'evidence'. A. P. Lerner in *The Economics of Control* (New York: Macmillan, 1947) later considered differing utility functions and 'probabilistic egalitarianism'.
100. *Papers*, II, p. 118.
101. See, for example, Pigou, *Public Finance*, p. 89.
102. *Papers*, II, p. 235.
103. One issue is Edgeworth's interpretation of Mill's famous paragraph quoted in *Papers*, II, pp. 115 and 237, where Mill seems to support both equal and minimum sacrifice. Edgeworth suggests that 'equal sacrifice is but a corrupt reading for equi-marginal sacrifice', and 'it may well be doubted whether Mill entertained the notion of proportional sacrifice' (*Papers*, II, p. 115). After considering Seligman's argument, Edgeworth said 'on reconsideration I am disposed to omit the word "well"' (*Papers*, II, p. 235). See also Schumpeter, *History*, p. 1071.
104. Pigou, a member of the 1920 Royal Commission, said 'there can be no question that . . . least aggregate sacrifice is an ultimate principle of taxation' (*Public Finance*, p. 43). For further references and discussion, see especially F. Shehab, *Progressive Taxation: A Study in the Development of the Progressive Principle in the British Public Tax* (Oxford: Oxford University Press, 1953), and W. J. Blum and K. Kalven Jr, *The Uneasy Case for Progressive Taxation* (Chicago: Chicago University Press, 1953).
105. *Papers*, II, p. 249.
106. *Papers*, II, p. 260. In *Papers*, II, p. 269, he considered $\alpha = 1$, that is $y = x^\beta$. Ironically, this tax schedule actually arises from equal

proportional sacrifice with a logarithmic utility function. For $u = \log x$ and a tax rate $t(x)$, the loss of utility, s, is equal to $-\log\{1 - t(x)\}$, and for constant $s/u = k$, then $t(x) = 1 - x^{-k}$ and $y = x^{1-k}$.

107. See E. S. Phelps (ed.), *Economic Justice* (Harmondsworth: Penguin, 1973) for references to this literature.

108. As Edgeworth was the first to acknowledge 'what is written . . . after a perusal of [Marshall's] privately circulated chapters . . . can make no claim to originality' (*Papers*, II, p. 46). Further, 'Mill's exposition of the general theory is still unsurpassed' (*Papers*, II, p. 20) even though he thought that the supplement of the 3rd edition was 'laborious and confusing'. For a contrary view see Schumpeter, *History*, p. 608 n 7.

109. First noted in his taxation paper, in which he held that his argument depended on taxes in kind. See also Pigou, *Public Finance*, p. 180. This subject was treated at length in A. P. Lerner, 'The Symmetry of Import and Export Taxes', *Economica*, n.s., III (1936) 308–13.

110. *Papers*, II, p. 5.

111. But Edgeworth did regard the existence of non-competing groups within a country as an argument for not lifting existing tariffs, because of the long term effect on employment.

112. *Papers*, II, p. 6.

113. *Papers*, II, p. 19.

114. *Papers*, II, p. 22.

115. *Papers*, II, p. 9.

116. Following J. Bhagwati, 'Immiserizing Growth: A Geometric Note', *Review of Economic Studies*, XXV (1958) 201–5.

117. He says only 'By combining properly the utility curves for all the individuals, we obtain what may be called a collective utility curve' (*Papers*, II, p. 293). See W. W. Leontieff, 'The Use of Indifference Curves in the Analysis of Foreign Trade', *QJE*, XLVII (1933) 493–503.

118. *Papers*, II, p. 32. F. Graham's criticism is in 'The Theory of International Values Re-examined', *QJE*, XXXVII (1923) 54–86. This is treated exhaustively by J. E. Meade, *A Geometry of International Trade* (London: Allen & Unwin, 1952). It may be noted here that J. Viner, *Studies in the Theory of International Trade* (London: Allen & Unwin, 1964) p. 546, criticises Edgeworth's diagram (in *Papers*, II, p. 32) for not including a straight line section in the offer curves to cover the case where the country does not trade. However, he does not realise that Edgeworth has simply shifted the origin, so that his axis refers to exports and imports rather than to the total output of 'exportables'. Viner (op. cit., p. 547 n 24) also wrongly interprets 'to generalise the theory' as meaning to allow for non-constant returns to scale.

119. *Papers*, II, p. 295.

120. *Papers*, II, p. 35.

121. See C. F. Bikerdike, 'The Theory of Incipient Taxes', *EJ*, XVI (1906), and A. C. Pigou, *Protective and Preferential Import Duties* (London: Macmillan, 1908).

122. *Papers*, II, p. 344.
123. For a later treatment of retaliation see H. G. Johnson, 'Optimum Tariffs and Retaliation', *Review of Economic Studies*, XXI (1953) 142–53.
124. *Papers*, II, p. 17 n 5.
125. Bowley, *Econometrica*, loc. cit., p. 114. It would be interesting to know how, and 'under what incentive' (Kendall, op. cit., p. 258), Edgeworth learnt his mathematics. Bowley (op. cit., p. 113) is the only person to suggest even that 'it may be presumed' that he studied mathematics in Dublin. It is very hard to believe that he was trained; see also note 51. In discussion of S. M. Stigler (op. cit., p. 318), Eisenhart suggests that Edgeworth's uncle (and grand-uncle!), Sir Francis Beaufort, may have had some influence, but this is doubtful. It is known that Edgeworth's grandfather (Richard Lovell Edgeworth) enjoyed working out arithmetical problems, but his father (Francis Beaufort Edgeworth) hated mathematics (see Butler and Butler, op. cit., p. 247). On Edgeworth's mathematics see also J. Creedy, 'The Early Use of Lagrange Multipliers in Economics', *EJ*, XC (1980) 371–76.
126. In G. J. Stigler, *Production and Distribution Theories* (London: Macmillan, 1941).
127. Reprinted in *Papers*, I, and first published in 1911.
128. G. J. Stigler, op. cit., p. 123.
129. 'The Mathematical Theory of Banking', *JRSS*, LI (1888) 113–27 concerned the transactions demand for cash.
130. Edgeworth was fond of quoting 'A mighty maze, but not without a plan'. Bowley (op. cit., p. 21) writes that 'To Edgeworth there was an underlying unity in the fundamental conceptions and in much of the method of economics and statistics.'
131. *MP*, p. 51.
132. He argued that other methods of arbitration, such as equal division, would be unstable because they were not on the contract curve. Edgeworth preferred the utilitarian to the competitive position, though the latter is also on the contract curve.
133. *EB*, p. 261.
134. *EB*, p. 263. There are signs that Edgeworth resented the popularity of others, even those he admired. In reviewing Marshall's 3rd edition of the *Principles* (1895) in *Papers* (III, p. 64) he says 'A feeling of relief and satisfaction may be experienced by another sort of susceptible *doctrinaire* when the *doyen* of English economists appears in a literary garb which can excite no suspicion of his being tainted with a form of error much condemned by those who have no mind to it – the inordinate use of reasoning.'
135. *Papers*, II, p. 261.
136. *Papers*, I, p. 11.

4 A. C. Pigou, 1877–1959

DAVID COLLARD

Introduction – biographia

Those of us who went up to Cambridge in the late 1950s remember Pigou as an eccentrically clad, unapproachable figure sitting in a deck chair on the grass of the front court of King's. At that time he refused to discuss economics and was reputed to read only comics and 'shockers'. Sartorial disarray was not, in Pigou's case, merely a product of old age for Marshall had complained to C. R. Fay, many years before: 'Fay, I do wish you'd speak to Pigou on a personal matter – a rather delicate matter. I saw him coming out of Bowes' shop in a Norfolk jacket with holes in both elbows. So bad for the Economics Tripos!'[1] Pigou's various eccentricities, closely linked to his shyness, had their attractive and unattractive aspects. He had a great sense of fun, particularly in his earlier years. Corrie reports

> If every one of his friends recounted their amusing recollections of the Prof it would fill a volume ... the remarkable thing about the Prof was the rapidity with which he could relax from serious work and plunge with boyish enjoyment into any sort of hair-brained [sic] scheme.[2]

Among such merry japes Corrie reports accidentally dropping lighted matches onto the Vice-Provost's head, singeing Corrie's eyebrows with a rocket and setting fire to a bridge in the Lake District. He was an enthusiastic and competent climber, encouraging the young and even including female undergraduates in his party. He had no time for foreigners or politicians and was extremely shy of women. Saltmarsh and Wilkinson report that when his memoir of Keynes appeared, 'Lydia Keynes kissed him: the only woman known to have done so since his childhood. After that it happened quite often, and the Prof seemed to like it.'[3]

He often affected a silly high pitched voice and, in his later years, pretended to be 'gaga'. There was something in him of the archetypal overgrown public schoolboy.

Life sketch[4]

Arthur Cecil Pigou was born at Ryde in the Isle of Wight in 1877. He was Head of School at Harrow and won a scholarship to King's where he took a First in the History Tripos and in Part II of the Moral Sciences Tripos (1901). He was tall, physically attractive and a brilliant debater and lecturer. From 1901 he gave lectures and was appointed to the Girdler's Lectureship in 1904, carrying much of the burden of teaching in the new Economics Tripos, established in 1903. Not surprisingly, in view of his academic background and his thesis title of 1900 (Browning as a Religious Teacher) he was regarded as something of a generalist and was called upon, presumably by Edgeworth, to write correspondingly generalist reviews.[5] But it was not long before Edgeworth 'spotted' him, as it were, as a promising young economist. Reviewing the *Riddle of the Tariff* he remarked that 'Mr. Pigou's close reasoning should be studied in connection with the demonstrations he has given in the January number of the Fortnightly Review and elsewhere. The power with which he wields the organon of economic theory is of the highest promise' and he compared Pigou's work with the early work of Clerk-Maxwell in physics.[6]

Marshall had the greatest confidence in Pigou who was appointed in 1908, at the extraordinary age of 30 and to the exclusion of Foxwell, to Marshall's Chair of Political Economy. Whether or not Pigou's position on free trade was decisive in bringing Marshall to campaign for him rather than Foxwell is not entirely clear. It is difficult to believe that Marshall could have entertained a definite preference for Pigou for the Chair before 1903 or that free trade swung the issue for Marshall, who believed Pigou to be an extraordinary genius, though it might have done so for some of the electors. If Foxwell's own account is to be trusted the vote was very narrow.[7]

A brilliant lecturing style (lost in later years), heavy involvement in the Tripos and closeness to Marshall, must have played their parts in his selection, for his publications list was, at that time, respectable though not impressive.[8] Much of his writing was associated with the tariff question about which he was a vigorous free trade campaigner but there were also a few short technical pieces on consumer surplus, import duties and dumping. From the standpoint of modern 'economic' theories of politics his two little pieces on the relationship between economics and politics are of interest. As with Edgeworth the *Riddle* won him somewhat wider recognition. However, his most ambitious book, prior to his appointment, was the *Principles and Methods of Industrial Peace* (1905) a rather discursive work based on Sidgwick and Edgeworth with a collaborative appendix, on bargaining diagrams, with J. M. Keynes – an astonishingly early collaboration. The book is frankly utilitarian in analysis but is remarkable for the pains taken over the nuts and bolts of industrial peace. But it could in no way be regarded as a really major work and the young Pigou was appointed to his Chair very much on promise rather than performance.

One should not in this pre-war period lose sight of Pigou the technician. He is seen at his best in a very brief *Economic Journal* note of 1910 on measuring elasticities of demand. Using *Blue Book* data he derives relative price elasticities for clothes and food on the assumption that utilities are independent and that each good forms only a small part of total expenditure.[9] The note was almost unnoticed until Friedman's critical discussion (1936) and Georgescu-Roegen's finding, as umpire, more or less in Pigou's favour.[10] Pigou's pioneering effort has won great praise from Deaton: 'still one of the best examples of indirect measurement by use of theory to be found outside of the physical and biological sciences'.[11]

Deaton christens as *Pigou's Law* the linear relationship between price and income elasticities under additivity. Pigou returned briefly to this line of work in 1930 and 1936 but neither he nor his colleagues pushed it very far. In view of his early interest it is hard not to feel that an opportunity had been missed.

His interests in industrial peace and unemployment were expanded into the major book *Wealth and Welfare* (1912).[12] As Johnson wrote: 'the remainder of Pigou's long working life can be regarded as largely occupied with strengthening the foundations laid in *Wealth and Welfare* and elaborating the superstructure laid upon them'.[13] To understand this, one must remember that economic welfare depended not merely on the size of the national dividend but also on its distribution and variability. The elaborations came in the four main editions of the *Economics of Welfare* (1920) and in *Industrial Fluctuations* (1927) and *A Study in Public Finance* (1928).[14] *The Economics of Stationary States* (1935)[15] is something of an anachronism; something very like it could have been written much earlier. But not all his subsequent work can be fitted into this picture of careful elaboration. His reactions to the onslaught of the Keynesians on unemployment, an interest of Pigou for decades, have to be treated separately. The principal working out of *Wealth and Welfare* was pretty well complete by 1928.

In view of Pigou's later writings on unemployment it is interesting that his little book *Unemployment* (1913),[16] based on *Industrial Peace* and on *Wealth and Welfare*, provides an early statement of his general position. That is that government intervention may be used to even out cycles (but not to increase demand over the cycle) and that 'plasticity' in wage-rates would ensure full-employment. The depth of Pigou's feeling on unemployment (see the concluding paragraph of his book) perhaps accounts for some of his hostility towards what he felt to be the Johnny-come-lately air of his future denigrators.

From about 1927 onwards ill-health took a heavy toll. He suffered from a debilitating heart disease which 'curtailed his climbing, impaired his vigour, and left him intermittently through the rest of his life in phases of debility. And with this, something was lost both from the liveliness of his lecturing and the vigour of his writing.'[17] This was most evident during his exchange with Keynes in 1937. The contrast with the brilliant young Edwardian is illustrated by the comment in a letter to Corrie: 'and so the days pass in Malebolge. We are dropping down the ladder rung by rung.'[18] What was it that turned 'the gay, joke-loving, sociable, hospitable young batchelor of the Edwardian period into the eccentric recluse of more recent times?'[19] War, politics and health all took their toll. Pigou the pacifist did not fight in the First World War but spent all his vacations in voluntary ambulance work at the Front. According to Robinson he deliberately chose the more dangerous tasks. Johnson reports Pigou's friend C. R. Fay as saying: 'World War I was a shock to him, and he was never the same afterwards.'[20]

Pigou's disillusionment with the fruit-bearing as opposed to light-shedding aspects of economics was a result both of his personal experiences of public service and of the abandonment of free trade. Though he served on the Cunliffe Committee of 1918–19, the Royal Commission on the Income Tax of 1919–20, and the Chamberlain Committee of 1924–5 he accepted that, unlike Keynes, he did not excel at such committees and retired (metaphorically) to cultivate his garden. But he was reluctant to let go of practical affairs completely and occasionally sniped from the sidelines. We also now know that he spent a considerable amount of time on the affairs of the Economic Advisory Council and that the policy advice he gave to the Macmillan Committee and in letters to *The Times* was substantially the same as that given by Keynes. For an extremely trenchant emphasis on this accord see the study by Hutchison.[21]

The Committee of Economists, consisting of Keynes (chairman), Pigou, Robbins, Stamp and Henderson, was split both on reflation and on the tariff issue.[22] Though Pigou joined Keynes in pressing for reflation it is interesting to note his reasons. Unless investment was due to lower interest or to technical progress it would be a purely monetary affair which would raise prices and lower real wages through 'friction, bamboozlements and so on'.[23] That is to say the employment effect would be through indirect real wage cuts. On the tariff issue Pigou continued to take the now minority view consistent with the campaigns of his youth and was greatly saddened by the abandonment of free trade in 1932.

Pigou's position *vis-à-vis* the Keynesians in Cambridge of the 1930s is discussed in some detail later. It suffices here to say that he and Robertson were tolerably close allies and that Pigou remained aloof from the younger Keynesians, particularly the now famous 'circus'. Engagement in discussion and debate was *not* Pigou's method of working.[24] The slow absorption and working through of new ideas in his own books was much better suited to his personality. Any hold that he might have had as 'leader' of the Cambridge economists was slipping away during the late twenties and early thirties. He seemed already to be a figure of the past.

At the onset of the Second World War, Pigou, despite his age and poor health, wished to make some contribution, offering his services in 1940 first (via Keynes) to the Government and then to the teaching of 'Hun, Frog and Wop' at Eton.[25] From what he called his 'funk-hole' at Buttermere he complained that he couldn't just sit there, eating the nation's food without any proofs to correct! This was a low point. Presumably the proofs referred to were of *Employment and Equilibrium* (1941) a truly remarkable work for a 64-year old.[26] Also from this period was his *Aspects of British Economic History* which, to his chagrin, the authorities insisted on treating as an official secret so it was not published until 1947.[27]

Luckily he was to revive in old age a facility for the short popular exposition of abstruse matters. The little book, *Socialism versus Capitalism* (1937)[28] had been a good example of this skill. *Income* (1946)[29] was outstandingly successful as a book, though, as Pigou admits in the sequel *Income Revisited* (1955),[30] student attendance at the lectures on which it was based dwindled to five! *Lapses from Full Employment* (1945)[31] is an excellent short compendium of Pigou's views and *The Veil of Money* (1949)[32] is good in parts. The best known of these miniatures is, of course, *Keynes' 'General Theory': A Retrospective View* (1950).[33] Their very lightness is a relief from some of the earlier pudding-like tomes and they provide a graceful end to a long and distinguished list of publications.[34]

Welfare economics

(i) *Welfare criteria*

In a 1907 review of the fifth edition of Marshall's *Principles* Pigou gave pride of place to *time* and to the national *dividend*. It is ironic that Pigou made rather a mess of time in his various discussions of increasing returns. But the national dividend was 'the nucleus to which all ends cohere ... a focus ... the kernel of economic theory'.[35] The great test of any policy, be it about trades unions or help for the poor, was its effect on the national dividend. Thus it was that the social dividend came to be central in, firstly, *Wealth and Welfare* (1912) and, secondly, in *The Economics of Welfare* (1920). Hicks's comment that 'in spite of its "welfare" colouring, the subject of his book was the Social Product',[36] nevertheless does only very rough justice. The social dividend was intended to be important not in its own right but as an indicator of welfare. Pigou clearly felt that he had some sort of duty to work the thing through. He had already in 1910 distinguished between private and 'collective' marginal supply and demand prices so it was a relatively straightforward step for him, building on Sidgwick's distinction, to show that, when such divergences arose, competition would not necessarily lead to an output maximising allocation of factors.

Pigou's technical discussions of the social dividend – its

definition, problem of base etc. – stood up reasonably well for many decades. Thus Keynes wrote to Kahn[37] that he had solved the problem of defining net income and that it had come out 'very near to the money value of the Prof's social dividend'. Notice that Pigou had, among other things, recognised the index-number paradox when tastes or distribution changed but had argued that it would not normally arise, i.e. one would *not* have C_2 better than C_1 at period 1 tastes and C_1 better than C_2 at period 2 tastes. Samuelson,[38] though commenting that it is as well that the rest of *The Economics of Welfare* did not depend on his discussion of the social dividend, referred to Pigou's treatment as masterly and classic. The reply was characteristic of Pigou the 'fruit-seeker': he was aware of the limitations of his method but was content for practical purposes with a rough measure. Something similar was true about his discussions of keeping capital intact (see *Wealth and Welfare* and the 3rd edition of *The Economics of Welfare*).[39] He was rebuked by Hayek[40] for taking too physical a view of capital but did not fully comprehend Hayek's point that the valuation of capital was itself part of the pricing process. Pigou's defence, again, was that he was after a rough and ready tool.[41] For his position on this Hicks has aptly dubbed him a materialist rather than a fundist.

The social dividend, then, was Pigou's measure of welfare. He was aware of snags in its measurement but prepared to compromise for the sake of a working definition. But this was only one leg of his welfare apparatus. The other was distributive in nature so that the whole welfare criterion (fluctuations apart) was the *double* one that:

1. welfare increased if the social dividend increased but the poor were no worse-off,
2. welfare increased if the absolute dividend going to the poor increased but there was no decrease in social dividend.

Like the notion of externality this was taken from Sidgwick.[42] In diagrammatic terms [Fig. 4.1(a)] the shaded region, including its boundaries, but excluding K_0 itself, may be said to be 'Pigou superior' to K_0. The question mark indicates ambiguity as to the effect on welfare of a redistribution in favour of the poor at the expense of some fall in the social dividend. (For simplicity, assume an equal number of rich and poor people.) Figures 4.1(a)–(c) enable Pigou's double criterion to be compared with a simple

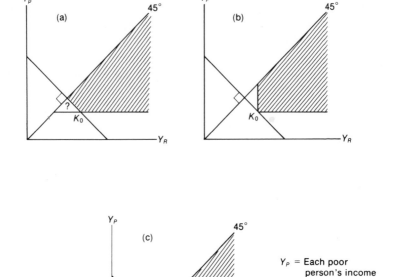

Fig. 4.1 Welfare criteria: (a) Pigou-superior allocations; (b) Pareto-superior allocations; and (c) Rawls-superior allocations

characterisation of two others, the Paretian and the Rawlsian criteria.

Taking, as he does, a utilitarian view, Pigou's double criterion is more 'inequality averse' than Pareto's but less so than Rawls'.

The intellectual basis for favouring more equality (*cet par*) was, of course, diminishing marginal utility. When it came to policy measures, however, Pigou's egalitarianism all but vanished. Following Marshall, he recognised that inequalities could be justified on grounds of differing needs as well as tastes: 'people bearing high responsibility and using their brains much, need, to keep them efficient, more house room, more quiet, more easily digested food, more change of scene, than unskilled workers.'[43]

His recommendations on redistribution were scarcely dramatic. Concentration on the incomes of the poor in his double criterion no doubt reflected Pigou's genuine concern with poverty. There is a most careful discussion of how the poor may be helped without reducing the dividend. Indeed the easiest cases of all are education, industrial training and medical attendance where 'there is reason to believe that the ordinary play of market forces tends unduly to contract investment in the persons of the normal poor, with the result that the marginal return to resources invested ... is higher than the marginal return to resources invested in machines'.[44] But in discussing ordinary transfers to the poor, Pigou distinguishes between those that encourage idleness and thriftiness and those that do not. 'Public parks for the collective use of the poor or flowers for their private use'[45] are mentioned with approval. The great principle throughout is that any transfer should be so arranged as to minimise damage to the social dividend. The idle are to be discouraged by activities like stone-breaking and actual detention and the best transfers are those depending not on work effort but on some characteristic such as age or motherhood.

Sometimes a clash between the two parts of the double criterion would be unavoidable. Pigou regarded minimum wage legislation as a good example – it would reduce the national dividend but raise the incomes of the poor. In such cases it was necessary to exercise judgement, a judgement which would, it seemed, normally come out in favour of the social dividend: 'in so far ... as social reformers rely upon improvements in the distribution of wealth, as distinguished from improvements in production, they are bound to chasten their hopes'.[46] In the end, it is the social dividend that really matters. Pigou gave thought not merely to the criteria themselves but to how they might be implemented. Suppose some act of policy is to be carried out because it will increase the social dividend. Should the losers be compensated? There was no illegality, argued Pigou, particularly if substantial notice had been given, in taking away property rights as these had in any case been granted by the State. When compensation was to be paid it should normally be based on market price (except for monopoly) and in the absence of market price one should use 'the money representative of the special value of the property right to its owner'.[47] Pigou does not say so, but if the poor lose as a result of policies to increase the national dividend they should presumably be compensated. The implied overall procedure is:

1. does the proposed policy lead to an unambiguous increase in national dividend?
2. if so, adopt but pay compensation if the losers are either poor *or* judged to have had their reasonable expectations thwarted *or* merit compassion.

He is clearly thinking of actual, not merely hypothetical, compensation. As to implementation of the second part of the criterion Pigou, after discussing voluntary transfers from the rich (benevolence, gifts to employees, the charity of local grandees, the awarding of 'gongs', etc.) recognises that these will have to be effected via taxation – voluntary transfers will be quite insufficient.[48]

His subsequent discussion of taxation, both here and in *A Study in Public Finance*, is an attempt to find some system of redistributive taxation which does not damage the social dividend, e.g. death duties. *Public Finance* is essentially an attempt to work out the tax implications of *The Economics of Welfare* more carefully and is discussed in more detail later.

(ii) *Externalities and returns*

Pigou's definition of externalities is classic:

the essence of the matter is that one person *A*, in the course of rendering some service, for which payment is made, to a second person *B*, incidentally also renders services or disservices to other persons ... of such a sort that payment cannot be extracted from the benefited parties or compensation enforced on behalf of the injured parties.[49]

Pigou was at great pains to stress the imperfection of *contractual* arrangements. Both here and in *Public Finance* he says astonishingly little, in view of subsequent discussion, about taxation as a means of correcting externalities. A difficulty is that Pigou discusses taxes and bounties not just in the case of 'real' externalities but also in the cases of generalised increasing and decreasing returns. For the present consider real externalities only. It is also interesting that many of his examples (lighthouses, parks, research) are pure public goods, analysed below. Though Coase rather overdid his famous attack on Pigou he was right about the lack of clarity: 'the main source of the obscurity is that Pigou had not thought his position through . . . not being clear it was never clearly wrong'.[50] Pigou, said Coase, had failed to take property rights and litigation fully into account. Existing property rights would affect the direction of payment but not the social optimum itself. Taking issue with Pigou's famous illustration of sparks from railway engines, Coase argued that it was *because* of state action that compensation did *not* have to be paid. Less importantly (and perhaps even pedantically) Coase showed that Pigou's grasp of institutional and legal facts was wanting. The power of the 'Coase theorem' is weakened by its requirement that property rights are well defined and negotiations more or less costless. But when these conditions hold the Pigovian tax actually prevents the attainment of a social optimum! Pigou was dimly aware of these difficulties but, as Coase says, he had failed to think them through, a failure which flourished for decades within the 'oral tradition'.

I turn now to the curious issue of increasing returns. Young, in his 1913 review of *Wealth and Welfare* had criticised Pigou's use of the marginal supply price curve, originating in his 1910 article. 'I fail to see that its use is appropriate in the analysis of the extent to which competition tends to secure the maximum national dividend'[51] or, in other words, Pigou was failing to distinguish real and pecuniary externalities: the difference between the supply curve and marginal supply price curve simply represented transfers. This criticism clearly caused Pigou some anxiety and, as Bharadwaj notes,[52] he corrected the decreasing returns case in the 1924 edition of *The Economics of Welfare* and in 1928 defined it so as to eliminate transfers. Marshall, it is now known, had great misgivings about Pigou's treatment, much preferring his own discussion in Appendix H of the *Principles*. Marshall's main complaint was that Pigou had pushed the tax-bounty argument too far – he was attempting an analysis of dynamic (and probably irreversible) changes with static tools. Marshall's failure to bring these criticisms to Pigou's notice is puzzling. It can hardly have been to protect Pigou from public criticism as a purely private discussion would have served. It is possible (though simply a speculation) that Marshall was unsure of his ground and reluctant to risk contradiction by his brilliant young successor. It is important to notice that the increasing/decreasing returns argument has nothing whatever to do with externalities and Pigou's proposal here for bounties and taxes has nothing to do with divergences between real social and private cost.

The increasing/decreasing returns distinction was, however, important to Marshall and Pigou and the latter felt obliged to reply, though somewhat lamely when his friend Clapham made a delightful assault upon it. Clapham rightly complained, in a rejoinder, that 'his suggestions towards filling the [empty economic] boxes are scantier than I had thought possible . . . now I am paid with a cheque drawn on the bank of an unknown Jevons'.[53] And despite his brilliant pioneering work on demand elasticities, neither Pigou nor his Cambridge contemporaries had anything to offer on cost curves or production functions.

Increasing returns also played a part in the well-known *Economic Journal* symposium on the representative firm. Even Robertson offered only a half-hearted defence of Pigou's reliance upon 'external–internal' economies; that is to say, external change (inventions?) leading to internal economies. Along with Robertson and even Shove, Pigou was on the losing side in this debate. Sraffa was especially devastating on Robertson's appalling analogies.[54] In spite of being on the wrong side Pigou's contribution is not without interest. After a rather thin piece[55] Pigou suggested the 'equilibrium firm' in place of the representative firm.[56] The former is in equilibrium when the industry is in equilibrium. His complex general case is where the costs of the equilibrium firm are a function of its own and the industry's output, $F_r(x_r, y)$ where x_r is the equilibrium firm's output and y the industry's.[57] Equilibrium industry price is equal to both the marginal and the average costs of the equilibrium firm (incidentally the definition of marginal cost is misprinted).[58] Clearly the equilibrium may hold yet industry supply price may be increasing, constant or decreasing. Pigou's very careful geometry of average and marginal curves must have been helpful in the subsequent discussion. 1933 already finds Pigou attempting an algebraic generalisation of Mrs Robinson's work and a measure of the degree of market imperfection.

$$\frac{\delta\psi(p, n)}{\delta p} \quad \text{or,}$$

'the rate of substitution, among one firm's customers, of product from the other firms when the price charged by the one firm, and by it alone, increases'.[59] n indicates number of firms and p price. This measure is infinite and negative in the case of perfect competition. Pigou's work on the firm and the industry is not of the first rank: it amounted to an ingenious rearguard action in defence of Marshall, overlaid by his habitual attempt to absorb new ideas into his own thinking. It is interesting that Kahn's frequent references, in this context, to Pigou are mainly to the earlier *The Economics of Welfare*.[60]

Public finance

The Study in Public Finance (1928), making use of Pigou's earlier *The Political Economy of War*,[61] of parts of *The Economics of Welfare* and of the 1925 compensation article,[62] may be divided into:

(i) the theory of public good provision
(ii) the theory of taxation.

(i) Where a charge was possible it should be the same for everyone and sufficient to cover aggregate cost (for neither here nor anywhere else was Pigou attracted to marginal cost pricing). But what principle may be used when no charge is possible? Pigou suggested the equi-marginal rule that: 'expenditure should be allocated between battleships and Poor Relief in such wise that the last shilling devoted to each of them yields the same return'.[63] The same principle, he suggested, may be applied to aggregate Government expenditure against consumption expenditure in general. But due to the 'indirect damage' done by taxation (unless there is lump-sum redistribution) government spending should not be pushed quite as far as marginal equivalence. This seems quite an acceptable intuition. However, Stiglitz and Dasgupta while accepting the rule that marginal benefit equals marginal cost *including* dead-weight loss from taxation, argue that the outcome need not follow Pigou's intuition: it could go either way. Pigou's rule is therefore not water-tight but the balance of probabilities rests with it.[64]

(ii) Pigou's ultimate principle of taxation was minimum aggregate sacrifice. By ignoring excess burden (which he calls 'announcement effects') one reaches the famous 'lopping-off' of top incomes doctrine, a doctrine which has to be modified, however, once announcement effects are allowed for. Regressive or proportional taxes are superior to progressive ones as far as announcement effects are concerned. Ideally one seeks a tax formula which minimises aggregate sacrifice taking into account both distributional and announcement effects: 'if levies conforming in *amounts* to the distributional ideal could be made in a *manner* conforming to the announcement ideal, we should have the optimum means of raising a tax revenue'.[65] How close one gets to this in practice depends on the number of lump-sum items there are, as well as on the distribution of income and other relevant economic conditions. To sort out these problems satisfactorily would require (as we now know!) 'extremely complicated mathematical analysis'. Because it is all so difficult and because he doubted the empirical importance of the work-disincentive effect he concluded that one should seek the best formula from the distributional point of view.

He was also able to refer to Ramsey's now famous paper on taxation[66] and the rule that, with commodity taxes, the production of all goods should be cut in the same proportion. Hence the inverse elasticity rule. But if work is inelastic a proportional tax on all commodities will do. As to distribution there is a nice passage[67] which includes a discussion of what we now call equivalence scales. In the light of recent discussion of tax reform it is interesting that Pigou entertains the notion of a consumption tax (which would not differentiate against saving) but dismisses it on the grounds of fraud,[68] and also because a *progressive* expenditure tax would be unworkable. The importance Pigou attached to a smoothly progressive tax structure may be gauged from his *Quarterly Journal of Economics* article of 1920.[69]

The 1928 book included a full discussion of families of tax formulae and the properties that each should have. One of these properties was that $\psi(0) = 0$ where ψ is the tax function, i.e. Pigou wishes to apply his minimum aggregate sacrifice principle to the raising of revenue, not to the whole tax/poverty problem. Modern optimal tax formulae, of course, have $\psi(0) < 0$, i.e. those with zero incomes pay negative taxes.

Money

Pigou's name is commonly associated with monetary theory in two ways. Firstly he articulated the Cambridge cash balance approach; secondly he 'invented' the *real balance* or Pigou effect. Money is also important in Pigou's scheme of things for its permissive role in so far as changes in the money supply are necessary to accommodate non-monetary changes. In his famous 1918 article following Marshall and Pantaleoni he specifically dichotomised his system into real and monetary parts: 'the value of all commodities other than money in terms of one another is determined independently of the value of money'.[70] As Patinkin has pointed out Pigou, like Marshall, conflated the demand curve and the equilibrium locus.[71] The Cambridge version of the quantity theory can be written as

$$P = \frac{kR}{M}$$

where P is the reciprocal of the price level, M the quantity of money, R money income and k the ratio of desired cash balances to income, so that where k and R are constants the equilibrium locus is a rectangular hyperbola. This, however, was a demand for titles to legal tender, not for legal tender itself. The more general relationship as introduced by Pigou is

$$M = \frac{kR}{p} (c + h(1 - c))$$

where p is the value of each unit of legal tender in terms of wheat, R is total resources expressed in wheat, c is the proportion of titles that the representative man chooses to keep in legal tender and h the proportion of legal tender kept by bankers. There follows a discussion of the various influences on k including price expectations. There undoubtedly *is* a muddle here about what the Cambridge quantity equations are supposed to be equations of but the article remains a classic one if only as a rare statement of the celebrated oral tradition. His discussion of the real balance effect is to be found in 'The Classical Stationary State'.[72] Here Pigou is concerned to counter Hansen's contention for a (more or less permanent) under-employment equilibrium. Pigou maintains that, when prices fall 'the stock of money, as valued in terms of real income, correspondingly rises'[73] so that consumers, and others, decide to save less. Formally, Pigou's system becomes

$$\phi(C, r) = 0 \qquad \text{(i) \quad investment}$$
$$f(C, x, r, T) = 0 \qquad \text{(ii) \quad saving}$$
$$x = X \qquad \text{(iii) \quad output}$$
$$r = g\left(\frac{T}{x}\right) \qquad \text{(iv) \quad interest}$$

where T is real money balances, C is capital stock, X is real income appropriate to full employment, x is real income and r is the rate of return on investment and equals the rate of time preference. In Pigou's curious equation (iv) it also balances the attractiveness of holding or not holding money – the less the quantity of real balances the more convenient it is to hold cash. In the stationary state, saving and investment are, of course, zero; and 'provided that wage-earners adopt a competitive wage policy [it] is always possible; indeed it is the goal towards which ... the economic system necessarily tends'.[74] As I understand it, the real balance effect preserves full employment only if wages are flexible. Otherwise it merely prevents endless disequilibrium. The empirical importance of the Pigou effect is generally acknowledged to be small and there is anecdotal evidence that Pigou himself attached little weight to it.[75] Finally, it has been shown by Leijonhufvud, that the effect depends heavily on 'high-powered' or 'outside' money.[76]

Money is also central to Pigou's analysis of unemployment and inflation in quite a different sense. He is absolutely emphatic in *The Theory of Unemployment* of 1933 that everything hangs on the monetary regime being assumed. His 'standard monetary system' is 'one so constructed that, for all sorts of movement in the real demand function for labour, or in the real rates of wages ... the aggregate money income is increased or diminished by precisely the difference made to the number of work-people ... at work multiplied by the original rate of money wages'.[77] Again in 1937, Pigou stressed that 'if nothing is known about banking policy, anything may happen'.[78] His normal banking system is therefore taken to be where,

(i) money supply is an increasing function of the rate of interest and
(ii) there is no credit rationing.

This perfectly straightforward pair of assumptions seems to have puzzled Keynes into thinking that Pigou was taking the *demand* for money to depend only on the rate of interest. I think it is correct to say that the supply of money plays an important *permissive* role in three important cases, (1) public works, (2) wage cuts and (3) post-war unemployment policies. But Pigou had in 1927 definitely rejected Hawtrey's view that 'the trade cycle is a purely monetary phenomenon' for if it were so public works would just be a piece of ritual.[79] Insisting on his view in a forceful rejoinder (1929) Hawtrey was unfortunately able to point out errors in Pigou's algebra – a budding multiplier analysis – of the employment effects of public expenditure.

In the three cases instanced:

(i) 'a small injection of money into the income-expenditure circuit in bad times in connection with carefully chosen public works, *might* lead to a progressive and far-reaching improvement in the employment situation'.[80]

(ii) Pigou conceded after criticism from Kaldor (see below) that a reduction in money wages would not affect unemployment except through the rate of interest. His view is summarised in his *Retrospective View*, ch. XIII, in which he baldly states that differences in the physical stock of money may have the same reactions on employment as do differences in the liquidity preference schedule, and in ch. XIV 'the implications of a lower value of money wages are the same as those of a larger income velocity of money, that is to say, of a lower schedule of liquidity preference'.[81] Although this term was not used in the 1918 article, Pigou put enormous emphasis throughout his writings on *income velocity*. Blaug reports that it was introduced in *Industrial Fluctuations*.[82] Money income could not change unless the rate of interest changes, as long as the quantity of money and income velocity were given, because income velocity itself is a function both of the interest rate and income distribution.[83]

(iii) Full employment pressures would, Pigou argued, create sustained inflation abetted by monetary expansion:

> in order to *maintain* full employment it is necessary that the money demand schedule for labour shall not merely be high, but shall be continually rising, spiralling upwards forever, so that it keeps ahead of the pursuing wage rate. This entails *progressive monetary inflation* and so, unless productive technique is improving at corresponding speed, continuously rising prices.[84]

The monetary inflation is necessary because of the pursuit of full employment. A few years earlier in a paper 'Types of War Inflation' he had attempted a distinction between *wage-induced* and *deficit-induced* inflation along similar lines. Provided full employment is being pursued 'deficit-induced inflation can be arrested by filling up the deficit, whereas wage-induced inflation, unless the chasing of wages after prices is prevented, cannot be arrested by *any means whatever*'.[85]

In all these matters money plays an important permissive role but is never a prime-mover.

Pigou and Keynes

First is is important to establish Pigou's position about wage-flexibility prior to the *General Theory*. His view may be distilled from *Industrial Fluctuations* and *The Theory of Unemployment*. The former is a compendious magisterial affair clearly regarded as important in its time. For example, Stamp in his 1927 review regarded it very highly and singled out his lagged correlations for praise: 'nowhere has the new method, so full of importance for the future of economic analysis been carried to such clear and definite usage'.[86] By modern standards Pigou's use of the 'new method' is at a pretty low level. It is a curiously unsatisfactory work, in particular his breath-taking statistical guesses are almost outrageous.

In view of later discussions it is necessary to set out Pigou's underlying theory. Unemployment is caused by deviation of the demand schedule for labour away from its general line of trend. This may come about *either* through changes in expectations *or* in the rate of discount. But the varying expectations of businessmen are the key to industrial fluctuations.[87] The main drift of Pigou's work on unemployment over this period may be illustrated by Fig. 4.2 which is not Pigou's but arises naturally out of his work. N is the number of would-be workers, D is the real demand function for labour and W is the real wage rate stipulated by labour. In *Industrial Fluctuations* Pigou was interested in the various causes of unemployment, resulting either from shifts in D or from changes in W or prices. Thus if the real demand for labour fell from D to D' there would be unemployment of u which could, in principle, be eliminated by allowing real wage to fall to W'. In *The Theory of Unemployment* he was interested in the elasticity of the real demand for labour, important because it would show how large a wage adjustment was necessary in the absence of policies for

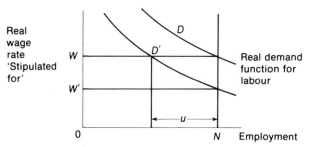

FIG. 4.2   Real wages and unemployment

raising D. Behind the diagram stands Pigou's work on the relationship between changes in money wages and the resulting change in real wages.

In *The Theory of Unemployment* the elasticity of the real demand curve for labour comes to the fore. Starting from microeconomic elasticities but having discussed interdependence and the dangers of aggregation Pigou moves[88] to a discussion of the elasticity of the real demand for labour as a whole. This is given by

$$E_r = x \, \frac{\phi'(x)}{\phi(x)} \, \eta$$

where x is employment in wage good industries; $\phi(x)$ is output of wage goods; and η is the elasticity of the real demand for labour in the wage good industries.

Pigou guessed that η was numerically large, perhaps -5 and estimated E_r at about -3. But the elasticity in respect of money wages (E_m) would be smaller than either of these, depending on the monetary system, say -1.5. Thus reductions in money wages would have a more than proportionate effect on employment.

Pigou was able to argue that the state of real demand did not affect employment but merely wages except in the short term. It is clear that Pigou's labour supply function was slightly unconventional. The number of 'would-be wage earners' is taken as given and there is a 'real rate of wages stipulated for'. This latter may be negotiated by unions or set by regulation. Pigou's supply function is ⌐___⌐ shaped but (see below) labour supply was not completely elastic below the stipulated wage. The reader is referred to Pigou's letter to Keynes of May 1937.[89] In Fig. 4.2 as the D curve falls there will be some real wage at which full employment may be achieved. His rationale for a non-zero elasticity of demand for labour was as follows. A fall in money wages would decrease money spending to a lesser degree, because non-wage incomes would not initially have fallen, so prices would fall by proportionately less than the money wage. But marginal cost will have fallen to the same degree as the initial wage reduction so existing output is at disequilibrium and is therefore expanded. It is noteworthy that Pigou and Robertson were at one over this.

In view of the Keynesians' reactions it is worth recalling the initial reception of *The Theory of Unemployment*. Despite one or two barbed criticisms Harrod saw it as a 'supreme intellectual achievement, a masterpiece of close and coherent reasoning' and praised 'the great beauty, the exquisite workmanship, the painstaking lucidity'.[90] Seymour Harris welcomed it as one of the great books of recent years though at the same time (and how one sympathises) asking for what Keynes was soon to supply, *completeness* and *simplicity*.[91] This reception is emphasised here to make the point that Pigou's book was not obviously or outrageously foolish. He had certainly taken a less extreme view on wages than had Hicks in his *The Theory of Wages* (1932). If wages exceed the competitive rate, Hicks had argued that 'very simple and familiar economic reasoning suggests at once the main answer – unemployment'. 'But even economists sometimes find a difficulty in seeing that what is admittedly true for each industry separately is also true for all industries taken together.'[92] Nevertheless, Pigou was very strongly attacked by the Keynesians. Thus Shove writes that Pigou's book is 'the worst book on economics that I had read for a long time – a good deal worse than Hicks'.[93] After attempting to make sense of Pigou he writes to Keynes 'I wish I could get out of the habit of thinking that there must be some defence for anything which the Professor says.'[94] At this stage Pigou and Keynes seem to have been on reasonably good terms, as they were to be later in the thirties. Their exchanges over the *Treatise* are unfortunately almost all lost[95] but led to no major differences once Keynes had translated his own language into Pigou's. Pigou stood aloof from the now famous 'circus' and Keynes had criticised *The Theory of Unemployment* in his Cambridge lectures. But his definitive critique is to be found in the *General Theory* itself and must have come as rather a blow. It is difficult not to feel that many of his criticisms were misplaced.

Thus he recognises that Pigou tried to incorporate fluctuations into his real demand function for labour but (oddly in view of the quotation from *Industrial Fluctuations*, earlier) complains that Pigou had omitted the unstable factor. He caricatures *The Theory of Unemployment* as 'mainly a study of what determines changes in the volume of employment, assuming that there is no involuntary unemployment'.[96] Keynes claims that

it is important to realise that the whole of Pigou's book is written on the assumption that any rise in the cost of living, however moderate, relatively to the money wage will cause the withdrawal from the labour market of a number of workers greater than that of all the existing unemployed.[97]

As was suggested earlier, this is a misinterpretation of Pigou's assumptions about the labour market.

Keynes's critique of Pigou also shows him to be rather imprisoned in his own framework of analysis. He alleged that changes in the money wage rate can affect output and employment only through Keynesian *C* or *I* and, therefore, only through the marginal propensity to consume, the marginal efficiency of capital or the rate of interest: 'there is no method of analysing the effect of a reduction in money wages, except by following up its possible effects on these three factors.'[98] This is surely not so. The whole thrust of Pigou's argument implies that money wage reductions could have an effect through the aggregate supply function. It is a pity that this aspect of the analysis disappeared from view in the later stages of the controversy. Keynes's well-known apologia for his attack – sharp, merciless and to some extent unfair – was that 'Pigou's *Theory of Unemployment* seems to me to get out of the Classical Theory all that can be got out of it'.[99] It is scarcely surprising that Pigou found this apologia less than convincing and his *Economica* review was correspondingly sharp:

Einstein actually did for Physics what Mr. Keynes believes himself to have done for Economics. He developed a far-reaching generalisation, under which Newton's results can be subsumed as a special case. But he did not, in announcing his discovery, insinuate through carefully barbed sentences, that Newton (Marshall!) and those who had hitherto followed his lead (Pigou?) were a gang of incompetent bunglers.[100]

This was strong stuff. Indeed the strength and resilience both of the 1935 review and of its 1950 sequel, *Retrospect*, seem to me to have been seriously underestimated. Admittedly Pigou entered the reservation, in two separate places, that he had not perhaps understood Keynes but he made several substantial points of criticism, (a) in defence of the 'incompetent bunglers' and (b) in attack on Keynes's theory:

(a) he rebutted Keynes's statement that he had not discussed changes in the position of the real demand function for labour and protested (perfectly reasonably) that the perfectly elastic labour supply function had been foisted upon the 'classics' by Keynes;

(b) he made a general attack on Keynes's obscurity and *loose and inconsistent use of terms*. He correctly fastened upon internal inconsistency in the treatment of investment, i.e. that capital equipment is assumed to be fixed yet net investment is going on: 'he is assuming a stationary state and at the same time a moving one'[101] which must have seemed a major offence to the recent author of the *Economics of Stationary States*. The multiplier process was criticised for assuming interest constant (Pigou repeatedly refused to leave interest out of the consumption function.) Whether or not saving would be a drain on aggregate demand would, he contended, depend on the banking policy being pursued. Similarly monetary policy would also govern whether or not a money wage reduction would lead to a real reduction – on any *normal* policy Pigou claimed that it would do. Finally on the abolition of unemployment he argues that even in Keynes's sustained boom 'wage earners would still have a choice between policies that promote respectively higher real wage rates *plus* less employment and lower real wages plus more employment'.[102]

On balance it is clear that Pigou seriously misjudged the impact the *General Theory* would have but that his review was not merely a hurt defence of Marshall. His specific criticisms were definitely non-trivial in nature and it is difficult to accept Keynes's complaint to Robertson that it was a 'profoundly frivolous' review.[103] Neither was the famous recantation of 1950 quite what it was reputed to have been. Austin Robinson writes

> Shortly before the end of his life he came to see more clearly the essentials of Keynes's arguments and, asking permission to give a public lecture, he said with great generosity that he had come with the passage of time to feel that he had failed earlier to appreciate some of the important things that Keynes was trying to say. It was the very noble act of a man who put truth before vanity and another's reputation beyond his own.[104]

Now it is true that Pigou here admitted to not having grasped the significance of Keynes's central passage on effective demand which contained an 'extremely successful germinal idea'. But it is clear, from a number of gentle but telling criticisms, that Pigou was anything but capitulating. I select from these the following:

(i) Keynes's book was a revolution only if one accepted the myth that earlier economists had ignored the part played by money in fluctuations. Indeed Robertson had earlier (February 1935) written to Keynes 'what is the monetary part of *Industrial Fluctuations* or *The Theory of Unemployment* but a study of effective demand?'[105]

(ii) Keynes does not deal with actual movements, it is a 'staccato . . . not a moving picture, but only a succession of stills'.[106]

(iii) Keynes provides an inadequate analysis of expectations – for example during the processes of money wage reduction and increased money supply. Pigou complains of a lack of any principle for the generation of expectations. Expectations had also been treated inadequately in his own work, of course, and Pigou is guilty of understating the extent to which Keynes discussed expectations. Nevertheless Pigou was correct to point to an analytical gap which subsequent economists have struggled to fill.

The remaining points in *A Retrospective View* cannot be discussed without noticing the controversial *Economic Journal* article of 1937[107] or Pigou's work during the 1940s, particularly in *Employment and Equilibrium*.

In August 1937 Keynes, having seen the page proofs, lamented that Robertson had passed for publication an article submitted by Pigou, 'Real and Money Wages in Relation to Unemployment'. Moggridge feels that Keynes 'first attempted to hold the article up, largely to protect Pigou, also a Fellow of King's, from embarrassment and to prevent an economist of Pigou's standing from looking foolish'.[108] Bear in mind that both Pigou and Keynes were suffering from heart attacks at the time so the traffic between them was through intermediaries.[109] Keynes held up publication and sent the article to Kahn, for his opinion, with a note of reply. Pigou had made his usual assumptions about the monetary system (see above) and Keynes claimed these were consistent only if the demand for money was a function of the rate of interest alone and that Pigou had elsewhere let the demand for cash depend on income velocity. There is, in fact, no contradiction in this part of Pigou's argument. I select the following from the ensuing exchanges

Keynes to Kahn:

> [the article is] the work of a sick man, which no one would print who was in his right mind.
>
> it would be unfair to him and humiliating to the whole tribe of economists if, in a state of sickness, the President of the Royal Economic Society were to print such stuff.

Austen Robinson to Keynes:

> I find an almost insuperable difficulty in balancing one's affection for Pigou against one's love of truth.

Joan Robinson to Keynes:

> He is gone so far that you have to rationalise him to some extent even to find a coherent error [she claims that Pigou is confusing the amount of money with its rate of increase].

Keynes to Robertson:

> It is outrageous rubbish beyond all possibility of redemption.
>
> . . . it would help if Pigou would start all over again, rather than try to discover whether he can save every other sentence.

Keynes to Kahn:

> why do they insist on maintaining theories from which their own practical conclusions cannot possibly follow? It is a sort of Society for the Preservation of Ancient Monuments.[110]

(Notice that Kahn had a different 'fundamental error' in mind, i.e. the equality of the rate of interest and the rate of time preference but that Keynes thought this was in order. In Keynes's correspondence with Kaldor Pigou's error was in not accepting the savings function. There was a lack of complete accord, it seems, in the Keynesian camp as to the precise nature of Pigou's crassness.)

By far the most useful and constructive contribution during this whole interchange, both in correspondence and in print, was Kaldor's. Let us first see what Pigou was saying in the 1937 article. Its whole point was that a cut in money wages cuts prime cost and leads to an expansion of output and employment. To cut through Pigou's argument (which is essentially a wage equals marginal value product equation) we have

$$w \, \frac{1}{\psi'(x)} = p/(1 + r)$$

(prime cost)   (marginal receipts)

over one production period, so prime cost must fall with w, at the existing output level. For equilibrium, $p/(1 + r)$ remaining unchanged, $\psi'(x)$ has to fall too so output expands. Pigou keeps p and r constant by the indirect argument that the quantity of money, income velocity and the rate of time preference are all constant. He concluded that the fall in wages is a definite cause in itself, *not* that it acts only through the interest rate.

In reply to the article which was indeed published, Keynes wrongly argued that Pigou's demand for money depended only on the rate of time preference and failed to appreciate his slightly odd mode of argument.[111] As Kaldor was to point out, Pigou was not assuming constant income and employment, merely that at *given* income and employment there would be a disequilibrium at lower money wage rates. Kaldor's view was much less severe.[112] He claimed merely that Pigou's article was badly phrased and incomplete. A fall in the rate of money wages lowers the demand for money which lowers the interest rate therefore savings fall and employment increases. This hinges, of course, on savings being a function of the rate of interest. Pigou seems to be assuming the special case where the marginal propensity to save is zero: this guarantees some wage rate that secures full employment.

Unfortunately for Pigou, Kaldor's mechanism is via the rate of interest and Pigou entirely accepted that a money wage cut operates only through the interest rate and that its effect is exactly the same as 'an increase in the quantity of money or a reduction in liquidity preference'.[113] Pigou continued to hold to this view but it is not entirely clear that he should have done so. Samuelson thought that he should not, but for different reasons to do with what we now know as the real balance effect.[114] As suggested above, Pigou's argument does make sense through the aggregate supply function depending on the monetary regime being assumed.

As a postscript to these controversies I offer this extract from an undated letter of Pigou to Keynes, written during the Second World War.

> Thoughts on the Tripos . . . the chief bad thing we found was that a very large number of people had been stuffed like sausages with bits of your stuff in such a way that (i) they were quite incapable of applying their own intelligence to it, and (ii) they perpetually dragged it in regardless of its relevance to the question. . . . My own guess – because there is no direct evidence – is that the parrot-like treatment of your stuff is due to the lectures and supervisions of the beautiful Mrs R – a magpie breeding innumerable parrots! I gather that she puts in the Tract, with an enormous T, with such Prussian efficiency that the wretched men become identical sausages without any minds of their own! Obviously there is nothing we can do about this at present, but I think, if peace ever comes, we ought to introduce some counter irritant into that territory. Even the muddle into which they got when Dennis and the beautiful lady were lecturing against one another seems better than this drill-sergeant business![115]

At the age of 64, having published in economics for 40 years, suffering from a debilitating illness since the early 1930s and no doubt exhausted by the Keynesian controversies we find Pigou publishing another major book on unemployment, *Employment and Equilibrium*, 1941. This book is important for two reasons.

Firstly Pigou chose to construct a simple macromodel of four unknowns (consumption goods, investment goods, the rate of interest and the money wage rate) but only three equations. He then proposed two alternative ways of closing the system – by assuming full employment (suitable for describing long run tendencies) or by assuming a given money wage (suitable for describing short run equilibrium). Kaldor's review, 1941, is again most useful.[116] The second major contribution of this book (heroic in view of Pigou's first reaction to Keynes's multiplier) was Pigou's construction of a number of multipliers. Pigou considered the comparative statics result of changing each of the basic variables so that, in all, he had seven multipliers each relating to income and employment. Only *one* of these, that corresponding to an increase in the 'demand function for labour for investment' on the assumption that saving is independent of interest, is the same as Keynes's multiplier. In a sense Pigou was the first post-Keynesian.[117]

It is interesting that Samuelson judged this book to be more important than *The Theory of Unemployment* and with respect to methodology almost ideal; it was 'one of the most important books of recent years' and the discussion of multipliers was long overdue.[118] Tsiang (1944) was quick to see that Pigou had opened the door for the return of his own apparatus! He also spotted slips (as is often the case with Pigou) in the technical analysis which Pigou acknowledged, with Champernowne's help in 1945.[119] A further defect of the book, as Kaldor noted, was its lack of signposts; it was difficult to see what was, and what was not, important. *Industrial Fluctuations* had been similarly defective and it is easy to see why *Employment and Equilibrium* was not widely read or discussed.

In the remainder of his macroeconomic writings, e.g. *Lapses from Full Employment* (1945), *The Veil of Money* (1947) and *Retrospect* (1950) Pigou sticks to this, his considered reformulation of his position following the Keynesian Revolution.

In spirit Pigou's neoclassical synthesis is very close to Friedman's 1971 article in which the missing equation is also discussed. Friedman concluded that 'the rigid price assumption of Keynes is entirely *deus ex machina* with no underpinning in economic theory'.[120]

One suspects that by the time he gave his *Retrospect* lectures the controversies of the *General Theory* must have seemed distant and irrelevant. He had, after all, in the meantime, moved on to higher things more in accord, as it happens, with the counter-revolution of the seventies than with the heady, revolutionary days of the thirties or the post-war years of Keynesian dominance.

Conclusion

Caught between the shadow of Marshall and the pyrotechnics of Keynes, Pigou's standing as an economist is elusive. By 1937 his reputation was at a low ebb, especially among the younger Keynesians. Yet he has fared reasonably well at the hands of historians of doctrine. Schumpeter's judgement was predominantly favourable. Thus *The Economics of Welfare* was 'the greatest venture into labour economics ever undertaken by a man who was primarily a theorist'.[121] Schumpeter's emphasis here is curious. Similarly odd is that he highlights Pigou's discussion of Pareto's Law and of industrial fluctuations and singles out the *Economics of Stationary States* as 'the crowning achievement in this line of analysis'.[122] Blaug's emphasis is more orthodox. He picks out Pigou's first explicit use of 'income velocity' and regards *Wealth and Welfare* as 'virtually a blue-print for the welfare state'.[123] This confirms Robinson's judgement that his welfare economics was his most solid contribution 'by which his ultimate standing will almost certainly be judged'.[124]

One is unable completely to repress the suspicion that Pigou's reputation in this area is due rather less to the intrinsic merits or originality of his book than to the resilience of its subject matter. His analytical tools and attitude to the subject were derived from Marshall, his generally utilitarian outlook from Sidgwick and Edgeworth and the structure of his welfare analysis from Sidgwick. He was prone to technical slips, some of which were discovered only after decades and some almost straight away, on which he was slow to accept correction. The judicious, magisterial style in which his larger books were written conveyed an authority and an impressiveness in which it was difficult to see what was important and what was not. And he lacked the personality to stimulate work and discussion with others or to give any clear direction to the post-Marshallian Cambridge School. While it remains broadly true that we judge him by *The Economics of Welfare*, it is also likely that Pigou's work on unemployment and wage flexibility will come to be more highly regarded the more successful the Keynesian counter-revolution is in establishing itself as the new orthodoxy.

Again, the modern revival of interest in the microeconomics of the labour market is very Pigovian in spirit and makes Schumpeter's judgement less odd than it must have seemed just a few years ago. Pigou, from his 1905 book on *Industrial Peace*, through *Wealth and Welfare* and successive editions of *The Economics of Welfare*, to *Industrial Fluctuations* and *The Theory of Unemployment*, paid painstaking attention to matters such as the pattern and duration of unemployment, wage regulation, labour mobility, regional markets and·labour supply.

I would like, in closing, to emphasise a rather neglected aspect of Pigou's work. Though, as I have already noted, he was prone to technical slips he was nevertheless a skilled technician (*vide*, his early work on demand elasticity and income definition, his painstaking attempts to define and estimate the elasticity of demand for labour as a whole and his late attempted integration of Keynes into the neoclassical framework). Given his character it is rather a pity that he was sitting at the Cambridge pinnacle during his most creative period rather than working away at sharpening his tools under the protection of a Marshallian umbrella.

Finally, the vitality of Pigou's work and outlook following the *General Theory* is nicely captured in a comment on Robertson: 'Dennis has been spending years meticulously examining and criticising Mr Keynes on this and that, instead of getting on, as I think would be much better, with constructive work of his own.'[125]

Indeed Pigou was very worried about the amount of space Keynes, as editor, was allowing for textual exegesis. As *Employment and Equilibrium* amply demonstrated, this chewing over of the past was not Pigou's way.

NOTES

1. J. Saltmarsh and P. Wilkinson, *Arthur Cecil Pigou, 1877–1959* (Cambridge: printed for King's College, 1960) [hereafter cited as *S&W*], p. 18.
2. Letter to Saltmarsh, 1960 (King's College Collection).
3. *S&W*, p. 14.
4. I am indebted to the admirable obituaries by Professor Austen Robinson in E. T. Williams and H. M. Palmer (eds), *Dictionary of National Biography, 1951–60* (Oxford: Oxford University Press, 1971) [hereafter cited as *DNB*], pp. 814–17; Harry Johnson, 'Arthur Cecil Pigou, 1877–1959', *Canadian Journal of Economics*, XXVI

(1960) 150–5; and David Champernowne, 'Obituary: Arthur Cecil Pigou, 1877–1959', *Journal of the Royal Statistical Society*, series A, CXXII (1959) 263–5. See also E. A. G. Robinson, 'Pigou, Arthur Cecil', *International Encyclopaedia of the Social Sciences*, vol. 12 (New York: Macmillan, 1968) pp. 90–7. There is a fascinating memoir by Saltmarsh and Wilkinson (op. cit.) and a very personal letter portrait by his friend D. W. Corrie (King's College Library). I am also grateful to King's College Library for letting me see unpublished Pigou–Keynes correspondence in the Keynes Papers.

5. Thus, we find him writing *Economic Journal* reviews in 1901 of *The Cely Papers*, *The Despatches and Correspondence of John, Second Earl of Buckinghamshire. . .* , *A Plain Examination of Socialism*, *Government in Switzerland*, *Social Justice* and a (devastatingly critical) review of *The Science of Civilisation*.

6. *Economic Journal* [hereafter cited as *EJ*], XIV (1904) 66.

7. This affair is felt by some to have done little for Marshall's reputation. The reader is invited to form a judgement after consulting R. H. Coase, 'The Appointment of Pigou as Marshall's Successor', *Journal of Law and Economics* [hereafter cited as *JLE*], XV (1972) 473–86; A. W Coats, 'Comment', ibid. (1972) 487–95; T. W. Jones, 'The Appointment of Pigou as Marshall's Successor: The Other Side of the Coin', *JLE*, XXI (1978) 235–43.

8. By 1908 Pigou had published the following items: a review of J. B. Clark, *The Control of Trusts*, *EJ*, XII (1902) 63–67; 'A Parallel between Economic and Political Theory', *EJ*, XII (1902) 274–7; 'A Point of Theory Connected with the Corn Tax', *EJ*, XII (1902) 415–20; 'Some Reflections on Utility', *EJ*, XIII (1903) 58–68; *The Riddle of the Tariff* (London: Brinley Johnson, 1903); 'Pure Theory and the Fiscal Controversy', *EJ*, XIV (1904) 29–33; a review of W. Graham's *Free Trade and the Empire*, *EJ*, XIV (1904) 267; 'Monopoly and Consumers' Surplus', *EJ*, XIV (1904) 388–94; *Principles and Methods of Industrial Peace* (London: Macmillan, 1905); 'Professor Dietzel on Dumping and Retaliation', *EJ*, XV (1905) 436–43; 'The Unity of Political and Economic Science', *EJ*, XVI (1906) 372–80; 'The Incidence of Import Duties', *EJ*, XVII (1907) 289–94; 'Social Improvement in the Light of Modern Biology', *EJ*, XVII (1907) 358–69; a review of Marshall's *Principles* (5th ed.), *EJ*, XVII (1907) 532–5; 'Equilibrium under Bilateral Monopoly', *EJ*, XVIII (1908) 204–20.

9. 'A Method of Determining the Numerical Value of Elasticities of Demand', *EJ*, XX (1910) 636–40. In the pre-war period, Pigou also published 'Producers' and Consumers' Surplus', *EJ*, XX (1910) 358–70; 'Railway Rates and Joint Cost', *Quarterly Journal of Economics* [hereafter cited as *QJE*] XXVII (1913) 535–6 and 687–92, as well as *Wealth and Welfare* (note 12 below) and *Unemployment* (note 16 below).

10. M. Friedman, 'Professor Pigou's Method for Measuring Elasticities of Demand from Budgetary Data', *QJE*, L (1936) 151–63; see also ibid., 532–3; N. Georgescu-Roegen, 'Marginal Utility of Money and Elasticities of Demand', ibid., 533–9.

11. A. S. Deaton, *Models and Projections of Demand in Post War Britain* (London: Chapman & Hall, 1975) p. 9.

12. *Wealth and Welfare* (London: Macmillan, 1912).

13. Op. cit., p. 153.

14. *The Economics of Welfare* (London: Macmillan, 1920) 2nd edn 1924, 3rd edn 1929, 4th edn 1932 [hereafter cited as *EW*]; *Industrial Fluctuations* (London: Macmillan, 1927); *A Study in Public Finance* (London: Macmillan, 1928) [hereafter cited as *SPF*].

15. *The Economics of Stationary States* (London: Macmillan, 1935).

16. *Unemployment* (London: Home University Library, 1913).

17. Robinson, *DNB*, p. 816.

18. King's College Library.

19. Johnson, op. cit., p. 153.

20. Ibid.

21. T. W. Hutchison, *On Revolutions and Progress in Economic Knowledge* (Cambridge: Cambridge University Press, 1978).

22. S. Howson and D. W. Winch, *The Economic Advisory Council 1930–49: A Study in Economic Advice During Depression and Recovery* (Cambridge: Cambridge University Press, 1977) pp. 46–72.

23. Ibid., p. 65.

24. See E. A. G. Robinson, 'Keynes and his Cambridge Colleagues', in D. Patinkin and J. Clark Leith (eds), *Keynes, Cambridge and the General Theory* (London: Macmillan, 1977) pp. 25–38.

25. *S&W*, p. 24.

26. *Employment and Equilibrium: A Theoretical Discussion* (London: Macmillan, 1941; 2nd rev. edn, 1947).

27. *Aspects of British Economic History 1918–25* (London: Frank Cass, 1947).

28. *Socialism versus Capitalism* (London: Macmillan, 1937).

29. *Income* (London: Macmillan, 1946).

30. *Income Revisited* (London: Macmillan, 1956).

31. *Lapses from Full Employment* (London: Macmillan, 1945). [Hereafter cited as *LFE*.]

32. *The Veil of Money* (London: Macmillan, 1949).

33. *Keynes's 'General Theory': A Retrospective View* (London: Macmillan, 1950). [Hereafter cited as *RV*.]

34. Other publications not otherwise referred to in this essay were 'The Burden of War and Future Generations', *QJE*, XXXIII (1919) 242–55; 'The Foreign Exchanges', *QJE*, XXXVII (1923) 52–74; 'Prices and Wages from 1896–1914', *EJ*, XXXIII (1923) 163–71; 'In Memoriam: Alfred Marshall' in A. C. Pigou (ed.), *Memorials of Alfred Marshall* (London: Macmillan, 1925); review of Edgeworth's *Collected Papers* in *EJ*, XXXV (1925) 177–85; 'A Contribution to the Theory of Credit', *EJ*, XXXVI (1926) 215–27; 'The Monetary Theory of the Trade Cycle', *EJ*, XXXIX (1929) 183–94; 'Comment on Hawtrey', *EJ*, XXXIX (1929) 642–3; 'The Statistical Derivation of Demand Curves', *EJ*, XL (1930) 384–400; *Economic Essays and Addresses* (with D. H. Robertson) (London: P. S. King, 1931); 'The Effect of Reparations on the Ratio of International Exchange', *EJ*,

XLII (1932) 532–43; 'The Elasticity of Substitution', *EJ*, XLIV (1934) 232–41; 'Marginal Utility of Money and Elasticities of Demand', *QJE*, L (1936) 532; review of S. and B. Webb, *Soviet Communism: A New Civilisation?*, *EJ*, XLVI (1936) 88–97; 'Money Wages in Relation to Unemployment: A Note', *EJ*, XLVIII (1938) 134–5; 'Presidential Address', *EJ*, XLIX (1939) 215–21; 'War Finance and Inflation', *EJ*, L (1940) 461–8; 'The Measurement of Real Income', *EJ*, L (1940) 524–5; 'Newspaper Reviewers, Economics and Mathematics', *EJ*, LI (1941) 277–80; 'Maintaining Capital Intact', *Economica*, n.s., VIII (1941) 271–5; 'Models of Short Period Equilibrium', *EJ*, LII (1942) 250–7; review of Hayek's *The Road to Serfdom*, *EJ*, LIV (1944) 217–19; 'John Maynard Keynes: Baron Keynes of Tilton, 1883–1946', *Proceedings of British Academy*, XXXII (1946) 395–414; 'Economic Progress in a Stable Environment', *Economica*, n.s., XIV (1947) 180–88; 'The Food Subsidies', *EJ*, LVIII (1948) 202–9; 'Unrequited Imports', *EJ*, LX (1950) 241–54; see also his reply to Johnson and Carter, ibid., 839; 'Professor Duesenberry on Income and Savings', *EJ*, LXI (1951) 883–5; 'The Transfer Problem and Transport Costs', *EJ*, LXII (1952) 939–41; 'Costs and Output', *EJ*, LXIII (1953) 181–4.

35. Review of Marshall's *Principles* (5th ed.), *EJ*, XVII (1907) 534.
36. J. R. Hicks, *Economic Perspectives: Further Essays on Money and Growth* (Oxford: Clarendon Press, 1977) p. 161.
37. J. M. Keynes, *Collected Writings*, vol. XIII (London: Macmillan for the Royal Economic Society, 1973) [hereafter cited as *CW*], p. 484.
38. P. A. Samuelson, 'Evaluation of the Real National Income', *Oxford Economic Papers*, n.s., II (1950) 1–29, at p. 28.
39. 'Real Income and Economic Welfare', ibid. (1951) 16–20, at pp. 17–18.
40. F. A. Hayek, 'The Maintenance of Capital', *Economica*, n.s., II (1935) 241–76, at pp. 245ff.
41. 'Net Income and Capital Depletion', *EJ*, XLV (1935) 235–41, at p. 240.
42. H. Sidgwick, *Principles of Political Economy* (London: Macmillan, 1883).
43. *Alfred Marshall and Current Thought* (London: Macmillan, 1953) at p. 51.
44. *EW*, 4th edn, p. 746.
45. Ibid., p. 726.
46. Ibid., p. 764.
47. 'Problems of Compensation', *EJ*, XXXV (1925) 568–82, at p. 574.
48. *EW*, 4th edn, p. 711.
49. Ibid., p. 183.
50. R. H. Coase, 'The Problem of Social Cost', *JLE*, III (1960) 1–44, at p. 39.
51. A. Young, 'Wealth and Welfare', *QJE*, XXVII (1913) 672–86, at p. 681.
52. K. Bharadwaj, 'Marshall on Pigou's *Wealth and Welfare*', *Economica*, n.s., XXXIX (1972) 32–46.

53. J. Clapham, 'A Rejoinder', *EJ*, XXXII (1922) 560–3, at p. 562. Pigou's contribution was 'Empty Economic Boxes: A reply', *EJ*, loc. cit., 458–65.
54. D. H. Robertson, 'Increasing Returns and the Representative Firm', *EJ*, XL (1930) 80–9; Sraffa's contribution is in ibid., pp. 89–93.
55. 'The Laws of Diminishing Returns and Increasing Cost', *EJ*, XXXVII (1927) 188–97.
56. 'An Analysis of Supply', *EJ*, XXXVIII (1928) 238–57.
57. At around this time Pigou was receiving help from Frank Ramsey.
58. *EJ* (1928) loc. cit., p. 243.
59. 'A Note on Imperfect Competition', *EJ*, XLIII (1933) 108–12, at pp. 108–9.
60. R. F. Kahn, 'Some Notes on Ideal Output', *EJ*, XLV (1935) 1–35.
61. *The Political Economy of War* (London: Macmillan, 1921).
62. See note 47 above.
63. *SPF*, p. 50.
64. J. E. Stiglitz and P. Dasgupta, 'Differential Taxation, Public Goods and Economic Efficiency', *Review of Economic Studies*, XXXVIII (1971) 151–74; see also A. B. Atkinson and N. H. Stern, 'Pigou, Taxation and Public Goods', ibid., XLI (1974) 119–28.
65. *SPF*, pp. 92–3.
66. 'A Contribution to the Theory of Taxation', *EJ*, XXXVII (1927) 47–61.
67. *SPF*, p. 129.
68. Ibid., p. 141
69. 'The Report of the Royal Commission on the British Income Tax', *QJE*, XXXIV (1920) 607–25.
70. 'The Value of Money', *QJE*, XXXII (1918) 38–65, at p. 40.
71. D. Patinkin, *Money, Interest and Prices*, 2nd edn (New York: Harper & Row, 1965) pp. 607–8.
72. *EJ*, LIII (1943) 343–51.
73. Ibid., 349.
74. Ibid., 350.
75. Professor Kahn in correspondence confirms that Pigou once asked him, at dinner, to explain the 'Pigou-effect'.
76. A. Leijonhufvud, *On Keynesian Economics and the Economics of Keynes* (New York: Oxford University Press, 1966) pp. 315–31.
77. *The Theory of Unemployment* (London: Macmillan, 1933) [hereafter cited as *TU*] pp. 205–6.
78. 'Real and Money Wage Rates in Relation to Unemployment', *EJ*, XLVII (1937) 405–22 at p. 408.
79. 'Wage Policy and Unemployment', *EJ*, XXXVII (1927) 355–68.
80. *TU*, p. 243.
81. Note 33 above, at p. 50.
82. M. Blaug, *Economic Theory in Retrospect*, 2nd edn (London: Heinemann, 1968) p. 615. For *Industrial Fluctuations*, see note 14 above.
83. *EJ* (1937), see note 78 above.
84. *LFE*, p. 39.

85. 'Types of War Inflation', *EJ*, LI (1941) pp. 439–48 at p. 442. Italics added.
86. *EJ*, XXXVII (1927) pp. 418–24 at p. 421.
87. See *Industrial Fluctuations*, pp. 33–4.
88. pp. 88 *et seq*.
89. *CW*, XIV (1973) p. 54.
90. R. F. Harrod, 'Professor Pigou's Theory of Unemployment', *EJ*, XLIV (1934) 19–32, at pp. 19–20.
91. S. E. Harris, 'Professor Pigou's Theory of Unemployment', *QJE*, XLIX (1935) 286–324, at p. 286.
92. J. R. Hicks, *The Theory of Wages* (London: Macmillan, 1932) pp. 179, 185.
93. *CW*, XIII, p. 321.
94. Ibid., p. 326.
95. Moggridge in ibid., p. 214.
96. *General Theory* (*CW*, VII, p. 190).
97. Ibid., p. 277.
98. Ibid., p. 262.
99. Ibid., p. 260.
100. 'Mr J. M. Keynes' General Theory of Employment, Interest and Money', *Economica*, n.s., III (1936) 115–32, at p. 115.
101. Ibid., p. 121.
102. Ibid., p. 131.
103. *CW*, XIV, p. 87.
104. Op. cit., p. 816.
105. *CW*, XIII, p. 505.
106. *RV*, p. 64.
107. See note 78 above.
108. *CW*, XIV, p. 234.
109. Professor Champernowne emphasises in correspondence that Pigou was not at all well over this period. See also *CW*, XIV, p. 256.
110. *CW*, XIV, pp. 238–9, 250, 254, 259.
111. J. M. Keynes, 'Professor Pigou on Money Wage Rates in Relation to Unemployment', *EJ*, XLVII (1937) 743–5.
112. N. Kaldor, 'Professor Pigou on Money Wages in Relation to Unemployment', *EJ*, XLVII (1937) 745–53.
113. *EJ*, XLVII (1937) 753.
114. P. A. Samuelson, 'Concerning Say's Law', in J. Stiglitz (ed.), *Collected Scientific Papers*, vol. II (Cambridge, Mass: MIT Press, 1966) [hereafter cited as *CSP*], p. 1182.
115. King's College Collection.
116. *EJ*, LI (1941) 458–73; see also note 26 above.
117. I owe this suggestion to Professor Donald Winch.
118. *CSP*, II, pp. 1183–90.
119. S. C. Tsiang, 'Professor Pigou on the Relative Movements of Real Wages and Employment', *EJ*, LIV (1944) 352–65; A. C. Pigou, 'Some Considerations on Stability Conditions, Employment and Real Wages', *EJ*, LV (1945) 346–56.
120. M. Friedman, 'A Theoretical Framework for Monetary Analysis', *Journal of Political Economy*, LXXVIII (1970) 193–238.

121. J. A. Schumpeter, *History of Economic Analysis* (London: Allen & Unwin, 1963) p. 948.
122. Ibid., p. 966.
123. Op. cit., p. 307.
124. Op. cit., p. 815.
125. Pigou to Keynes, July 1938 (Keynes Papers, Marshall Library, Cambridge).

5   A. L. Bowley, 1869–1957

ADRIAN DARNELL

Introduction – biographia

Arthur Lyon Bowley[1] was born on 6 November 1869 in Bristol. The family had settled there five years earlier when his father, James William Lyon Bowley, was appointed vicar of St Philip and St Jacob, Bristol. They originated from London where James was born in 1826. He first took employment in a smith's shop, then as a clerk in a drapery and in 1846, after much private study, was appointed as assistant master at a Totteridge school. He clearly had great reserves of energy and self-discipline (qualities his son inherited) for once installed in his teaching position he furthered his quest for greater learning by early morning study of the classics.

Study of the classics was the first step towards ordination; he obtained a grant and received his Masters degree from Durham University in June 1854. Two years later he married Ann Jackson (having become engaged some eight years earlier) but after just five years of marriage and three children (James, Mary and Florence) she unfortunately died. Meanwhile, James had obtained a curacy at Lambeth which he left after disagreeing with the vicar on doctrinal grounds and then took various appointments as a tutor.

He was remarried in 1863 having met his bride, Maria Johnson, at Isleworth Naval College where he was then the chaplain. When he died of colitis at the early age of 44 Maria was left a widow with seven children (the oldest 13, the youngest, Arthur Lyon, 1).

The family position would have been very difficult but for a sum of £2100 collected by the Mayor and local Bristol businessmen which was invested in breweries, ironworks and railway wagon works and produced an annual income of about £200. Maria was evidently an excellent household manageress for the children were well-fed, well-clothed and the household never in debt.

Bowley was educated at Christ's Hospital, Newgate Street from 1879 to 1888 and from there went to Trinity, Cambridge on a first mathematics scholarship. His schoolmaster believed that in Bowley his long held ambition of educating a Senior Wrangler would be relised, but Bowley's poor health prevented this achievement. The tutors and dons of Cambridge financed a 'recuperative' voyage to Egypt, but after the trip a lengthy stay at Bournemouth was necessary! Nevertheless, he sat his finals in 1891 and was placed a most creditable tenth in the first class, although in order to take his degree he had to keep one more term. From October 1891 to March 1892 he studied physics, chemistry and economics. He worked in the Cavendish Laboratory at the natural sciences, and his study of economics was advanced by his tutor, the Rev. R. Appleton, who introduced him to Alfred Marshall. This was the start of a long friendship, with Marshall often giving fatherly advice. (On publication of *Elements of Statistics* Marshall wrote 'I told you I thought there was too much mathematics in your excellent book . . . having now brought out this great and successful book . . . leave mathematics for a little on one side'.)[2]

On Marshall's suggestion he entered for and won the Cobden Essay Prize in 1892 on the subject Changes in the Volume, Character and Geographical Distribution of England's Foreign Trade in the XIXth Century and Their Causes.[3] The work subsequently became a successful publication, and is to be noted for its detailed analysis of the balance of trade. This early promise was confirmed in 1894 when he won the Adam Smith Prize with a paper on changes in average wages. With Marshall's help, Bowley was transformed from mathematician to economic statistician. From 1892 to 1899 Bowley was a mathematics school teacher, first at Brighton, then Leatherhead and finally at Clifton. Whilst at Leatherhead Bowley was appointed to the newly founded London School of Economics as part-time Lecturer in Statistics. This position was almost certainly gained on Marshall's recommendation. He taught at the LSE continuously from 1895 to his retirement in 1936.

In 1900 Bowley was appointed as Lecturer in Mathematics at Reading College, where he became Professor of Mathematics and Economics in 1907. There he met Julia Hilliam, 'Instructor in Wood Carving', whom he married in 1904. At 29 she was one of the most accomplished women carvers in the country. The marriage was a fine combination of the scientist and the artist.

Three daughters were born to Arthur and Julia, Ruth, Agatha and Marian who appeared at regular two-year intervals from 1907 to 1911.

Whilst at Reading Bowley maintained his part-time appointment at the LSE and was promoted to Reader at London in 1908 having added mathematics to the curriculum there. In 1913 he resigned his Reading post and at the end of the war the family moved to Harpenden. In 1915 he was yet again promoted, this time to a chair, and four years later was appointed to the newly created Chair in Statistics. This was the first ever chair in statistics in the social sciences. The year after his retirement (in 1936) he was awarded the CBE and in 1950 he was honoured again, being made Knight Bachelor.

His academic honours are countless, perhaps one of the most notable being the award of both the Silver and Gold Guy Medals by the Royal Statistical Society (an honour shared by only three people). He was invited out of retirement in 1940 to become acting-director of the Oxford Institute of Statistics. Although then over 70 he was far from a figurehead, devoting great energy to the post. He retired (for a second time) in December 1944 and 'left the Institute a vigorous and going concern'.[4]

After a short illness he died in 1957. A memorial service, arranged jointly by the LSE and the Royal Statistical Society, was held at St Martin-in-the-Fields on 11 February 1957. His widow died two years later.

He was a most conscientious enquirer in all that he studied. He spread his talents widely, as teacher and research worker in economics, statistics and economic statistics. He was editor and member of the Executive Committee of the London and Cambridge Economic Service from its foundation in 1923 to 1945 (his final contribution was in 1953), Fellow of the Royal Economic Society from 1893 (elected to Council in 1901), and a founder member of the Econometric Society in 1933.

His major contributions to economics were made as a collector and compiler of economic statistics (particularly on wages and national income), as a pioneer of statistical techniques in the social sciences, in the development of mathematical economics and econometrics and, most notably, as a pioneer of sampling techniques. These contributions are discussed in the remaining sections of this chapter.

Wage and national income statistics

Bowley's work on wages and National Income accounting is well known, if only through the unfortunately named 'Bowley's Law'.[5] His life-long interest in the subject began in 1894 when he won the Adam Smith prize with the essay 'Changes in Average Wages in the United Kingdom Between 1860 and 1891'. When a revised version of the paper was read to the Royal Statistical Society on 19 March 1895, Marshall commented that he 'had been struck by the brilliancy of the plan by which Mr. Bowley proposed to extract some information from the great mass of wage statistics which had hitherto been almost useless because of its fragmentary nature'.[6]

Bowley's object was not to obtain figures of wages which would represent the facts with 'mathematical accuracy' for that 'would have been impossible'. His intention was rather to 'tabulate all the figures accessible . . . to find what changes of wages are indicated by the scanty statistical information available, and to give the results in such a form that further or more reliable information can correct them'.[7] Given the numerous sources of information which he consulted, Bowley was faced with a severe problem of comparability, for the figures available related to different years in different trades, had been compiled using different methods, the exact period and locality were often unknown and finally the relationship between the reported and actual earnings was doubtful. Because of these difficulties, it was necessary for Bowley to devise a method capable of yielding an accurate account of general wage movements.

The plan, like all brilliant plans, was extremely simple in conception. The method was Jevonian, employing not the 'static' techniques of Charles Booth or the Board of Trade, but the 'kinetic' technique of constructing index numbers. The two special characteristics of the method were that two statements of wages were never compared unless they originated from the same source, and ratios rather than levels of wages were used. In ample justification of his procedure, Bowley remarked 'Without this possibility the inquiry would break down at the start for want of comparable figures; and I see no other way of making full use of figures that do exist, other than that I have chosen'.[8]

The minute attention to detail which characterises Bowley's work was evident in this, his first contribution to the Royal

Statistical Society. The potential errors inherent in the method were analysed, and on the question of using weighted index numbers to describe the movement of the national average wage (where proxies were used for the unknown weights and aggregation required that the individual trades be treated as if they all received identical remunerations in the base year) Bowley concluded his defence of this practice by saying 'It appears at first sight as if this must vitiate the result, but both by experiment and theory it is found that the error introduced into the result is exceedingly small.'[9] In further support of this statement Bowley wrote a most detailed paper which appeared in 1897, showing that 'in general the total error due to weight is less than that due to quantity' and adds the necessary (yet often ignored) caveat that 'Their relative importance depends on the special circumstances of each investigation.'[10]

The general approach in his essay on wages was thoroughly original and great care had been taken with errors. Moreover, Bowley had painstakingly worked through the mass of primary statistics himself, for his position at the time did not warrant any kind of assistance.[11] It should also be remembered that the tedious work was completed without the aid of a computer. The paper was rightly hailed by the chairman of the meeting as:

one of the most novel, interesting, and valuable which the Society had had for a long time ... [it] ... had struck out a method by which an accumulation of statistical observations hitherto lying waste might be utilised ... and ... the scientific and theoretical portions of the propositions contained in the paper seemed completely established.[12]

In later years Bowley developed his work on wages, and between 1898 and 1906, published in the *Journal of the Royal Statistical Society* a 14 part saga entitled 'The Statistics of Wages in the United Kingdom during the Last Hundred Years'. The first nine parts were produced by his sole authorship; the last five concerned the Engineering and Shipbuilding trades and were in joint authorship with Mr G. H. Wood. The statistical techniques used, and the economic concepts employed, became more refined in the later parts. In the first essay it is at times difficult to distinguish between Bowley's various concepts of wage rates, earnings and the total national wage bill, but by 1921, when

Bowley published his study of wages and prices under wartime conditions, *Prices and Wages in the United Kingdom, 1914–1920*, we find precise definitions of all expressions. Furthermore, there is a detailed explanation of why changes in earnings would diverge from those of wage rates. Although he does not use the term 'wage-drift', Bowley was the first to draw attention to this important phenomenon. Thus, while his wages work was of a primarily statistical character, the economic content may be seen to grow over the years. Indeed, Bowley's causal economic analysis of changes in wages concentrates on the changes in the demand for labour, the increasing market power of combined workers and labour's increasing efficiency.[13]

Not only did Bowley use his method to analyse the position in the UK but he also produced comparative results for the UK, the USA and France.[14] His results have since been used in various contexts; for example by Phillips in his famous 1958 paper on wages and prices. While Bowley did his best in his lifetime to safeguard statistics from abuse there was little he could do after his death!

Bowley's work on wages naturally led him into three related areas; the theory of index numbers, an examination of national income statistics, and investigations of poverty, unemployment and social change. While Bowley's work on the first of these topics was to some extent overshadowed by the work of others such as Fisher and Edgeworth, it is worth noting that the index christened by Frisch as the 'Bowley Index' had in fact been proposed earlier by both Marshall and Edgeworth. But the index number now known as 'Fisher's Ideal Index Number' (proposed by Fisher in 1926) had been suggested by Bowley as early as 1899 in Palgrave's *Dictionary of Political Economy*.[15] At the practical level Bowley advocated the use of index numbers to evaluate the 'cost-of-living' adjustments in sliding scale wage agreements.[16]

His concern with wages became a motivating force in his inter-war work on national income estimation.[17] The early papers used rudimentary principles and unsophisticated techniques, but as the work progressed to the 1927 joint publication with Sir Josiah Stamp, *The National Income, 1924,* we can observe the refinement of concepts, definitions and methods. Indeed, the first official estimates of National Income, made during the Second World War, depended heavily upon the pioneering work of Bowley and Stamp. This work examined nearly all the problems encountered today.

Bowley's 1922 paper 'The Definition of National Income' is a landmark, containing the distinction between market price and factor cost evaluations, and the term 'transfer payments' is explicitly introduced. The treatment of taxation was also clarified, and one need only examine the 1927 essay to appreciate the methodological sophistication of the later work of Bowley and Stamp. It was their work which moulded the subject into its modern form and one cannot over-estimate our debt to them.

The clearest statement of Bowley's work in the field of social change is to be found in *The Measurement of Social Phenomena* (1915). This contains a systematic and comprehensive research programme for a complete socioeconomic analysis of society. The emphasis on dynamics is surprising for such an early work, and of particular interest is the analysis of intergenerational mobility. This book is still worth detailed study.

Bowley was genuinely concerned about matters of wages, national income, unemployment and poverty;[18] he applied his scientific, statistical, mind to such problems, and those who work in these areas today will find the extent to which their methods, procedures and definitions first found expression in Bowley's early contributions. The development of these areas was frustrated in Bowley's day by the lack of data, and much of his time and effort was devoted to attempting to remedy this situation. This aspect of his work will be considered later.

The role of statistics in economics

For a full appreciation of Bowley's work as a collector of statistics, it is important to cast him in historical perspective and to examine the attitude of the professional economists to the role of statistics in economics. Elementary statistics was not taught as a component of an economics degree until the late nineteenth century, and even in those cases where such a course did exist, students were not 'pressed to go, and were encouraged in the belief that a little common sense could easily take the place of regular training with tables of numbers'.[19] In this respect the LSE was unique. From its foundation in 1895 it has had a systematic course of lectures on the elements of statistics. Bowley's first lecturing appointment was to deliver this course, cycling up on his free Wednesday afternoons from Leatherhead.[20]

In 1901 Bowley published his very successful *Elements of*

Statistics, which was the first English text on the subject. The credit for the book should go not only to Bowley but also to the LSE, for it is doubtful whether it would have been written had the school not introduced its lecture course. The book was very well received and went through six editions, the last being published in 1937. Sanger, reviewing the first edition, said, 'this book is the best book on the Elements of Statistics written in English, French, German or Italian'.[21] In it we find Bowley's statement that:

> The statistician furnishes the political economist with the facts, by which he tests his theories or on which he bases them ... it may be held to be the business of the statistician to collect, arrange and describe, like a careful experimentist, but to draw no conclusions; even in an investigation relating to cause and effect, to present evidence but not conclusions.[22]

In Bowley's second text on statistics, the *Elementary Manual of Statistics,* published in 1910 and going through seven editions by 1951, he says

> Three of the principal uses of statistics are (i) to give correct views, based on facts, as to what happened in the past; how, when and under what circumstances, population, trade, wealth, etc., have grown; and by comparison and analysis to search for the causes of changes that have taken place; (ii) to afford materials for estimates of the present ... (iii) to make possible a forecast for the near future; for this purpose we study the changes that have taken place in the recent past, by the light of relations between phenomena that comparative statistical analysis reveals.[23]

In this early section of the book, Bowley makes two points to which he often returns in a number of later papers; first, that 'There is urgent need for more systematic and more complete national statistics', and secondly, that 'Statistics only furnish a tool, necessary though imperfect, which is dangerous in the hands of those who do not know its use and deficiencies. A knowledge of methods and limitations is necessary, if only to avoid being misled by unscrupulous or unscientific arguments.'[24]

Bowley's conception of the role of statistics is clearly in accord with that of the founders of the Royal Statistical Society, for in the introduction to that body's first journal issue we find the following:

> The science of statistics differs from Political Economy, because, although it has the same end in view, it does not discuss causes, nor reason upon probable effects; it seeks only to collect, arrange and compare, that class of facts which alone can form the basis of correct conclusions with respect to social and political government.[25]

He does not, of course, deny that the statistician, as a collector of information, may also draw conclusions; but he views this process as that of a man changing his hat from that of statistician to that of political economist. Even though Bowley acknowledges that the statistician may furnish the facts by which the economist may test his theories this was a most underdeveloped role of statistics at that time.[26] It is more often the case that the economist would base his theories on statistics rather than use them as a means of verification of deductive reasoning.

This methodological standpoint is supported by J. N. Keynes writing in his *Scope and Method of Political Economy,* first published in 1890, where he says of the dual roles of deduction and induction:

> The functions of history and statistics in economic enquiries are very important and various . . . namely, as constituting the basis of inductive generalisations. . . . It follows that even when we rely primarily on induction, it is of great importance that our conclusions should be confirmed and interpreted by deductive reasoning . . ∴ the induction may usefully precede the deduction.[27]

It is interesting to note that Keynes's view is almost identical to that expressed some 47 years earlier by J. S. Mill in one passage of *A System of Logic* where Mill remarks that

> instead of deducing our conclusions by reasoning, and verifying them by observation, we in some cases begin by obtaining them provisionally from specific experience, and afterwards connect them with the principles of human nature by *a priori* reasonings, which reasonings are thus a real verification.[28]

Bowley rarely approached statistics with the intention of verifying *a priori* theory. Rather he approached data with two objectives, first to process the information and present it in a meaningful way and secondly to examine it in an exploratory way. It would seem as if Bowley's maxim was 'Let the data speak for itself.' Concerning the process of verification, Bowley's position may be gleaned from an examination of the studies he made of national progress. His first essay on this subject appeared in the *Economic Journal* in 1903. It begins with the words,

> So many writers and speakers are making use of statistical arguments, in dealing with the current fiscal controversy, to support such inconsistent and confusing conclusions, that an analysis of the kinds of error involved and the suggestion of some rules of criticism will not be out of place.

He goes on to argue that the most general fault lies in the province of logic, not of statistics, in that a theory based on deductive reasoning which is in accord with observations is often quoted as 'proved by the infallible test of statistics'. On this widely-held misconception, Bowley comments

> But if the *a priori* proof is complete, statistics are not necessary to confirm it, though they may give a useful complementary quantitative measurement; if it is incomplete, and therefore an appeal is made to facts, the statistics must be examined as strictly as if the whole burden of proof rested upon them. The two methods are not of mutual assistance like two strings supporting a picture, but alternative as two bridges over a river.[29]

This is an extreme view which is difficult to grasp as Bowley leaves undefined his concept of 'completeness'. However, one may interpret Bowley as arguing that deductive and inductive reasoning are strict substitutes, not complements.

This methodological stand is in direct opposition to that expounded by Keynes and is less satisfactory. Keynes expresses what may be termed a more modern view in the statement

> If pure induction is inadequate, pure deduction is equally inadequate. The mistake of setting up these methods in mutual

opposition, as if the employment of either of them excluded the employment of the other, is unfortunately very common.[30]

Bowley makes precisely the mistake noted by Keynes for he argues that confirmatory statistical analysis has a useful role if and only if the deductive reasoning is unsatisfactory in respect of completeness and then may only be used if the statistics are wholly acceptable and thus permit a purely empirical or inductive proof. However, Bowley does not carry this view over to the role of exploratory statistical analysis where he is quite content to use statistical observation, both to provide the initial premises from which deduction can proceed, and to provide empirical generalisations which then require the substantiation of deductive reasoning.

This somewhat paradoxical use of statistics was common to the majority of British economists at that time. This may be contrasted with the work being done in the US at the beginning of this century, where the names of Mitchell, Moore and Persons figure largely in the field of testing economic theory by use of available statistics. It is fair to say that confirmatory analysis and testing of a theory's predictions did not gain widespread acknowledgement in the UK until the post-war years. The reasons for this difference cannot, unfortunately, be examined here, but suffice it to say that Bowley's work as a collector of statistics was typical of British statisticians in aim, though not in execution. His meticulous care and attention to detail were exceptional.

The contribution of statistics to economic science depends crucially upon the scope, nature and continuity of the available data; and at a time when no official body existed to co-ordinate collection it was left to individuals, such as Bowley, to make available the quantitative information. In this role, Bowley may be seen as fulfilling the aim of his original economics teacher, Marshall. In the *Principles,* Marshall pointed out the need for a body of data to aid our understanding of economic affairs when he wrote:

> The rapid growth of collective interests, and the growing tendency towards collective action in economic affairs, make it every day more important that we should know what quantitative measures of public interests are most needed and what statistics are required for them, and that *we should set ourselves to obtain these statistics* (author's emphasis).[31]

Later, in 1907, when addressing the Royal Economic Society he said

> qualitative analysis has done the greater part of its work. ...
> Much less progress has indeed been made towards the
> *quantitative* determination of the relative strength of different
> economic forces. That higher and more difficult task must await
> upon the slow growth of thorough realistic statistics.[32]

Clearly Marshall appreciated and supported the work which Bowley
and others were doing in the collection of statistics. One may suggest
that Bowley was simply extending the application of Marshallian
economics and hence conjecture that one of the reasons for a lack of
confirmatory statistical analysis in the UK at this time was because
the able men were doing the all-important and essential job of
collecting statistics and thus preparing the ground for later
confirmatory statisticians.

The improvement of official statistics

Bowley, the collector of statistics, took great care over the
accumulation of data and paid considerable attention to the detail of
errors. The criteria for the acceptability of statistics are first to be
found in the pamphlet *Statistical Studies relating to National Progress
... A Plea for Further Enquiry* (1904), in which five stringent tests
of the worthiness of statistics are proposed. First, the statistics used
must be comprehensive; secondly they should correspond to the
theoretical concepts which we wish to measure; thirdly, close
attention should be paid, in the case of time series, to both trend and
fluctuation; fourthly, in measuring units in terms of money, real not
nominal measurements need to be taken; lastly, in considering a
significant change in an aggregate measure it is most important to
examine closely the underlying changes in the constituent parts.
Having put many of the available statistics through these tests and
having found, not surprisingly, that many failed, Bowley commented
sadly:

> It is humiliating to have to admit that our positive knowledge is so
> limited, and it is natural to ask whether more cannot be done in the
> way of official enquiry or private investigation. There is doubtless a
> wide field for the latter, but the unofficial student is constantly

handicapped by the absence of essential data which the Government only can collect. The fault, if fault there be, must be attributed to the general public, who have made no effective demand for more complete information, and to the successive Governments, who have not recognised our stupendous ignorance of matters of vital importance as an evil calling for a remedy.[33]

This was a theme to which Bowley was to return.

On 16 June 1908, he read a paper to the Royal Statistical Society entitled 'The Improvement of Official Statistics'. The paper was very different to those normally read before that body and Bowley, recognising this, began by explaining the 'unusual nature of this paper. ... It is rather a paper with an object, that of exciting interest for the further improvement of our official statistics'. Repeating his previous argument for the need to increase public pressure he asserted that

> In 1903 statisticians . . . suddenly found their neglected wares in demand, and . . . both public departments and private investigators were . . . unprepared to meet the strain on their resources. . . . It was not then, is not now, and will not be, till an intelligent public opinion forces the development, the business of any . . . department to prepare . . . measurements of national or industrial development.[34]

Bowley's argument that public pressure was essential to this much needed improvement is less than compelling though he did point to the eagerness of the media to publish statistical tables whenever they might be relevant as indicating an interest on the part of the newspaper-reading public.[35]

In the discussion which followed Bowley's paper it was suggested by Chiozza Money that the lobby should come from the Society itself. In fact, the Society had on previous occasions attempted a similar move and had met with little success. Indeed, it is, perhaps, surprising that a body of such eminent statisticians should have had so little influence on the publication of statistics by government, and this leads one to suspect that Bowley's plea for greater public demands would have had a similar lack of success. The failure of the Society to effect reform may in part have been due to the implied criticism of government statisticians as typified by Bowley's remark that 'the official view is that everything published under the Government's authority is accurate, that the facts are just so', which was quickly followed by 'Every statistician knows that the true meaning of published official statistics is quite different from their face meaning',[36] suggesting, it would seem, that those working in Government departments do not merit the worthy title of statistician!

The subject had first been raised by Bowley in his Presidential Address to Section F of the British Association in York in 1906 when he said of official publications

> It is a sad reflection that, while so much care and labour are spent in accumulating and printing statistical tables, so few of them are of any real importance, and so few are intelligible, even to one who studies them carefully.[37]

Bowley complained bitterly of the lack of coordination between the various Government departments, and declared 'We need a central thinking department in statistics.'[38] He was also extremely critical of the official view that no figure should be reported unless it was an ascertained fact and could be sustained as exact in a court of law. This pursuit of accuracy not only delayed the publication of new figures but also made their collection unnecessarily complicated. Furthermore, Bowley pointed out that the very field of study precludes numerical exactness. Perhaps most importantly, this over-riding preoccupation with numerical accuracy led to the production of useless statistics, for the published figures failed to correspond with any meaningful measure. The scientific enquirer, Bowley said 'is left in the position of a man who inquires a distance in France, and is told that it is 8.543 kilometres along the high road, and then some way along the path; the precision of the first measure is useless to him'.[39]

Much of the problem was due to the fact that those Civil Servants dealing with statistics were ill-trained and ill-prepared for their work. The departmental view was that 'technical methods are best studied in the departments themselves'. The entrance qualification was merely a test in non-specialised education.

The theme of the insufficiency of official statistics recurs many times in Bowley's writings. Because of his growing reputation in the field of wages and prices, Bowley was naturally invited to participate in many official enquiries, and one may conjecture that this contact enabled him to further his aim. Bowley's own preoccupation with the fundamentals may seem less important today, but questions concerning definitions, methods of tabulation, coverage of the population, comparability and accuracy which are now commonplace needed to be stressed by someone, and no-one seems to have made such an explicit and systematic exposition of these issues prior to Bowley.[40] The lobby for reform of official statistics grew throughout the early part of this century and while Bowley's voice was one of many it was certainly one of the loudest and clearest. There were two main demands for the means of reform; one being the creation of a Central Statistical Office and the other being the creation of a professionally trained statistical officer class in the Civil Service.

These ideas were brought together in the form of a petition presented to His Majesty's Government in the Autumn of 1919, signed by the President and a number of members of the Royal Statistical Society, and by members of other statistical societies, which called for a public enquiry into the current state of official statistics. However, the committee of officials to whom the petition was referred took it as an attack on them rather than, as Bowley put it, as an attack on 'the system under which it was their misfortune to find their efforts frustrated'.[41]

The report of the committee, which was presented to the Cabinet, was published in June 1921. It denied that the Government had a responsibility to provide statistics covering all aspects of social and economic life; and by reference to a former official committee of 1877 it proceeded to show that the establishment of a Central Statistical Office was impracticable. Needless to say, Bowley was far from pleased by this report and immediately wrote a short note for *Economica* entitled 'Recent Official Statistical Publications'. This was most critical of the report, but welcomed the setting up of a permanent Consultative Committee of statistical officers as a good thing, even though 'the inquisitive public is carefully warned off the official preserve and must continue to be satisfied with such information as the Department functioning behind closed doors chooses to give them'.[42] The criticism of UK statistics on which Bowley concentrated was that the self-governing dominions had recognised the need for a central office while the home country had not. He concluded on the mournful note that in the UK 'The frequent repetition of the same figures . . . tends to give them an appearance of completeness, relevance and accuracy to which they have little title, and the whole mass of statistics may be dangerously misleading to those who have not the opportunity or ability to criticise them at their source.'[43]

Despite this apparent failure, the cause was never abandoned. It progressed slowly during the inter-war years but received great impetus in 1941 with the establishment of the Central Statistical Office which, despite its many shortcomings, has become an effective and useful institution. The process of reform was the result of many people's efforts and it is difficult to apportion credit. Nonetheless it is fair to credit Bowley with playing a vital role. He published at least half a dozen articles explicitly on the subject, almost certainly used his influence with those officials with whom he made contact, and generally expended a great deal of time and energy in what he felt was a most essential and immediate issue.

Mathematical economics and econometrics

In 1924, Bowley published his text *The Mathematical Groundwork of Economics*. The book is a landmark in many senses. Not only does it represent the first English text which presents the theories of economics since Marshall in a mathematical form but it also represents the vehicle by which a number of techniques came to be generally accepted. Bowley's intention was 'to reduce to a uniform notation, and to present as a properly related whole, the main part of the mathematical methods used by Cournot, Jevons, Pareto, Edgeworth, Marshall, Pigou and Johnson . . .' and he goes on to state with typical modesty: 'I have not intended to advance any new theories in economics, nor do I claim any originality in mathematical results. . . . Perhaps, however, there is in my analysis a more definite attempt than has been usual to deal equally with the hypotheses of competition and of monopoly . . .'[44]

The book was reviewed in what was to be Wicksell's last publication. This interesting review ends with a long list of inaccuracies and typographical errors which he says 'can make an already complicated book unnecessarily difficult . . . [and] . . . will probably have completely disappeared when, as I hope, a new edition of this excellent work is shown to be necessary'.[45] The *Groundwork* was, in fact, never to be published in a second edition, and errors spotted by Wicksell remained. It should, perhaps, be noted that Wicksell's list is itself bedevilled by a number of typographical errors! Furthermore, one could both add to and subtract from Wicksell's list.

The text was designed with postgraduates and professional economists in mind and was not designed as a course text book. It represents, rather, an attempt by Bowley to facilitate the dissemination of mathematical economics within the profession.

Bowley was a trained mathematician and it was, therefore, most fitting that he should have written such a book. It was a path-breaking text, a true first. The earliest text which may properly be called mathematical economics is Laundhart (1885),[46] and before the *Groundwork* there was no introductory treatise in English. As Schumpeter says of those earlier publications, there was 'nothing that will stand comparison with Bowley's *MG* . . .'[47]

At the time of Bowley's writing, mathematical economics was in its infancy. Nevertheless, the contribution which mathematics could make to the development of economic theory had been recognised for many years; indeed, in 1913 whilst still at Reading, Bowley published what seems to be the first text on pure mathematics designed for students of the social sciences, *A General Course of Pure Mathematics*. In the preface, Bowley wrote 'It has been the intention to include the bulk of the results obtained in pure mathematics which . . . are needed by those who use pure mathematics as an instrument in mechanics, engineering, physics, chemistry and economics.'[48]

The text was the result of lectures given by Bowley and was, like the *Groundwork*, intended as a synthesis of known results. It was welcomed by Whittaker of Edinburgh University who wrote to Bowley, saying 'I shall have much pleasure in recommending the book to my own students',[49] but was not so well received by the pure mathematician, Hardy, in the *Contemporary Review*. Bowley reacted to the review by writing to Hardy defending his work, and received a 12 page epistle in reply. In it, Hardy remarked 'What I felt about the whole of your treatment was that it was so far from rigorous that it would have been much better to be content with a few vague explanations of a geometrical kind . . . it was an attempt to do what is simply not possible for anyone but a professional mathematician in the strict sense.'[50] In a further six-page letter, Hardy responded with a full retraction on one point of dispute by writing 'On one point I was clearly wrong, and I apologise for my mistake. . . . Your proof of the multiplication theorem therefore, is, I think, substantially correct. . . . As my review was, in one point definitely unjust, I propose to send a note to the *C.R.* withdrawing that particular criticism.'[51] Hardy was, at the time, the foremost pure mathematician in the country, and for Bowley to have successfully defended himself against Hardy's censure on one point at least is no little achievement. Clearly the high hopes of his early schoolmaster were not ill-founded. Bowley's text in pure mathematics stands careful examination today and illustrates his diversity. Not only was he a most gifted and capable social scientist but he was also a mathematician of the highest rank.

Returning to the *Groundwork,* we find his mathematical ability in evidence at several points. As Tappan said in his review of the book: 'Professor Bowley, needless to say, knows what he is about; and what others have been about becomes clear as the disguises . . . fall away in his hands.'[52] The main achievement of the text was to enable other, less mathematically able, economists to appreciate the value of such work, and to make known certain concepts best approached through the language of mathematics. For example, the indifference curve, the contract curve, and the derivation of properties of the demand curve, appear in the first chapter alone. It should be added that in deriving the slope of the demand curve Bowley, followed by Marshall, thought in terms of the response of price to quantity. On the other hand, the formulation of Slutsky's equation is expressed in terms of the response of quantities to prices. Were one to invert Bowley's expression for dp/dq to obtain dq/dp then Slutsky's equation may, with some algebraic manipulations, be obtained. Bowley, however, did not actually attempt to break up quantity responses into substitution and income effects.

The point should be made that Bowley's mathematics did in fact, at certain points, take him beyond the current state of economic knowledge. The Slutsky equation is perhaps the most notable example, but one could also point to Bowley's use of the offer curve or to his treatment of duopoly where, in order to obtain a solution, he stated 'We should need to know x_2 [the output of firm 2] as a function of x_1 [the output of firm 1] and this depends on what each producer thinks the other is likely to do.'[53] Here we see both the reaction curve and the concept of conjectural variations. Bowley's intention is to suggest that the variations may well be non-zero (in contrast to Cournot's analysis of 1838) and while it was Edgeworth who had first introduced the concept explicitly in 1897, it is not certain whether Bowley was aware of this work as it was only made available in English in 1925.[54]

Bowley, quite typically, is concerned with the conditions of solutions to practical problems; this is illustrated most admirably by his analysis of production and exchange under various market structures, from perfect competition at one extreme to monopoly at the other. Furthermore, his analysis extends to both product and factor markets. This section of the book is most original in presentation and content, representing as it does a complete and uniform coverage of the topic, and may be found to contain many perceptive remarks. For example, his interpretation of Pigou's 'marginal supply price' is not that of the original author, for Bowley treats the concept as identical to marginal cost. Bowley's work also represents a departure from Marshall's in avoiding the use of the 'representative firm'. Bowley assumes all firms in a competitive industry to operate under identical technical conditions.

It is a remarkable book and it is a great pity that it should never have been developed into a second, revised edition. Nonetheless, the text achieved more than Bowley's aim of presenting results, for it goes beyond synthesis of known analysis, and as Tappan commented

> By selection, by improved variant forms of analysis, by the ordering of the matter of the various authors whom he names, he has made a whole which is more than the sum of its parts.[55]

The text was also reviewed by Edgeworth who remarked that

> A long-felt want is satisfied by this clear, concise and correct statement of the leading propositions and methods which mathematics contributes to Political Economy. . . . By steps that are neither violently abrupt nor tediously circuitous he reaches the heights from which the mutual dependence of all economic quantities can best be contemplated.

However, he rightly went on to point out particular difficulties which would face a 'tiro' were he to read the book, not least of which was the original notation used by Bowley to express the differential calculus. But the praise was unqualified when he said 'The authorship of the treatise guarantees the importance of the subject.'[56] Wicksell, too, welcomed the book warmly, saying that 'it is well worth while for any economist to make its acquaintance if he can spare sufficient time to work through its few but well packed pages'; but regarding the 'few' pages he remarked 'Bowley belongs to those who love conciseness more than is desirable for the average reader.'[57] No doubt Bowley's answer would have been that the book was not written to be read by the 'average reader'!

In the same year, 1924, Bowley also used his mathematical abilities in reply to a short paper on consumer's surplus by his good friend and colleague, Professor Edwin Cannan,[58] and again two years later in reply to Wicksell's criticisms of his treatment of bilateral monopoly.[59]

Bowley's major contribution to econometrics was the path-breaking text *Family Expenditure* (1935) which he wrote in collaboration with R. D. G. Allen. The work is an exemplary piece of econometrics, the purpose of which was

> to discover how far the expenditure of individual families . . . can be described by rules and formulae, to relate any rules that are found to the postulates of economic theory and to describe the variations from the averages that result from the different choices of individual families.[60]

The primary aim, therefore, was the discovery of empirical 'laws' and the related aim was then to account for observed behaviour within an analytical framework. The methodology was strictly 'measurement before theory' which is quite in accord with Bowley's general use of 'exploratory analysis', namely the use of empirical generalisations as the initial premises of pure deduction. Thus 'In so far as these formulae are of general application, they should not only have immediate practical use but should also provide economists with fundamental material for theoretical analysis.'[61] Furthermore, having eliminated temporal effects by their use of cross-section data and fitted Engel Curves (by eye) to scatter diagrams of family expenditures on various goods against family income, they remarked 'we can formulate and examine these results objectively without any theoretical basis'. The aberrations from the observed linear relationship for food were found in the highest income ranges and were 'probably due to the larger numbers of children in the families in this range'.[62]

On the basis of this (not unreasonable) assertion, Allen and Bowley proceeded to divide expenditures into two categories, namely those common to the family as a unit and those specific to individuals within the unit. Clearly, the family's expenditures on the former items (such as rent, fuel and lighting) are less sensitive to family size than expenditures on the latter items (especially food and clothing). For expenditures in the first category their method was simply to introduce additively a family size term to the expenditure–income relationship, but for the second category it was felt 'more appropriate to divide each expenditure by the number of persons. This number should be, not the actual number of individuals, but a number based on a scale of needs in which allowance is made for age and sex.'[63] For both categories we have, then the use of equivalent adult scales. Such scales may be constructed in one of three ways: so as to reflect individual (typically nutritional) needs, or from observed market behaviour, or one might simply pluck them from the air. Allen and Bowley employed all three possibilities but concluded 'the various scales appear to give nearly the same results'.[64] Such words have been echoed by many researchers since!

In order to test the use of equivalent scales, they plotted expenditure per equivalent adult against income per equivalent adult and, having observed linearity, concluded that the 'modified linear law' was applicable. Furthermore, in the analysis of a complete set of linear Engel Curves, economic theory imposes certain restrictions on the parameters. Allen and Bowley tested these restrictions in good econometric fashion, finding general acceptance of their model and then proceeded to carry out various diagnostic specification tests and used a chi-squared goodness of fit test to support their results. Great stress was laid upon the distribution of expenditures. This part was work which grew out of a paper by Bowley in the first issue of *Econometrica* which examined the applicability of the normal distribution to such variables. In fact, the samples used by Allen and Bowley reflected Gibrat's law of *'effet proportionnel'* namely that it is the logarithm of income not income *per se*, which is normally distributed.

In the Appendix, there is a theoretical analysis of expenditure distributions which is notable for its use of both a quadratic utility function and directly additive utility functions. Concerning the latter the authors concluded, like many later workers, 'All that we can do is to assume independence on *a priori* grounds, a step we are scarcely prepared to take. The case of independent goods would appear to be of little practical interest.'[65]

It should be clear from what has been said that Bowley made notable contributions to mathematical economics and to econometrics. In the *Groundwork* he innovated and popularised various concepts and used mathematics to great effect in clarifying the issues at stake in the analysis of consumer's surplus and bilateral monopoly. Furthermore, with R. D. G. Allen, he produced a monograph which serves as the foundation stone of the modern econometric studies of family behaviour. It should be remembered that Bowley was 66 when *Family Expenditure* was published! The book uses a wholly original style of analysis within the (then) new 'econometric' mould and it is, therefore, of interest to note that Bowley was not too old to learn new methods and to produce such a path-breaking study even in his last years before retirement.

The development of sampling

In order to appreciate fully Bowley's contribution to sampling it is necessary to examine briefly the history of the subject. A technique known as the 'Inverse Method', apparently first used by Laplace,[66] dominated early sampling theory. The approach is essentially Bayesian, and while Laplace's work does not fit such a framework and was based on incorrect assumptions, the very principle of sampling seems to have been largely ignored by nineteenth century statisticians. The Inverse Method was, however, to re-appear in the late nineteenth century, particularly in the work of Edgeworth. Between Laplace and the re-emergence of the Inverse Method of sampling we find a period in which the principle of total enumeration reigned supreme. Demographic studies using population censuses produced an ill-founded sense of security in those working in the field. Indeed the apparent certainty yielded by such studies was so overwhelming that the aim became one of investigation by complete census of as many variables as possible. Those late nineteenth and early twentieth century advocates of the representative method in sampling had, therefore, first to win the battle against the prevailing dogma that reliable, precise results were only possible by the route of exhaustive (and exhausting!) enumeration.

Bowley was one of the early crusaders for the sampling technique, first drawing attention to the method in his 1906 Presidential address to the British Association for the Advancement of Science where he stated that

> The simple method of samples . . . for which all the materials have existed for at least twenty years . . . has been completely ignored . . . progress in the development of theory has . . . been rapid . . but there has been remarkably little application to practical statistical

problems. The attention of mathematical statisticians has been mainly directed to theory . . . it is time that it was brought to bear on the . . . analysis of existing industrial statistics.[67]

The recent developments had been the result of the work done by such men as Edgeworth, Pearson and Yule. Edgeworth's work, in particular, was of a theoretical rather than practical nature, and Bowley's remarks may perhaps have been directed towards him. In his 1934 tribute to Edgeworth, Bowley wrote 'Edgeworth was the philosopher of statistics rather than the practitioner.'[68] Bowley, of course, was the practitioner rather than the philosopher.

When Bowley was first appointed to the LSE as part-time Lecturer in Statistics in 1895 he wrote to Edgeworth (on Marshall's advice) asking for recommended reading on the nature and literature of statistics. It was through this introduction that Bowley's methodological view of statistical theory coincided so closely with that of Edgeworth.[69]

Thus it was that in 1906 Bowley impressed his audience with a number of well-worked examples of the sampling method, stressing the vital element of the technique, namely that 'the chances [of inclusion] are the same for all the items of the group to be sampled'[70] and emphasising the great advantage and virtue of the technique in that the investigator can not only obtain a measure of the precision attained by sampling but also set the level of precision required and thus determine the corresponding sample size. Professor W. F. Maunder in his inaugural lecture in 1972 said of Bowley 'It was a subject which occupied him through the greater part of his active career; it almost became a King Charles' head, and no opportunity was lost to draw attention to its potential whatever the topic on which he was writing.'[71]

Bowley was the most successful practitioner of sampling in his day. In his appreciation of the care required at all stages of a survey, in planning the project, in questionnaire design, in field-working, in proper instruction of interviewers, and in scientific interpretation and analysis of the results, he set an exemplary standard. Bowley's first sample survey, of Reading in 1912, still provides a model from which a great deal can be learnt. It should be noted that the 1912 study was the first serious attempt made by any investigator to apply statistical theory to the design and interpretation of sample surveys. Nevertheless, Bowley was well aware of the potential problems and fully appreciated the many dangers inherent in supplying 'cookbook' rules in the matter. In 1910, writing in the *Manual*, Bowley stated forcibly 'No formal rules can replace judgement and experience in the selection of samples.'[72]

The Reading enquiry was quickly followed by similar surveys of Northampton, Warrington, Stanley and Bolton, which were brought together in the famous Five Towns Survey, *Livelihood and Poverty* (1915). This experience placed Bowley at the forefront of practical sampling and it was only natural that the pre-war study should be followed up in the 1920s. One of the primary objectives of the first surveys was to examine the incidence of poverty, and having obtained the relevant estimates (with their associated levels of precision) the post-war question 'Has Poverty Diminished?' remained. The question became the title for the sequel to *Livelihood and Poverty* and was answered in the affirmative. Each of the five towns was re-surveyed in 1924 and it was found that, due mainly to the increased earnings of the unskilled and smaller families, significant advances in the alleviation of poverty had taken place over the 12 years.

By the mid 1920s, therefore, Bowley was one of the recognised world leaders in this newly developing field of sampling. Not only had he practised the art extensively but he had also contributed fundamentally to its dissemination by including sections on the topic in his two best-selling statistics textbooks. His pioneering work on both the practical and theoretical aspects of sampling made him ideally suited to membership of a committee set up by the International Statistical Institute in 1924 to study the representative method in sampling. It is of interest to note that Bowley was elected to the Institute in 1903, the year in which that body endorsed the use of the representative method of sampling as proposed by the Norwegian statistician A. N. Kiaer.

The main report of the 1924 committee was penned by Jensen which recommended that sample survey investigations 'should be so arranged ... as to allow of a mathematical statement of the precision of the results, and that with these results should be given an indication of the extent of the error to which they are liable'.[73] In order to provide the necessary theoretical foundation for this statement, and to provide the formulae and reasoning to achieve its end, Bowley wrote a separate (62 page) report entitled *Measurement of the Precision Attained in Sampling* in which he set out all the mathematical theory of sampling known to him. The significance of this report cannot be over-stated. Bowley's concern was not only with simple summary statistics, but also with the functional form of distributions, a concern born of a Bayesian standpoint.

Bayesian statistical inference treats population parameters as random variables rather than as unknown constants and requires the investigator to hold particular *a priori* beliefs about the distribution of the parameters. Given a sample of observations the prior distribution is modified to yield the posterior distribution from which inferences are then drawn. Thus it is ultimately sensible for Bowley to speak of 'the chance that the average was', and thus state the posterior distribution of the average. However, for a non-Bayesian to attach a probability to a population parameter is nonsense; and such a statistician would form what we know today as a 'Confidence Interval' and speak of the probability that an interval contains the parameter. To those not versed in statistics the differences may appear at first sight to be of little consequence but they reflect fundamentally opposing views of the world. As Theil says 'What is random in the Bayesian approach is always viewed as a fixed number in the non-Bayesian approach and vice versa.'[74] Thus Bowley's work on the 'Inverse Problem' is essentially Bayesian, and although he was equally aware of the non-Bayesian approach (what Bowley calls the 'Direct Problem') his applications of inferential sampling invariably display a Bayesian framework.

That Bowley took a Bayesian stand-point is of no surprise considering that his introduction to the philosophy of statistics was through Edgeworth who 'gave careful consideration to the objective frequentist . . . view, but in the end adopted the inverse probability or Bayesian view'.[75] Equally, Bowley's text *The Elements of Statistics* displays his reliance on Edgeworthian theoretical statistics, and furthermore it should be noted that, prior to the publication of the *Elements,* Edgeworth's 1885 articles served as the reference points for those interested in statistical techniques but were succeeded by Bowley's book. Indeed, Bowley (modestly) made little attempt to claim originality in the *Elements,* and expressed in the Preface his indebtedness to Edgeworth, Pearson, Sheppard and Yule saying 'It will be evident that there is little that is wholly original . . . in this book.'[76]

Bowley's 1925 report is, then, essentially Bayesian in flavour and three features deserve particular attention. The first is his demonstration of the superiority of stratified random sampling over simple random sampling. In this analysis he followed the method to be found in Yule's *An Introduction to the Theory of Statistics*[77] but the conclusion that 'stratification therefore improves the precision of the sample'[78] was well worth reiterating. The second feature is his weak postulate regarding the *a priori* distribution required for the Bayesian Inverse Method. Bowley, following Edgeworth, typically used a uniform prior but regularly made use of a weaker assumption.[79]

The last feature to note is Bowley's analysis of 'purposive selection' in survey sampling. Despite his recognition of the importance of strictly non-systematic, i.e. random, selection of a sample he developed a theory of purposive selection. The unit of selection is itself an aggregate and it is assumed that the quantity under investigation is correlated with certain other variables called 'controls'. Selection of the sample is then made such that the characteristics of the sample in terms of controls coincide with those of the universe. By this method of selection it was hoped that the resulting sample would be representative in respect of the quantity under investigation. However, it became apparent that Bowley's technique was deficient on theoretical and practical grounds. In 1928 Gini and Galvani used the technique to estimate the natural rate of increase of the Italian population but found the estimate unsatisfactory and in 1934, on theoretical considerations, Neyman said 'it is a special case of stratified random sampling by groups' and went on to point out that estimators so obtained are neither consistent nor efficient. Incidentally, even though the purposive selection technique was first described in theoretical terms by Bowley in the addendum to the main 1925 report, and in spite of that report treating the representative and the purposive methods on equal terms, Bowley never used the latter in practice. It, thus, never gained that seal of approval and after Neyman's remarks seems to have disappeared from discussions on sampling.

Neyman's 1934 paper read to the Royal Statistical Society is of importance however, not only because it represents the final nail in the coffin of purposive selection (a method which Bowley stated in discussion he had distrusted even in 1925) but also because it illustrates the subtle yet crucial difference between Bowley as a Bayesian statistician and Neyman as a non-Bayesian. Neyman introduced the concept of a 'Confidence Interval' in his paper upon which Bowley, in his vote of thanks, remarked

I am not at all sure that the "confidence" is not a "confidence trick". . . . Does it really lead us towards what we need – the chance that in the universe we are sampling the proportion is within these certain limits? I think it does not. . . . The statement of the theory is not convincing, and until I am convinced I am doubtful of its validity.[80]

Neyman, in reply, pointed out quite rightly that Bowley's question

contains the statement of the problem of estimation in the form of Bayes . . . the solution of this problem must depend on the probability law *a priori*

and assured his audience that if Bowley's question were all that required to be answered then we could go no further than was already known. But, he confirmed

The present progress is connected with . . . solving some other mathematical problem . . . which has a solution independent of . . . the probability law *a priori*. . . . Both (approaches) are dealing with probabilities, but these probabilities apply to different events.[81]

Here we have Neyman's appreciation of the difference between the two solutions, namely that they are answering different questions born of different conceptions of what is random and what is not.

This fundamental difference between Bayesians and non-Bayesians raised its head at the next meeting of the Society on 18 December 1934 (Neyman's paper was read on 19 June 1934). At the December meeting, R. A. Fisher read a paper entitled 'The Logic of Inductive Inference' to which Bowley, yet again, proposed a vote of thanks. Caustic wit was rarely an element in Bowley's armoury but it came to the fore on this occasion. He first thanked Fisher

not so much for the paper that he has just read to us, as for his contribution to statistics in general. . . . I found the treatment to be very obscure. I took it as a weekend problem, and first tried it as an acrostic, but I found that I could not satisfy all the 'lights'. I tried it then as a crossword puzzle, but I have not the facility of Sir Josiah Stamp for solving such conundrums. Next I took it as an anagram, remembering that Hooke stated his law of elasticity in that form, but when I found that there were only two vowels to eleven consonants, some of which were Greek capitals, I came to the conclusion that it might be Polish or Russian, and therefore better left to Dr. Neyman or Dr. Isserlis. Finally I thought it must be a cypher, and after a great deal of investigation, decided that Professor Fisher had hidden the key in former papers, as is his custom, and I gave up. But in so doing I remembered that Professor Edgeworth had written a good deal on a kindred subject, and I turned to his studies. . . . We are therefore left very much where we were.[82]

Isserlis, seconding the vote of thanks, commented

no doubt . . . Professor Fisher, like other fond parents, may perhaps see in his offspring qualities which to his mind no other children possess; others, however, may consider that the offspring are not unique.[83]

Fisher, in a written reply, was equally abrasive

The acerbity, to use no stronger term, with which the customary vote of thanks has been moved and seconded . . . does not, I confess, surprise me. . . . However true it may be that Professor Bowley is left very much where he was . . . at least Dr. Neyman and myself have not been left in his company.[84]

Bowley's reference to Edgeworth's work requires further examination, but this is not the place for a detailed discussion. Edgeworth's concept of 'genuine inverse probability' and the non-Bayesian 'maximum likelihood' concept are very similar. Indeed, the mathematical manipulations are identical in a number of respects, but the difference in approach remains. Edgeworth's work is fundamentally Bayesian, as is Bowley's, and this stands in stark contrast to that of Neyman and Fisher. We should not, then, be surprised at the vociferousness with which these differences were aired at the Royal Statistical Society. Hence, the description of these differences given by Maunder when he says

The trouble was, of course, that throughout his life he [Bowley] had been seeking the answer to the wrong question (or, rather quite correctly knew that there was no answer but still thought one was wanted) and could not adjust readily to those who produced an answer to another, more useful question[85]

cannot be accepted. From a Bayesian point of view Bowley's question is the question to answer, and furthermore an answer exists. It is no less useful than the non-Bayesian question and to suggest that Bowley knew there was no answer but still provided one is surely a misconception.

Bowley was the driving force in the early sampling movement, especially on a practical level. His work cleared and paved much of the way for later investigators. He gave direction to, and instilled life into, the quantitative investigation of social phenomena at a time most crucial to the evolution of this complement to pure economics. He gave more than a lead, however; he gave the example to follow. His exactingly high standards still provide guidance and inspiration to anyone interested in quantitative research today.

Conclusion

Arthur Bowley was an economic statistician of the highest rank. His work was motivated by a genuine concern for his fellow man; there was nothing he did that was without practical, or at least a potentially practical, application. Shy and retiring in personal relationships he was rarely so in academic matters: always a model of modesty he was quick to correct others (especially on statistical issues) and equally quick to protect, preserve and promote those areas, techniques and methodologies of economics and statistics which had the great benefit of his patronage.

All his work is connected by the common theme of social enquiry with the goal of change for the better. Indeed, Bowley himself felt that the pinnacle of his career was reached on the publication of the massive sample survey *New Survey of London Life and Labour, 1930–35*. This monumental work bears his unmistakable imprint.

He viewed life as one long education, and we can do no better than to close with his own words, spoken in 1909 when addressing a group of Irish bankers

it is not the things ... learnt that [are] so important ... the essential thing [is] the development of the intellectual habit of receptivity and of wide and sympathetic observation, the habit which [will] force people to continue their education so long as their mental vigour lasts, and which [will] give them the elasticity of mind and the power of adaptability to changing conditions.[86]

Here was a most admirable man – a humane, scrupulous scientist possessed of many rare qualities not the least of which was that he practiced what he preached.

NOTES

1. He was christened Arthur Lyon because his mother admired Tennyson's 'King Arthur' and Lyon was a paternal family name. See A. Bowley, *A Memoir of Professor Sir Arthur Lyon Bowley (1869–1957) and his Family* (privately printed, 1970) for a detailed and fascinating account of the Bowley family. [Hereafter cited as *ALB*.]
2. Marshall to Bowley, 21 February 1901, at the Royal Statistical Society Library. [Hereafter cited as *RSSL*.]
3. International trade became one of Bowley's lesser interests; but see his 'Import and Export Index Numbers', *Economic Journal* [hereafter cited as *EJ*], VII (1897) 274–8; 'Changes of Prices of Imports and Exports since 1881', *Journal of the Royal Statistical Society* [hereafter cited as *JRSS*], LX (1897) 437–9, and *The Effect of the War on the External Trade of the United Kingdom* (Cambridge: Cambridge University Press, 1915).
4. F. A. Burchardt and G. D. N. Worswick, 'Sir Arthur Lyon Bowley', *Bulletin of the Oxford Institute of Statistics*, XIX (1957) 1–2, at p. 2.
5. The earliest reference to the 'law' (which refers to the alleged constancy of the wage share in national income) of which I know is P. A. Samuelson, *Economics*, 6th edn (London: McGraw-Hill, 1964) p. 736. It is interesting to note that Samuelson does *not* use the expression 'Bowley's Law' in any of the first five editions of the book.
6. 'Changes in Average Wages (Nominal and Real) in the United Kingdom between 1860 and 1891' and 'Discussion', *JRSS*, LVIII (1895) 223–85, at p. 279. [Hereafter cited as *Wages*, I.] Marshall had been one of the examiners of Bowley's Adam Smith essay.
7. *Wages*, I, 225 and 226.
8. *Wages*, I, 230. Bowley's paper was heavily criticised by one discussant, Chadwick (see *Wages*, I, 281), but he seems to have misunderstood its purpose.
9. *Wages*, I, 236.
10. 'Relations between the Accuracy of an Average and that of its Constituent Parts', *JRSS*, LX (1897) 855–66, at p. 861. The 'special circumstances' of Bowley's 1895 work ensured that the errors in that

investigation were small. It should also be noted that the results of the 1897 paper were first given by Bowley in the 1897 Newmarch lectures.

11. Bowley was then the Senior Mathematics Master at St John's School, Leatherhead.

12. The chairman was Hendricks, one of the senior members of the Royal Statistical Society (he was Vice President in 1880/1). See *Wages*, I, 285.

13. See N. Jha, *The Age of Marshall*, 2nd edn (London: Frank Cass, 1973) who writes: 'One can observe the typically Marshallian concepts of the normal and market price behind these statistical investigations' (p. 113).

14. It is interesting to note that Bowley's 1898 *EJ* article does not appear in the bibliography given by R. G. D. Allen and R. F. George, 'Professor Sir Arthur Lyon Bowley', *JRSS*, CXX (1957) 236–41. This is, no doubt, because the index of the 1898 *EJ* records a contribution by *D*owley.

15. See R. Frisch, 'The Problem of Index Numbers', *Econometrica*, IV (1936) 1–38, esp. at pp. 27 and 28, and 'Wages Nominal and Real' in Palgrave's *Dictionary of Political Economy*, vol. III (London: Macmillan, 1926) pp. 639–41.

16. See, for example, 'Wages and Cost of Living in Germany: The Board of Trade and Mr. Ellis Baker', *EJ*, XVIII (1908) 657–62; 'The Measurement of Changes in the Cost of Living', *JRSS*, LXXXII (1919) 343–61; 'Cost of Living and Wage Determination', *EJ*, XXX (1920) 114–17; 'The Labour Report on the Cost of Living', *EJ*, XXXI (1921) 406–11.

17. See 'The Census of Production and the National Dividend', *EJ*, XXIII (1913) 53–61; *The Division of the Product of Industry* (Oxford: Clarendon Press, 1919); *The Change in the Distribution of the National Income* (Oxford: Clarendon Press, 1920); 'The Definition of the National Income', *EJ*, XXXII (1922) 1–11; *Studies in the National Income 1924–1938* (Cambridge: Cambridge University Press, 1942); A. L. Bowley and J. Stamp, *The National Income 1924* (Oxford: Clarendon Press, 1927) and *Three Studies on the National Income* (London: London School of Economics Reprints of Scarce Works on Political Economy, 1938).

18. 'In particular I was doubtful of the socialist's statement that the rich were getting richer and the poor poorer. If the contrary were true, poverty would diminish without revolution. This question led to a greater part of my statistical work after 1892', *ALB*, p. 33. See *Wages in the United Kingdom in the Nineteenth Century* (Cambridge: Cambridge University Press, 1900); 'Notes on Mr. Wilson Fox's Paper (on Agricultural Wages)', *JRSS*, LXVI (1903) 303–12; 'The Measurement of Unemployment', *JRSS*, LXXV (1912) 791–822; (with A. R. Burnett-Hurst) *Livelihood and Poverty* (London: Bell, 1915); 'Conditions of Employment of Dock Labour', *EJ*, XXX (1920) 272–5; 'Earners and Dependents in English Towns in 1911', *Economica*, I (1921) 101–12; (with M. H. Hogg) *Has Poverty Diminished?*

(London: P. S. King, 1925); 'Methods of Investigating the Economic and Social Conditions of a Great City', *Révue de l'Institut International de Statistiques*, I (1933) 7–18; 'The New Survey of London Life and Labour: Effect of Modifying the Poverty Line', *JRSS*, XCIX (1936) 364–6; J. J. Aston *et al.*, *The Third Winter of Unemployment* (London: P. S. King, 1923); and *Is Unemployment Inevitable?* (London: Macmillan, 1924).

19. C. P. Sanger, 'Review of *Elements of Statistics*', *EJ*, XI (1901) 193–7, at p. 193. For brief biographical details of Sanger (1871–1930), see J. M. Keynes, *Essays in Biography* (London: Macmillan for the Royal Economic Society, 1972) ch. 25.

20. Bowley was a keen cyclist and was often accompanied by Cannan and Edgeworth.

21. *Elements of Statistics* (London: P. S. King, 1901) [hereafter cited as *Els*] p. 193.

22. *Els*, pp. 8, 9.

23. *An Elementary Manual of Statistics* (London: P. S. King, 1910) [hereafter cited as *Manual*] pp. 4, 5.

24. *Manual*, p. 5. Bowley echoes Marshall's thoughts on this point: 'many of the worst fallacies involved in the misapplications of statistics are definite and can be definitely exposed, till at last no one ventures to repeat them even when addressing an uninstructed audience' *Principles of Economics*, 9th (Variorum) edn (London: Macmillan, 1961) [hereafter cited as *G.I*], Book V, ch. XIV, s8, p. 492.

25. *JRSS*, I (1838) p. 1.

26. There was, in fact, little early empirical work on economic *functions*; there was 'a general failure to recognise that economic functions, as well as quantities, could be determined empirically': G. J. Stigler, 'The Early History of Empirical Studies of Consumer Behaviour', *Journal of Political Economy*, XLII (1954), repr. in G. J. Stigler, *Essays on the History of Economics* (Chicago: Chicago University Press, 1965) 198–233, at p. 232.

27. J. N. Keynes, *The Scope and Method of Political Economy*, 4th edn (London: Macmillan, 1917) [hereafter cited as *SMPE*] pp. 203, 208.

28. J. S. Mill, *A System of Logic*, new edn (Toronto: Toronto University Press, 1974) Book VI, ch. IX, s1, p. 897.

29. 'Statistical Methods and the Fiscal Controversry', *EJ*, XIII (1903) 303–12, at p. 303.

30. *SMPE*, p. 172.

31. *G.I*, Book V, ch. XIV, s8, p. 492.

32. A. Marshall, 'The Social Possibilities of Economic Chivalry', *EJ*, XVII (1907) 7–29, at pp. 7, 8.

33. *Statistical Studies Relating to National Progress in Wealth and Trade Since 1882: A Plea for Further Enquiry* (London: P. S. King, 1904) pp. xii, xiii.

34. 'The Improvement of Official Statistics' and 'Discussion' [hereafter cited as *IOS*] *JRSS*, LXXI (1908) 460–95, at pp. 459, 460.

35. 'editors . . . gauge . . . the tastes of their readers', *IOS*, p. 461.

36. *IOS*, p. 475. Chiozza Money (1870–1944) was a Liberal MP from 1906 to 1918.
37. 'Presidential Address to Section F of the British Association' [hereafter cited as *Address*], *JRSS*, LXIX (1906) 540–58, at p. 542.
38. *Address*, p. 543.
39. Ibid.
40. Perhaps it is over-optimistic to suggest that such principles are commonplace. The fundamental principles of good statistical practice cannot be overstressed.
41. 'Recent Official Statistical Publications' [hereafter cited as *ROSP*], *Economica*, I (1921) 302–6, at p. 302.
42. *ROSP*, p. 303.
43. *ROSP*, p. 306.
44. *The Mathematical Groundwork of Economics: An Introductory Treatise* (Oxford: Clarendon Press, 1924) [hereafter cited as *MG*] pp. v, vi.
45. K. Wicksell, 'Matematisk nationalekonomi', *Ekonomisk Tidskrift* (1925) 103–25, at p. 123. I am most grateful to Mrs B. M. Walwork of Durham University Library for translating this work from the original Swedish.
46. See J. A. Schumpeter, *History of Economic Analysis* (New York: Oxford University Press, 1954) [hereafter cited as *History*] p. 957.
47. *History*, p. 958.
48. *A General Course of Pure Mathematics* (Oxford: Clarendon Press, 1913) p. iii. In *ALB*, p. 30 it is recorded that Bowley's early unpublished essay 'In Praise of Mathematics' states that 'the importance of mathematics is to be measured by its use to the engineer, the physicist, the chemist and others'. By 1913 'others' was made more specific and became 'economists'.
49. Whittaker to Bowley 25 March 1914 at RSSL. Sir Edmund Taylor Whittaker (1873–1956) was Professor of Mathematics at Edinburgh from 1912 to 1946.
50. G. H. Hardy to Bowley, 8 May 1914 at RSSL.
51. G. H. Hardy to Bowley, n.d., at RSSL.
52. M. Tappan, 'Review of *The Mathematical Groundwork*', *Economica*, V (1925) 334–8, at p. 334. Tappan had in fact been taught by Bowley at the LSE.
53. *MG*, p. 38.
54. The concept of 'conjectural variations' is explicitly introduced by F. Y. Edgeworth in *Papers Relating to Political Economy* (London: Macmillan, 1925). The material was first published in 1897 in Italian and one may conjecture that Bowley was aware of its contents before 1925 owing to his close association with Edgeworth.
55. Note 52, p. 338.
56. F. Y. Edgeworth, 'Review of *The Mathematical Groundwork*', *EJ*, XXXIV (1924) 430–4, at p. 430.
57. Note 45, p. 209.
58. See E. Cannan, '"Total Utility" and "Consumer's Surplus"', *Economica*, IV (1924) 21–6 and the two replies: D. H. MacGregor, 'Consumer's Surplus: A Reply', ibid., 131–4, and A. L. Bowley,

'Does Mathematical Analysis Explain? A Note on Consumer's Surplus', ibid., 135–9. See also the correspondence between Bowley and Cannan: Cannan to Bowley 27 March 1924, Bowley to Cannan 31 March 1924 and Cannan to Bowley 7 April 1924 at the British Library of Political and Economic Science.

59. For Wicksell's criticism see note 45, esp. at p. 216 where Wicksell says 'Bowley's treatment of this problem does not seem to me to be completely satisfactory'. In his reply, 'Bilaterial Monopoly', *EJ*, XXXVIII (1928) 651–9, Bowley remarked quite rightly, 'Wicksell's solution is one-sided' (p. 651).

60. R. D. G. Allen and A. L. Bowley, *Family Expenditure* (London: P. S. King, 1935) [hereafter cited as *FE*] p. 1.

61. *FE*, p. 4.

62. *FE*, p. 8.

63. *FE*, p. 19.

64. *FE*, p. 20.

65. *FE*, p. 115. It is interesting to note that A. Deaton, 'A Reconsideration of the Empirical Implications of Additive Preferences', *EJ*, LXXXIV (1974) 338–48 also dismisses additivity saying 'if the price to be paid for theoretical consistency of demand models is the necessity of assuming additive preferences, then the price is too high' (p. 346).

66. P. S. Laplace, 'Sur les naissances, les mariages et lest morts à Paris depuis 1771 jusqu'en 1784, et dans toute l'etandue de la France, pendant les années 1781 et 1782', *Histoire et Mémoirs de l'Académie Science de Paris* (1786) 693–702.

67. *Address*, pp. 548, 549.

68. 'Francis Ysidro Edgeworth', *Econometrica*, II (1934) 113–24, at p. 116.

69. It is of note that Edgeworth's only joint paper was with Bowley: 'Methods of Representing Statistics of Wages and Other Groups not Fulfilling the Normal Law of Error', *JRSS*, LXV (1902) 325–54.

70. *Address*, p. 551.

71. W. F. Maunder, *Sir Arthur Lyon Bowley* (Exeter: Exeter University, 1972) p. 22. [Hereafter cited as *MALB*.]

72. *Manual*, p. 62.

73. A. Jensen, 'Report on the Representative Method', *Bulletin de l'Institut International de Statistique*, XXII (1926) 359–80, at p. 378.

74. H. Theil, *Introduction to Econometrics* (London: Prentice-Hall, 1978) p. 252.

75. S. M. Stigler, 'Francis Ysidro Edgeworth, Statistician', *JRSS*, CXLI (1978) 287–313, at p. 296.

76. *Els*, p. viii.

77. *An Introduction to the Theory of Statistics* (London: Griffin, 1911).

78. 'Measurement of the Precision Attained in Sampling', *Bulletin de l'Institut International de Statistique*, XXII (1926) 1–62, at p. 30. See also his 'The Precision of Measurements Estimated from Samples', *Metron*, II (1923) 494–500.

79. For example, in the case of references about a proportion, Bowley merely required that the prior distribution be continuous and such

that the products of the derivatives with $1/n$ (where n is the sample size) vanish in the neighbourhood of $P = p$ (where P and p represent the population proportion, a random variable, and the observed sample proportion, a fixed number respectively). Such an approach, while employing weaker assumptions than a uniform prior is, of course, only valid in large samples, and this reliance on large sample theory is, in fact, a characteristic weakness of this period of Bayesian statistics.

80. J. Neyman, 'On Two Different Aspects of the Representative Method' and 'Discussion', *JRSS*, xcvii (1934) 558–625 [hereafter cited as *Rep. Meth.*] at p. 609.
81. *Rep. Meth.*, pp. 623, 624.
82. R. A. Fisher, 'The Logic of Inductive Inference' and 'Discussion', *JRSS*, xcviii (1935) 39–82 [hereafter cited as *Logic*], at pp. 55, 56.
83. *Logic*, p. 57.
84. *Logic*, p. 76.
85. *MALB*, pp. 21, 22,
86. 'Education and Business', *The Dublin Daily Express*, 14 January 1909.

6 D. H. Robertson, 1890–1963

JOHN R. PRESLEY

Introduction – biographia

There is little doubt that Robertson would be somewhat flattered, and perhaps even amused, to find himself regarded as a pioneer of economics. He always regarded Alfred Marshall as being the explorer, the advance guard in economics, paving the way for the troops to follow. He thought of himself as one of the more disciplined troops, keeping to the Marshallian tradition and anxious to prevent his fellow troops, particularly J. M. Keynes, from breaking ranks. Yet Robertson was able to lead the troops in one *important* direction in which Marshall had rarely sought adventure[1] – in the development of a theory of industrial fluctuation. Commenting upon the subject matter of fluctuation, money, credit and employment, Robertson wrote: 'this has always been to me the most interesting part of economics – the only part to which I can hope to be remembered as having made any personal contribition'.[2] This erroneously omits his contribution to economics over a wide range of subjects, particularly in the field of international trade and the theory of the firm;[3] but in truth such contributions are small in relation to that which Robertson gave to the study of industrial fluctuation.

Born in 1890, the youngest of six children, Robertson spent much of his early childhood in Whittlesford, Cambridgeshire learning classics under the supervision of his father who then was a country parson.[4] At the age of 12 he went to Eton and from there gained a classical scholarship to Trinity, Cambridge. Despite considerable success as a classical scholar,[5] he turned to the Economics Tripos in 1910 and gained a first in that tripos in 1912.

Although not taught by Marshall at Cambridge, Robertson was immersed in Marshallian economics at the hands of A. C. Pigou and his director of studies, the young J. M. Keynes. This marked the beginning of a long and very productive partnership between Robertson and Keynes which flourished until the mid-1930s and which only perished in the heat of the Keynesian Revolution. Robertson gained a Trinity Fellowship in 1914 on the basis of a thesis which was to become, a year later, his *novum organum*[6] – *A Study of Industrial Fluctuation*.[7] He remained an academic in Cambridge throughout his lifetime, the only major interruptions being army service in Egypt and Palestine during the First World War,[8] one year spent as Professor of Banking at the London School of Economics in 1938 and several years during the Second World War as Economic Adviser in the Treasury. He succeeded to the Chair of Economics in Cambridge on the retirement of A. C. Pigou in 1947, a post he held to his own retirement in 1957.

Robertson is perhaps best known to the student of economics for his Cambridge Economic Handbook, *Money*,[9] but his academic reputation had a solid base not only in the real analysis of his *Study* but in *Banking Policy and the Price Level*,[10] a complex and difficult book[11] which attempted to extend the real analysis of the *Study* and to establish the operation of monetary forces in the trade cycle. He devoted much of his later life to his lectures in Cambridge which became *Lectures on Economic Principles*,[12] and to work on less theoretical and more policy-orientated issues than those which preoccupied most economists in the interwar period. From 1944 to 1946 he was a leading member of the Royal Commission on Equal Pay and in 1957–8 he became the only economist on the Cohen Council on Prices, Productivity and Incomes. In total he wrote over 100 articles, 30 of which were published in the *Economic Journal*, and 15 books[13] covering most areas of study within economics.

Clearly it would be unrealistic to claim that such a volume of literature could be adequately surveyed and assessed in one chapter.[14] The inevitable specialisation brings a division into two sections. After an examination of the theory of industrial fluctuation, we will consider the positive contributions to the saving/investment debate of the interwar period. This will include reference to the economic policy aspects of Robertson's work.

Industrial fluctuation

Robertson was the first British economist to emphasise the view that real factors, inherent in any capitalist society, were responsible for industrial fluctuation; as such his theory represented a non-monetary, over-investment explanation of the macroeconomic cycle.

In considering the nature of fluctuations Robertson stressed those fluctuations which occurred not only in prices and credit but in output and employment. His review of Tugan-Baranowski's *Les Crises Industrielles en Angleterre*[15] was critical of its lack of discussion of variations in output and consumption and its preoccupation with the circulation of credit.[16] The major concern of his *Study* was with the cycle in real national income; although he claimed no great originality for this,[17] he was aware of post-war criticisms from Keynesian economists who implied that output did not 'attract the attention of economists until the 1930s'.[18] He described industrial fluctuation as 'a quasi-rhythmical movement in the level of prices, in the level of money profits, and the level of employment',[19] and continued by arguing that such movements implied the existence of movements in the volume of production and consumption. All of his main works on fluctuation recognised that cycles may differ between kinds of production,[20] more pronounced cycles taking place in construction good industries with consumption goods being less affected; in fact in a depression Robertson suggested that consumer good production may not decline.[21] These were the common features of most cycles. But Robertson did stress that cycles exhibit different characteristics at different times; all cycles do not have an identical form. This was the basis of his assertion that there may be more than one possible cause of industrial fluctuation.

(i) *The recovery*

During the course of the preparation of his *Study* he had been encouraged by Pigou to 'dig down behind monetary appearances to real facts'.[22] The work of Hawtrey, as well as that of Tugan-Baranowski,[23] was criticised for its failure to get behind the monetary exterior of the cycle to the underlying real causes. In addition, in 1913, Robertson accused new work on economic crises of having a 'determination to burrow below mere monetary phenomena followed by the same relapse into monetary terms at all critical stages of the argument'.[24] A paper read by Robertson to the Royal Statistical Society in 1913 chose to concentrate upon the gestation period and the longevity of investment within important industries within the UK.[25] It was not surprising therefore that when the *Study* eventually appeared in 1915 it was to blame the real features of the capitalist system of production for the cyclical nature of output, employment and prices.

It was most crucial for Robertson to explain the upturn of the cycle. The downturn was less important for he believed that the boom breeds its own destruction.[26] Depression would come to an end when an increase occurred in either the supply of effort, or the average productivity of effort of the labour force. This, in turn, resulted primarily from an upward revision of the marginal utility attached to expenditure on construction or capital goods. This 'increased attractiveness to investment' brought about the additional demand necessary for the revival. Clearly Robertson needed to explain why such a revision in the marginal utility of capital goods may take place. The *Study* isolated three possible causes. Exceptionally good crops in the agricultural sector might boost confidence and inspire more demand for construction goods. The need to replace an 'unusually large number of the instruments of production in some important trade or group of trades' could bring the revival; but of most significance the occurrence of an invention might be responsible for the upturn.[27] Pigou saw fit to write of the part played by inventions in Robertson's thesis on fluctuation 'this strikes me – the stress laid on that (invention) and its working out – as the most important original contribution in this book'.[28]

Invention works on the revival in activity in two ways. It not only tends to lower the real operating costs of production, in so doing raising the productivity of effort expended, but it also acts on the demand side, increasing the desire to buy capital goods. For invention to guarantee a general revival it must be widely applicable to industry; revival will not occur unless at least one major sector of the economy can gain from innovation. The good fortune of one sector will not be at the expense of a diminution in output and employment in other sectors. Robertson saw industries prospering side by side, bringing a net addition to total output rather than a redistribution of a fixed output between sectors.[29]

This kind of emphasis upon the role of invention was new to British literature. Marshall too had observed that fluctuation in capital good production dominated the cycle and went so far as to suggest that the cycle may be caused 'by good and bad harvest, and by the alternate opening out of promising new enterprises';[30]

but the over-riding cause of fluctuation in Marshallian theory was to be found in the psychological forces, especially in the variability of business confidence.[31] Robertson's thesis was stimulated by the mass of empirical evidence he had accumulated for the *Study*. He was able to point to the booms prompted by innovations associated with railways (1872), the steel industry (1882) and the electrical industry (1902–7). Later, in *Banking*, he could add to this list the boom created by innovation relating to oil power in 1912.

Historians of economic thought now tend to associate this emphasis upon innovation as the cause of recovery with the name of J. A. Schumpeter.[32] Although Robertson was familiar with some continental literature at the time of writing the *Study*, in particular the work of A. Aftalion and M. Tugan-Baranowski,[33] he had not read Schumpeter. It was not until the second edition of *Money* in 1928[34] that reference was made to Schumpeter's work on the cycle, and this was most probably stimulated by an article written by Schumpeter in English as late as 1927.[35] There is a striking resemblance between their respective theories. Both make a clear distinction between invention and innovation, the application of invention to production techniques. The revival is characterised by a burst of innovation. This, Schumpeter argues, results from a few bold investments by some entrepreneurs which create a 'herd-like' movement of innovation by other entrepreneurs.[36] Robertson too in the *Study* portrayed entrepreneurs as sheep who will follow the more courageous entrepreneur to innovation, but this argument is not employed with the same conviction as that displayed by Schumpeter.[37] As Robertson was to later remark 'I think that in 1914, blissfully ignorant of a great mass of continental literature, I felt quite brave in awarding the prize apple for trouble-making to the twin goddesses of investment/invention and innovation, or at any rate splitting it between them and the god of weather.'[38]

The second major possible cause of the upturn, as the above quotation indicates, was to be found in a good harvest – again a real as opposed to monetary force acting on the cycle. Approximately one third of the *Study* explored the empirical relationship between crop production and industrial activity. As T. S. Ashton remarked, this was a bold, but not original, step by Robertson for 'to exhibit any leaning towards celestial or crop theories was indeed to invite the suggestion that one ought to go to see a doctor'.[39] Robertson had a great respect for the work of W. S. Jevons. He regarded his work as a more constructive contribution to trade cycle theory than that of Aftalion, an economist for whom, as we shall see later, Robertson had the highest regard.[40] Jevons based his view of the cycle upon the strong correlation he had found between the length of the industrial cycle and the sunspot cycle.[41] But Robertson was not convinced that the industrial cycle was permanently linked to a sunspot cycle. By 1915 the sunspot theory had in any case floundered on new scientific evidence relating to the sunspot cycle. This however did not lead Robertson to believe that there need be no significant effect of agricultural variation upon an industrial revival. He instead adopted and developed an approach which he encountered in the work of Piatt-Andrew.[42] Agricultural variation was one possible cause of the industrial cycle, but not the cause of all cycles. There was no attempt to establish that an agricultural cycle existed. The *Study* concentrated upon the empirical support for the argument that a change in crop volumes would alter farm incomes, which, in turn, would have repercussions upon the demand for capital equipment.[43] Invariably Robertson found that, with the exception of the building industry, increased farm incomes were associated with an improved demand for capital goods in Britain in the period 1869 to 1913. He concluded that agricultural abundance would in general stimulate total production, and that agricultural shortages would have a depressive effect (although agricultural shortage was not accepted as one of the *major* causes of recession).

In later work less attention was paid to the role of agricultural variation. In *Banking* Robertson concluded that agricultural periods 'do not furnish a complete explanation of the periodicity of industrial output', rather they merely help determine the timing and amplitude of the various phases of the cycle.[44] Despite the diminishing contribution of agricultural output to total production throughout the twentieth century, Robertson still saw fit to write in his *Lectures* 'It [revival] may occur to meet a demand arising out of abundant harvests, either directly, through the farmers' purchases of *equipment*, or indirectly via the pressure on railway and shipping capacity, or more indirectly still, through the optimism generated as to the prospects of the producing areas.'[45]

Haberler has given Robertson some credit for recognising the acceleration principle and incorporating it in his theory of fluctuation.[46] Amongst British literature, the *Study* was the first, alongside the work of F. Bickerdike,[47] to assess thoroughly the role of the accelerator in the cycle. By 1914 Robertson had encountered the accelerator in the work of A. Aftalion.[48] He gave it a mixed reception. Although he went to some length to defend it as a possible explanation of the upturn, recognising that a small change in consumer demand could have large repercussions on the capital good industries, in the *Study* he concluded that the principle may be attempting to make 'something out of nothing'.[49] The crux of the matter appeared to be in the variability of the marginal utility of consumer goods. Robertson was adamant that this remained fairly constant over the cycle.[50] The explanation of the cycle was to be found in those factors which caused the marginal utility of *capital* goods to change – and these were invention and agricultural change, not a small change in consumer demand.

Later work by Robertson, however, was not disposed to dismiss the accelerator so lightly. In 1937 he went so far as to argue 'the principle of acceleration deserves pride of place in any analysis of the trade cycle', and commended Harrod for the importance that he gave to the accelerator in his theory of fluctuation.[51] This change of position is best demonstrated by his radio broadcasts in 1937 in which the accelerator was taken to be at the heart of fluctuation.[52] At the same time Robertson was aware of the limiting features of the principle – its failure to operate where excess capacity existed and its neglect of all the other factors, notably the rate of interest and invention, working upon the level of investment. He was also critical of Keynes for his failure to utilise the accelerator in the *General Theory*; and in the post-war period he displayed a continued faith in the accelerator, culminating in a declaration in his *Lectures* that it had *always* taken the central role in his explanation of the cycle. Despite this, Robertson was never blind to the other forces acting upon the level of investment.[53] The *Study* saw recovery beginning in the capital good industries and from there being transmitted to the consumer good industries. The *Lectures* envisaged expansion starting in either capital or consumer good industries, and being passed on to other industries.

This apparent about-turn on the accelerator is an untypical feature of Robertsonian literature. In general, once Robertson adopted a certain standpoint on theory or policy matters, he never moved his position. This will be best illustrated in a later section where we find Robertson unmoved by the Keynesian Revolution.

(ii) *The recession*

In Tugan-Baranowski's work, Robertson had read of the boom coming to an end due to the excessive demand for capital goods in relation to the available supply of credit needed to finance the purchase of those capital goods.[54] In the work of both M. Labordère and A. Spiethoff he had also encountered, by 1913, an over-investment theory where the crisis was brought about by an inadequacy in the stock of consumer goods required to support investment in the boom.[55] Although he did have some sympathy for this real *saving* thesis (and no sympathy for Tugan-Baranowski's thesis), he was more impressed by the over-investment theory propounded by Aftalion. It was this theory which, after much detailed empirical support, provided Robertson's explanation of the recession in the *Study*. Aftalion believed that too much investment was a consequence of the demand for capital goods falling short of the current supply of such goods at the end of the boom. This was reflected in a decline in the marginal utility of capital goods. In evidence to the Macmillan Committee Robertson stated 'among the causes of industrial depression I attach leading importance to the temporary gluttability of large groups of particular human wants'.[56] Gluttability was later defined in oral evidence as meaning 'saturation';[57] in other words over-investment yielded over-production in relation to particular demands. As was customary with Robertson this was followed by reference to specific examples: 'anybody ought to have been able to see in 1920 that the world was so clogged with ships that the shipbuilding industry was not in for two years of depression but for a dozen'.[58] What Robertson needed to do in the *Study* was to discover why this downward revision in the demand for capital goods should take place.

In this respect also Robertson proved to be a disciple of A. Aftalion; here therefore he gave nothing new to economic literature, except that published in the English language. The main causes of over-investment were to be found in the *real* features of the 'capitalist' (i.e. decentralised), system of production; in particular the gestation period of investment, defined as 'the length of time necessary to construct and prepare for use the requisite instruments of production',[59] led investment beyond the *appropriate* level.[60] During the recovery prices will rise. The increased profitability of investment will act so as to induce investment. The time lag until this investment materialises will help maintain the high level of prices, and encourage more investment. Thus, a situation might arise where all producers are inclined to react to high prices by investing. The lack of knowledge on the part of the individual producer as to what investment is being undertaken by competing producers may create a general over-investment. The ultimate production and utilisation of this excessive investment must bring a decline in prices and a recession. Robertson concluded 'the longer therefore this period of gestation, the longer will the period of high prices continue, the greater will be over-investment and the more severe the subsequent depression'.[61] Empirical evidence in the *Study* on the gestation periods in the coal, pig iron, shipping, coffee and cotton industries supported the significance of the gestation period in causing over-investment and in determining the intensity and duration of several phases of the trade cycle in the late nineteenth and early twentieth century.

Two further features of the investment process worked so as to aggravate the extent of the cycle. These were what Robertson referred to as the 'imperfect divisibility and intractability of the instrument' and the 'longevity of the instrument'.[62] The scale of production and the large size of the unit of investment often necessary, may tempt the producer to enlarge his capacity to a greater extent than that required to meet known or anticipated demand. Similarly, the inability to withdraw previous investment because of the time period required to close down and then reopen, and the cost involved, would aggravate the depression.

The interference of the longevity of capital upon the cycle has always been associated with Karl Marx.[63] A ten-year cycle was the consequence of an average life of capital of ten years. The theoretical support of this was not strong; in particular, if the lifespan of capital varied from industry to industry, there was no guarantee that bursts of replacement investment would recur every ten years. Robertson saw this weakness, but nevertheless was keen to appeal to the facts. Investment was not evenly distributed over the cycle, but was congested during the recovery phase. Clearly if most industries showed little deviation from the average life of capital, one burst of investment, for whatever reason, e.g. invention, may be followed by recurrent bursts of replacement investment. The evidence was inconclusive, although it did, in Robertson's view, provide some support for Marx.[64] The average life of capital in two major industries at that time – railways and cotton spinning – did appear to be ten years; but in the case of other industries, notably shipbuilding, this was not so. What did, he believed, tend to support Marx was the finding that past peaks in investment activity had been largely peaks in replacement and not net investment. Investment activity in railways, cotton, wool and shipbuilding had a close correlation with the lifespan of capital equipment in those industries. Whilst disputing the theoretical soundness of his argument, Robertson was prompted by the empirical evidence to offer some support to Marx that the longevity of capital may be yet another contributory factor to the wide fluctuations in macroeconomic activity that take place in capitalist societies.

(iii) *The role of psychological and monetary forces in the trade cycle*

In marked contrast to conventional wisdom Robertson displayed a belief in the *Study*, and in all later work, that industrial fluctuation was an *inevitable* feature of a capitalistic society. Full employment was not a normal feature of an economic system based on an investment process which exhibited large units of capital, varying gestation periods of investment, and durable capital equipment. His evidence to the Macmillan Committee stressed 'A feature of modern industrial progress, partly aggravated by avoidable causes but partly inevitable, is that it proceeds discontinuously – in lumps and by jumps.'[65] Industrial fluctuation was a price which had to be paid for long-term economic progress, for 'out of the welter of industrial dislocation the great permanent riches of the future are generated'.[66] Without giving a clear definition of the terms, Robertson distinguished between appropriate and inappropriate, desirable and undesirable fluctuation.[67] The former in either case is associated with the real features of capitalism, the latter being brought about primarily by the actions of psychological and monetary forces on the cycle.

But such undesirable forces were not *active* in creating the cycle, they merely responded to the real changes taking place. Hence Robertson was opposed to the emphasis of Hawtrey's argument that the trade cycle was entirely the result of monetary disturbances and to the concentration of Pigou's explanation upon the errors of the business community in reaching their investment decisions. Given the absence of errors of optimism and pessimism, and of monetary excesses, industrial fluctuation would still arise.[68] Nevertheless Robertson was anxious not to overstate his differences with the monetary and psychological theories. Errors of judgement were important in the cycle, and were encouraged by the imperfect knowledge existing during the gestation period of investment. Together with excessive monetary expansion. they could contribute to the over-investment of the boom. Equally pessimism and monetary contraction, may exaggerate the recession and depression. It was the role of monetary policy to act upon these excesses: 'people try to behave recklessly and greedily, but this is not the cause of the downturn since the government can act as schoolmaster and bank lending can be controlled'.[69]

Saving, investment and economic policy

There is a widespread tendency in modern macroeconomic textbooks to tar most economists writings before 1936 with the same classical brush.[70] The approach in this section is to examine whether Robertson deserves to be tarred in this fashion, or whether his work before the *General Theory* did add sufficient to distinguish it from 'classical economics'. Comment will also be made on the Robertson–Keynes debate of the interwar period insofar as it helps to distinguish between Robertson, Keynes and the classical strawman. Space does not permit me to examine whether the classical strawman is typical of classical economics in general. There is strong evidence to suggest he is not.[71] But what cannot be denied is that thousands of post-war graduates in economics have been led to believe that he is typical.

It is not too alarming a claim to regard Robertson as the father of the study of macroeconomic dynamics in Britain. The comparative static approach of the classical model, and the later work of Keynes, was alien to Robertson's view of economic analysis. The major problems of the day were dynamic in nature, and needed to be analysed in a dynamic manner. Comparative statics were misleading and largely unhelpful in finding solutions to the cyclical problem of unemployment. *Banking* was the first major work in Britain, not only to seek to establish the meanings of saving and investment, which had previously been terms loosely employed, but to explore thoroughly the relationship between saving and investment using period analysis – the step-by-step approach which typifies later work on the trade cycle and economic growth. Indeed, Robbins has gone so far as to suggest that Robertson anticipated the Domar equations.[72]

Much of Robertson's later disaffection for Keynes's work can be blamed upon the failure of Keynes to utilise the dynamic analysis of *Banking*. This is especially demonstrated by Robertson's critical response to the multiplier and, to some extent, the liquidity preference theory of interest. He was bitterly disappointed that his step-by-step analysis never 'got under his [Keynes's] skin'.[73] Commenting on the drafts of the *General Theory* Robertson wrote

> Equations of the type of those on p. 63 are unsuitable for application to heterogenous slices of time within which income is changing because they obscure the time element . . . and obscure instead of clarifying what happens when an act of investment takes place . . . why should one be expected to hold that short period equilibrium, any more than long period equilibrium is established as it were instantaneously by magic.[74]

In the *Study* he had recognised the output lag – the lagged response of output to a change in spending. This was evident in his discussion of the gestation period of investment. His article 'Saving and Hoarding' had utilised the lag between receiving income and spending it – now commonly called the Robertsonian lag.[75] Period analysis provided for Robertson a more detailed and accurate picture of the working of the economy; but it also provided a more complex analysis for Robertson's readers to understand, and left the vast majority exhausted after their attempt.[76]

Parallel with this prime concern with dynamics was Robertson's disposition to study disequilibria. Such was the normal state of affairs, not the equilibria of both Keynesian and classical analysis. Although there may be a tendency to move towards equilibrium, it may never be reached as parameters change and consequently equilibria change. Hence Robertson believed that a study of the process of change, rather than of the position of stability, was more fruitful.

At the foundation of the classical strawman model is Say's Law, and the belief that in the long run, in a perfectly competitive economy, there need be no unemployment. Clearly, from what has been said already, this is not a part of Robertsonian analysis. Theories of industrial fluctuation grew out of a disrespect for Say's Law. The over-investment theory of crisis, in particular, saw the economy producing more capital goods than would be demanded. There *could* be over-production of such goods. But Robertson went even further than this in agreeing with Aftalion that over-investment could in turn bring a general over-production.[77] The cycle was an *inevitable* feature of capitalism, and so must be, to varying degrees over the cycle, the existence of unemployment.

(i) *The theory of interest*

The arm of the classical strawman which was subjected to most pulling and twisting in Keynes's *General Theory* was that which exhibited a strong and simple relation between voluntary saving and investment via the rate of interest. Robertson too put forward a loanable funds type theory of interest prior to 1936[78] but this was considerably less simplistic than that of the classical model in several important respects:

(1) The supply of loanable funds in any period was not comprised entirely of voluntary saving, but also of net dishoarding by the public and net additions to the supply of money created by the commercial banks.[79]

Voluntary saving did have a strong, direct and 'classical' link with the rate of interest, but it was also dependent upon the level of disposable income. Current saving is determined partly by the received income of the preceding period, determined by the 'margin of income over necessary, or at all events customary expenditure'.[80] In the Robertsonian dynamic analysis there was no stable relation between voluntary saving and the rate of interest. Income was not assumed to be constant, but changing over time, such that the classical savings curve would be continuously moving. Thus, Robertson did not dispute Keynes's later claim that there would be a different natural rate of interest for every level of income;[81] indeed he had strongly argued the point himself two years before the *General Theory* appeared.[82]

Net dishoarding too was related to the rate of interest. An increase in the rate of interest would raise the marginal disutility of hoarding and encourage the release of past savings on to the money markets. In the *General Theory*, Keynes was to introduce the concept of liquidity preference; this led to much debate on the similarity of hoarding and liquidity preference;[83] Robertson did concede that the liquidity preference theory was superior in one respect – that is in the greater emphasis it placed upon the psychological forces acting upon the demand for money. But net dishoarding was not dependent entirely upon the rate of interest. It could be induced by changes in the price level, or by expectations of price changes, which, in turn, stem from the third source of supply of loanable funds, net additions to the money supply.[84]

This third source has an elevated importance in the Robertsonian system. It is independent of the savings decisions of individuals in the economy, being determined by the Bank of England and the commercial banks. It is hence not subject to the same influences as voluntary saving. It is also responsible for the forced and induced saving process (see below), and for the possible divergence between the actual market rate of interest and what Robertson calls the quasi-natural rate of interest.

(2) It was not until 1938 that Robertson saw the demand for loanable funds coming from beyond that needed to finance investment. In this respect, therefore, he adopted a classical stance; but clearly in the short-run the rate of interest could not be relied upon to bring about the equality of voluntary saving and investment, due to the interference of net dishoarding and net additions to the money supply in the market for loanable funds. Even in the long run, where the monetary forces might conveniently disappear, the rate of interest and the equality of saving and investment may not be entirely dependent upon the classical forces of productivity and thrift. The apparently short-run monetary forces may have long-run implications for the distribution of income, and the propensity to spend.[85]

(3) This takes us to yet another feature which the classical strawman does not possess: a natural or quasi-natural rate of interest as well as a market rate of interest.[86] Robertson was familiar with the natural rate of interest found in the works of Wicksell, Hayek and Keynes.[87] But he disputed that a natural rate of interest could exist which would bring both price stability and full employment. The capital stock would never be constant; consequently, output, employment and prices would be continuously changing. There could not be a static equilibrium at a constant natural rate of interest. There would always be forces operating to change the quasi-natural rate, principally the classical forces of productivity and thrift; there was little possibility that the market and natural rates could be equated for any length of time as endogenous forces were always working to alter the quasi-natural rate; Robertson also viewed the quasi-natural rate as dominant, pulling the market rate towards it. Although this divergence between the two rates of interest was a feature of the trade cycle, Robertson disputed the Hayekian proposition that

this divergence was the *cause* of fluctuation; it was merely a symptom of the underlying real causes.

(4) The mechanism by which Robertson sought to relate price and interest theory was developed most fully in *Banking* (1926). It is to be found in the occurrence of automatic and induced 'lacking' throughout the cycle; this not only yields a fundamental divide between Robertson and the classics, but also between Robertson and Keynesian analysis.

The automatic lacking process, although Robertson was not aware of it at that time, was not new to economic literature. It had been utilised by several of the early classical writers[88] in what is now referred to as the 'forced saving' doctrine. (It has not, however, been deemed so significant as to be included in the classical strawman model.) As one might expect, automatic lacking arises from the dynamic nature of the Robertsonian system. In a very simplified form this process is as follows: during the upswing the marginal productivity of capital may increase. This will raise the demand for loanable funds needed to undertake investment. In the immediate period there will be insufficient voluntary saving to support this investment, hence businessmen will look to the commercial banks for credit. If the expansion of credit takes place, the output of *capital* goods will be stimulated. The wage bill in the capital good industries will rise, heightening the demand for consumer goods; but the output of consumer goods is fixed in the short-run, that is until the upsurge in capital good production materialises and can be utilised to boost the output of consumer goods; supply is unable immediately to match this increased demand for consumer goods. The consequence must be an increase in prices. Those on fixed incomes are forced to lack, to consume less than they would have done without the rise in prices. They shoulder the burden of financing the increased investment which is taking place.[89]

'Induced lacking', unlike the above, was not to be found in early literature. This lacking again arises from an increase in the money stream; but in contrast to automatic lacking it is voluntary and designed. As the money stream expands, and prices rise, so the real value of the individual's money stock may decline. He may be *induced* to 'lack' in order to restore the real value of his money stock. Here we have the beginnings of a 'real cash balance effect', later to be associated with A. C. Pigou and D. Patinkin,[90] but surprisingly introduced by Robertson in 1926 largely as a result of

Keynes's inspiration.[91] Whether or not the individual sought to restore the real value of his money stock to the level existing before the price rise depended mainly upon the behaviour of interest rates during this expansionary phase, and upon the influence of price expectations; higher interest rates might encourage a greater real money stock, by increasing the reward for saving. Expectations of yet further price rises may diminish the desire to reach the initial real value of the money stock and encourage greater spending.

Keynes in the *General Theory* was to regard the forced saving process as one of 'the worst muddles of all',[92] despite his approval of Robertson's approach, and his joint work with Robertson on 'lacking' in 1926.[93] The key to the dispute between Keynes and Robertson over the *General Theory* lay in the basic difference of approach. Using a comparative static framework there would be no need for forced, or induced, lacking to support additional investment. 'The logical theory of a multiplier, which holds good continuously, without time-lag, at all moments of time'[94] would guarantee that sufficient *voluntary* saving would be created to finance any addition to investment; neither would there be any need for the rate of interest to rise as the demand for capital goods expanded. An increase in the marginal efficiency of capital would not alter the rate of interest, it would simply lead to more investment occurring at a *given* rate of interest. A change in the productivity of investment, or for that matter a change in thrift, would, Keynes held, have no effect upon the rate of interest. The multiplier process could always be relied upon to provide the finance, in the form of voluntary saving, for any addition to investment, without the need, in doing so, to resort to a rise in the rate of interest to attract additional finance.[95]

Robertson's reaction to this attack on the forced saving thesis, and the theory of interest, was predictable. He counter-attacked by criticising the lack of realism in Keynes's argument. The real world was dynamic; economic problems had to be solved using dynamic analysis. The multiplier was no more than a 'potentially useful little brick',[96] not the solid base upon which policy recommendations, and theoretical judgements, could confidently rest. It would take time for voluntary saving to be manufactured by the multiplier process; there were lags between receiving income and spending it (Robertsonian lag), and between additional spending and output (gestation period). In the meantime investment had to be financed, and businessmen had to resort to borrowing from the banking sector; in a dynamic world there was still the need for forced saving.

This argument was reinforced by Robertson's regard for the acceleration principle. Any voluntary saving generated by the multiplier process may not be used to finance the *original* increment in investment of that process, but instead may be employed in financing new investment projects stimulated by increased consumer demand.

Keynes himself was beginning to acknowledge the limitations of the static multiplier theory when war interrupted the post-*General Theory* debate. He was moving towards the development of a 'concept of finance' which would explain the financing of investment in the absence of voluntary saving, and in a dynamic world.[97]

Similarly, Robertson came to the defence of the classics against Keynes in arguing that productivity and thrift did help to determine the rate of interest; if the productivity of investment increased it might be necessary for the rate of interest to rise to tempt people to part with money balances: the interest rate was not solely determined by the monetary forces contained in the liquidity preference theory of interest.[98]

Keynes had accused the classics of focusing upon the relation between saving and the rate of interest; Robertson believed Keynes to be guilty of the same over-simplification by concentrating upon the influence of current income upon current saving and consumption. Saving was not only determined by current income, but by past income, by the rate of interest, and by the individual's stock of wealth; the propensity to spend out of income was not stable. Hence the multiplier process grossly over-simplified the link between additional spending and output in portraying a constant multiplier value. In the post-war period, Robertson believed this criticism to be further supported by the empirical studies of consumption, and by the new theories of J. Duesenberry and others.[99] This is best illustrated by his pronouncement to A. Hansen

I did not, so far as I know, in 1936 or at any time, commit myself to the view that current saving is a single-valued function of 'yesterday's' income. On the contrary, I think it may be influenced by expectations of future income (see EMT, p. 7, line 1)

or perhaps a la Duesenberry by previously attained income, as well as by the rate of interest, liquid assets etc. (it was not I who invented an over-simplified consumption function).[100]

(5) The final major difference between Robertson and the classical strawman model on interest theory is Keynesian in nature. In 1929 Robertson supported a view put forward by Cassel that there may be a minimum positive rate of interest.[101] At very low interest rates the regard for saving is so minimal that the desire to reach any fixed saving objective may be abandoned, and hence saving may become zero at a positive interest rate. Keynes's liquidity preference theory was later to suggest a minimum level below which the rate of interest would not sink, but the reason for it not doing so, in contrast to Robertson's theory, relied upon expectations relating to future movements in interest rates.

(ii) *The theory of prices*

The classical strawman model incorporates a crude quantity theory of money which depicts a proportional relationship between the money supply and the price level. This is justified on the grounds of a constant velocity of circulation of money, and a full employment level of real output.

Robertson was not happy about the proportionality argument. In *Money* (1923) he approached price determination as a 'special case of the general theory of value'.[102] The general price level is fixed by the demand for and supply of money. But these are not independent; hence an increase in the money supply may not bring about an equal percentage increase in the general price level. In the later edition of *Money* (1928) proportionality is upheld through a real balance effect. As prices rise, so the real value of money balances will decline; people will react by attempting to restore this real value, that is to restore the value of K (the ratio of cash balances held in any period to the level of money income), to that level existing before prices changed. By the end of the forced saving process 'the volume of bank loans has permanently increased by, let us say, 10 per cent and so has the volume of money in the hands of the public. But since prices have risen by 10 per cent, the aggregate real value of the public's money supply is no greater than it was before.'[103]

This apparent conflict is resolved in *Banking*. Here Robertson makes a clear distinction between periods of moderate inflation, where proportionality might prevail, and periods of 'rapid and violent inflation' (as in the case of the German hyper-inflation of 1923) where proportionality will not exist. The latter is most interesting for it isolates the reason for the instability of K and V in Robertsonian literature. This brings us back once more to induced lacking which can be seen as a change in the value of K. Price increases, resulting from additions to the money supply, reduce the real value of money balances held by the public; but the public may not wish to *restore* the initial real level of their money stock. Price rises may breed expectations of further rises and lead to an acceleration in spending and to a reduction in the desirable real level of the individual's money stock. There must also be a redistribution of income as a consequence of the inflationary process. Given that the propensity to hoard and to spend vary from one individual to the next, the aggregate demand for money balances, and hence K, is altered.[104]

Additionally, in 1926, Robertson was keen to explore the likely consequences of a change in the rate of interest, which may follow a movement in the money supply, upon the desire to hold money balances. During expansion the rate of interest will rise under the pressure of the demand for capital. This may increase the desire to hoard; it may encourage businessmen to use past profits to finance future expenditures rather than to resort to bank lending, and it may diminish the demand for circulating capital which is financed through the commercial banks.[105]

Little need be said on the assumption of the quantity theory that real output is constant. The first section of this chapter fully indicates Robertson's view on this. It was never a feature of Robertsonian literature to assume constancy of real output; fluctuation continually occurred in any capitalist society – as we have seen, it was an inherent feature of any economy relying heavily upon private sector investment.

As to Robertson's methodology in discussing price determination one can again witness his concern with economic dynamics. Although he did use the equation of exchange developed in the quantity theory approach, and in particular, from 1926 onwards, the Cambridge equation which focussed upon the demand for money, he was still primarily concerned with the transmission mechanism taking the economy from one price level to the next. Even as early as *Money* (1923) he was anxious to attempt to integrate monetary theory with saving–investment analysis through the forced saving process; and he made a much more sophisticated attempt in *Banking* in 1926.

Economic policy

The most popular of Keynesian myths – that fiscal policy was first advocated in 1936 by J. M. Keynes – can be quickly destroyed by reference to Robertson's early work. Friedman has remarked 'by comparison with my own extremely libertarian position, Robertson clearly had a great belief in individualism, but so did Keynes. And when it came to economic intervention . . . Robertson had a good deal of tolerance of it'.[106] This is very much true of Robertson from the *Study* onwards. He continually advocated a policy mix approach; fiscal and monetary policy should operate side by side whether it be to cure unemployment or inflation.

However Robertson doubted the potential effectiveness that many economists later claimed for both monetary and fiscal policy in bringing economic stability. Not all economic fluctuation was undesirable. The real features of the capitalist system of production brought an inevitable fluctuation, and it was necessary for the Government only to 'limit the turbulence without destroying the vitality'.[107] Samuelson interprets Robertson as wanting to do little about unemployment.[108] In fact, Robertson was worried only by the encouragement which some economists gave government to take employment to too high a level such that inflationary pressures were created; he suggested that a small pool of unemployed resources should be permanently held in order to cushion the impact of any sudden burst of expenditure. Indeed he warned of the inflationary dangers of low unemployment long before the appearance of the Phillips Curve and he alarmed many economists in 1957 by welcoming the abatement of rising employment, declaring 'if we want to prevent the continuance or recrudescence of inflation we should not try to work our industrial system with such a small margin of unemployment of this kind [transitional unemployment] as we have been doing in recent years'.[109] But it must be stressed that this was not a call to do nothing about unemployment.

In 1915 Robertson had been very much concerned with the problem of unemployment. The *Study*, in proposing an over-investment theory of fluctuation, saw the cause of unemployment as a short-fall in the demand for capital goods. Economic policy therefore was required to create 'an artificial elevation in the demand for constructional goods'.[110] This was best achieved through public works policies, which would allow private investment enough time to recover. He strongly supported the proposal of the minority report of the Poor Law Commissioners that Government contracts for structural work should be concentrated in times of bad trade. In so doing an attack was launched upon the 'Treasury view' which held that public investment must be at the expense of private sector investment. Robertson disputed that during a depression private investment would otherwise utilise the saving taken up by public investment.

His most forceful recommendation of fiscal action came in his evidence to the Macmillan Committee in 1930.[111] Unemployment resulted from the 'temporary gluttability of wants' – an over-production of capital goods in that the existing demand for such goods is saturated. The following corrective measure was proposed

> public bodies, central and local, as well as semi-public bodies such as railway companies, electricity commissioners and so forth should intervene to organise and express a collective need for instruments and structures – rolling stock, pylons, lavoratories and whatnot – at times when the ordinary commercial demand for instruments and structures is in a condition of temporary saturation.[112]

But there was not at this time, or later, any firm preference for tax changes as opposed to expenditure changes. Later Robertson doubted that tax changes could be administered fairly and with consistency, and believed that their role in the pursuit of economic stability should be subservient to that of achieving a redistribution of income, or a reallocation of resources.[113] Fiscal policy, in whatever form, had its disadvantages. It was 'somewhat cumbrous and unwieldy ... working with a pronounced lag and difficult to set moving more than once or at utmost twice a year'.[114] As such it should not be entirely relied upon; that is it should not be imposed without the support of monetary policy.

During a depression fiscal policy must be the senior partner in the Robertsonian policy mix. In the severe depression of the interwar period monetary policy was regarded as a 'blunt and clumsy weapon'.[115] Robertson doubted that any rate of interest, no matter how low, would entice businessmen to invest. He was critical of Keynes on the Macmillan Committee for arguing that the reverse was true.[116] More moderate depressions, however, may be countered by monetary policy. Investment here would be sensitive to interest rate changes. Later Robertson became critical of the Keynesian pessimism on the effectiveness of interest rate policy, and the over-emphasis upon fiscal policy. He maintained, in response to the Radcliffe Report, that a wide margin of transactions existed which were influenced by interest rate changes.[117] This final statement on monetary policy confirmed his earlier views; credit easing, and the reduced cost of finance, could boost investment under normal circumstances. It was only where business confidence was at its lowest ebb that it could do little to increase spending.[118] Monetary policy was therefore no panacea during depression. It merely had a role to play alongside fiscal policy.[119]

In 1915 Robertson proposed the introduction of a system of investment planning in support of fiscal and monetary policies. Such planning was indicative rather than direct. Its aim was to seek to eliminate the imperfect knowledge surrounding the private investment decision. In so doing it might prevent over-investment from arising by providing a central information bureau to create a pool of knowledge on which businessmen could draw when deciding whether or not to invest. It was hence a means to secure economic stability, rather than a policy designed to foster economic growth. Indeed Robertson thought that investment planning may involve the sacrifice of economic growth on the 'altar of stability'.[120]

In contrast, the policy mix for controlling inflation required a dominant element of monetary policy. Whatever the initial cause of inflation, Robertson believed that prices could only continue to rise if the monetary flow continued to expand.[121] He was very critical of the Keynesian post-war reliance upon fiscal policy where demand was high. He attacked the post-war cheap money policy in the UK and called for an increase in interest rates and restrictions on credit expansion. (Such a policy was adopted in 1951–2.) Monetary policy had to be forceful in times of over-expansion, not hesistant and indecisive. He was not surprised by the Radcliffe Report's conclusion that monetary policy had been impotent in the 1950s – during an inflationary period. But he believed that it need not have been so if larger changes in Bank Rate had been imposed, and more stringent credit restrictions introduced. But a strong restrictive monetary policy did not provide all the answers to inflation. The control of the money supply would not guarantee the prevention of the inflationary process. Prices may rise owing not only to an increased money supply but also by virtue of a change in the velocity of circulation of a fixed money supply – and this was beyond the control of monetary policy. As a member of the Cohen Council, Robertson stressed that 'even if the quantity of money is not increased, the stream of monetary demand can be fed'.[122]

Fiscal policy was basically inappropriate in the fight against inflation. It could be seen only as a possible cure for inflation not as preventive medicine. True it was a means to limit the excessive monetary demand which fuelled inflation, but it was 'in the nature of a *pis aller* and by no means a perfect substitute for measures designed to prevent the spilling of the milk in the first place'.[123] Again Robertson was concerned that fiscal changes to cure inflation should not interfere with the other objectives to be achieved through taxation.[124]

All this is a very long way from the advocacy of the classical strawman. In relation to macroeconomic policy, there is no evidence in Robertson's pre-1936 writings to suggest that wage reduction is an effective means of eliminating unemployment. The key to the success of such a policy in any case depended upon the influence of wage changes upon the level of spending. In evidence to the Macmillan Committee, Robertson emphasised that the demand for labour would be inelastic in a period of severe depression; even large reductions in money wages would not succeed in raising employment. He illustrated his argument with reference to the shipbuilding industry. No amount of wage reduction could lead to an increase in the demand for shipping tonnage, and to increased employment in that industry. Later on, after 1936, he was less certain that wage reductions would in fact damage spending.[125]

Conclusion

It would be erroneous to claim for Robertson the supreme pioneering nature of Marshall or Jevons, but this chapter has shown his fundamental contribution to the study of industrial fluctuation. In this respect one cannot fail to be impressed by his early attention to the relation between saving and investment which became a focus of discussion in the 1930s and his continuous use of economic dynamics and his faith in, and advocacy of, that explanation of fluctuation which concentrated upon real factors – particularly the role of invention and innovation, and the characteristics of the capitalist system of production. This approach was very much against the tide in Britain in 1915, a time when monetary theories of the trade cycle dominated.

Robertson was not alone in forwarding a real theory of the cycle. Indeed, as we have observed, a good many of the ideas he expressed were derived from continental literature, particularly the works of A. Aftalion and M. Tugan-Baranowski. Robertson developed these ideas so that he was able to make a considerable impact on the way British economists thought about the trade cycle and the problems of unemployment and inflation associated with cyclical fluctuation; most significantly he had a profound influence upon the development of J. M. Keynes's thoughts in the 1920s, and without a doubt Keynes was one of the greatest pioneers of all.

NOTES

1. See, however, A. Marshall, *Principles of Economics* (London: Macmillan, 1890; 8th edn 1920) pp. 709–11 and the same author's *Economics of Industry* as well as *Money, Credit and Commerce* (London: Macmillan, 1923). See also ch. 2.
2. *Lectures on Economic Principles* (London: Fontana Library, 1963) [hereafter cited as *LEP*] p. 325.
3. See, for example, 'Increasing Returns and the Representative Firm', *Economic Journal* [hereafter cited as *EJ*], XL (1930) 78–89 and 92–3; and 'The Future of International Trade', *EJ*, XLVIII (1938) 1–14.
4. He had been a master at Rugby School and was later headmaster of Haileybury School.
5. Gaining a 1:i in the Part 1 Classics Tripos.
6. A description employed by T. S. Ashton in his review of the reprint of *Study*. *Economica*, n.s., XVIII (1951) 298.
7. *A Study of Industrial Fluctuation* (London: P. S. King, 1915). Reprinted with a new introduction in *Reprints of Scarce Works on Political Economy* (London: The London School of Economics and Political Science, 1948). [Hereafter cited as *SIF*.]

8. He was awarded the Military Cross.
9. *Money* (London: Nisbet, Cambridge Economic Handbooks, 1923); rev. edn 1924; repr. 1924, 1926, 1927; rev. edn 1928; repr. 1930, 1932, 1935, 1937 (with new preface), 1940, 1941, 1943, 1944, 1945, 1946; new edn 1948 (two new chapters); trans. into Portuguese, Spanish and Japanese.
10. *Banking Policy and the Price Level* (London: P. S. King, 1926); repr. 1926; repr. with rev. 1932; repr. in the USA in 1949 (new preface) (New York: Augustus M. Kelley). [Hereafter cited as *BPPL*.]
11. See J. M. Keynes's comment in a letter to Robertson 10 November 1925 in *The Collected Writings of John Maynard Keynes*, vol. XIII (London: Macmillan for Royal Economic Society, 1973) [hereafter cited as *CW*], pp. 40–1.
12. Three volumes (London: Staples Press, 1957–9); trans. into Italian, Spanish and Japanese.
13. Nine books of original material plus six books comprising collections of previously published works. For fuller details see J. R. Presley, *Robertsonian Economics* (London: Macmillan, 1978) pp. 310–15.
14. For a detailed treatment see ibid., Pts I, II and III.
15. M. Tugan-Baranowski, 'Review of *Les Crises Industrielles en Angleterre*', *EJ*, XXIV (1914) 81–89.
16. Ibid., p. 82.
17. He gave the credit to A. C. Pigou, *Wealth and Welfare* (London: Macmillan, 1912) pt IV, which he had read prior to writing the *Study*.
18. *SIF* (1948 edn), Preface, p. ix.
19. *BPPL* (1926 edn), p. 6.
20. See, for example, *SIF* (1915 edn), ch. 1; *BPPL* (1926 edn), p. 7.
21. *BPPL* (1926 edn), p. 7.
22. Letter from Pigou to Robertson (dated 1913) in private possession.
23. Reviews of M. Tugan-Baranowski, op. cit., and of R. G. Hawtrey's *Good and Bad Trade*, *Cambridge Review*, 27 November 1913.
24. Review of Hawtrey, loc. cit.
25. 'Some Material for a Study of Trade Fluctuations', *Journal of the Royal Statistical Society*, LXXVII (1914) 159–73.
26. See J. R. Presley, op. cit., Pt I, ch. 4.
27. *SIF* (1948 edn), p. 157.
28. Letter from Pigou to Robertson (dated 1916) in private possession.
29. *SIF* (1948 edn), p. 127.
30. E. Eshag, *From Marshall to Keynes* (Oxford: Blackwell, 1963) p. 6.
31. A. Marshall, *The Economics of Industry*, p. 154. Pigou, who, in general, exerted most influence upon Robertson (excluding Marshall) was in fact criticised by Robertson for underestimating the importance of invention. *SIF* (1948 edn), p. ix.
32. See, for example, G. Haberler, *Prosperity and Depression* (New York: League of Nations, 1937, 3rd edn 1946) p. 81.
33. Robertson had reviewed the work of A. Aftalion as well as that of M. Tugan-Baranowski in *EJ*, XXIV (1914) 81–9.
34. *Money* (1928 edn), p. 156.

35. J. A. Schumpeter, 'The Explanation of the Business Cycle', *Economica*, VII (1927) 286–311.
36. J. A. Schumpeter, *Business Cycles* (New York: McGraw-Hill, 1939) pp. 87ff.
37. *SIF* (1948 edn), p. 39.
38. *Economic Commentaries* (London: Staples Press, 1956) [hereafter cited as *EC*], p. 89.
39. T. S. Ashton, op. cit., pp. 298–302.
40. Review of A. Aftalion, op. cit., p. 88.
41. W. S. Jevons, *Investigations in Currency and Finance* (London: Macmillan, 1884).
42. A. Piatt-Andrew, 'The Influence of the Crops upon Business in America', *Quarterly Journal of Economics* [hereafter cited as *QJE*], XX (1906) 322–55.
43. *SIF* (1948 edn), pt 1, ch. 5.
44. *BPPL*, pp. 14ff.
45. *LEP* (1963 edn), p. 409.
46. G. Haberler, op. cit., p. 87.
47. F. Bickerdike, 'A Non-monetary Cause of Fluctuations in Employment', *EJ*, XXIV (1914) 427–9. It is most probable that *SIF* had gone to print *before* this article appeared.
48. A. Aftalion, *Les Crises périodiques de Surproduction* (Paris: Rivière, 1913).
49. *SIF*, p. 125, see also pp. 122–4.
50. Although it would not follow that the demand for consumer goods would consequently be stable. It would change, for example, with the level of income.
51. *Essays in Monetary Theory* (London: P. S. King, 1940) p. 179.
52. *The Listener*, 28 July 1937.
53. *EC*, pp. 72–4.
54. M. Tugan-Baranowski, *Les Crises industrielles en Angleterre*, 2nd ed. (Paris: Giard & Brière, 1913).
55. M. Labordère, 'Autour de la crise américaine de 1907', *Revue de Paris*, 1 February 1908. Robertson read of A. Spiethoff's work in W. Mitchell, *Business Cycles* (New York: Burt Franklin, 1913).
56. Report of the Committee on Finance and Industry, *Parliamentary Papers 1930–1*, Cmnd 3897, xiii [hereafter cited as *Macmillan*]. Minutes of Evidence, Section 1, para. 11, p. 323.
57. Ibid., para 4702, oral evidence, p. 327.
58. Ibid., Section 1, para. 11, p. 323.
59. *SIF* (1948 edn), p. 13.
60. The use of 'Appropriate' will be explained later.
61. *SIF* (1948 edn), p. 13.
62. Ibid., ch. 11.
63. K. Marx, *Das Capital*, vol. II, pt ii, ch. 9, English edn (London: Allen & Unwin, 1938) vi, p. 211.
64. *SIF*, pp. 165ff.
65. *Macmillan* (n 56 above) loc. cit.
66. *SIF*, p. 254.

67. See, for example, *BPPL* (preface to 1949 edn, p. viii).
68. *BPPL*, p. 2.
69. 'Is Another Slump Coming?', *The Listener*, 28 July 1937.
70. See, for example, E. Shapiro, *Macroeconomic Analysis*, 3rd International edn (New York: Harcourt, Brace, Jovanovich, 1974) ch. 17.
71. See, for example, D. P. O'Brien, *The Classical Economists* (Oxford: Clarendon Press, 1975).
72. L. Robbins, *The Evolution of Modern Economic Theory and Other Papers in the History of Economic Thought* (London: Macmillan, 1970).
73. *BPPL* (1949 edn), Preface, p. xi.
74. Letter from Robertson to Keynes, 3 February 1935; see *CW*, XIV, p. 424.
75. 'Saving and Hoarding', *EJ*, XLIII (1933) 399–413.
76. Keynes commented 'You'll be lucky to get five understanding readers within two years'. Letter to Robertson, 10 November 1925, in private possession.
77. *SIF*, pp. 200–5.
78. See especially 'Industrial Fluctuation and the Natural Rate of Interest', *EJ*, XLIV (1934) 650–6.
79. Which gave rise to Forced Saving (see below). This is evident from the first edition of *Money* (1923) onwards.
80. A quotation taken from *LEP* (1963 edn), p. 231, but typical of his pre-1936 approach.
81. See J. R. Presley, op. cit., pp. 210–11.
82. *EJ*, XLIV (1934) 650–6. (But this was under the influence of the early drafts of Keynes' *General Theory*.)
83. *CW*, XIV.
84. See below for a discussion of 'induced lacking'.
85. *Essays in Money and Interest* (London: Fontana, 1966) pp. 68–9.
86. This is a dubious omission from the classical strawman model since even the early classical writers saw the interference of monetary forces with the market rate of interest in the short-run and recognised a long-run natural rate of interest. See J. R. Presley, op. cit., ch. 9.
87. J. R. Presley, ibid., pp. 154ff.
88. See F. A. Hayek, 'A Note on the Development of the Doctrine of "Forced Saving"', *QJE*, XLVII (1932–3) 123–33.
89. See J. R. Presley, op. cit., Pt. II, ch. 4 for a fuller discussion.
90. D. Patinkin, *Money, Interest and Prices* (New York: Harper & Row, 1956).
91. *BPPL* (1949 edn), p. 49.
92. *General Theory of Employment, Interest and Money*, *CW*, VII (1973) p. 183. [Hereafter cited as *GT*.]
93. *BPPL*, Preface.
94. Op. cit., p. 122.
95. IS/LM curve analysis did however eventually show that an increase in the productivity of investment would raise the rate of interest if the LM curve was upward sloping.

96. *Money* (1948) p. 212.
97. 'The "Ex Ante" Theory of the Rate of Interest', *EJ*, XLVII (1937) 663–9.
98. For further development see J. R. Presley, op. cit., pt. II.
99. See J. Duesenberry, *Income, Saving and the Theory of Consumer Behaviour* (Harvard: Harvard University Press, 1949); see also A. J. Westaway and T. Weyman-Jones, *Macroeconomics* (London: Longmans, 1978).
100. Letter from Robertson to A. Hansen, 23 September 1953, in private possession.
101. For comment see *LEP* (1963) p. 247.
102. *Money* (1923 edn), Preface, p. vii.
103. Ibid. (1928 edn), p. 92.
104. *BPPL* (1926 edn), p. 60; see also J. R. Hicks, *Value and Capital*, 2nd edn (Oxford: Clarendon Press, 1946) ch. XX.
105. *BPPL*, pp. 76–7.
106. Letter from M. Friedman to the author, 30 November 1972.
107. Review of E. Durbin's *Purchasing Power and Trade Depression: A Critique of Under-consumption Theories*, *EJ*, XLIII (1933) 281–3.
108. P. Samuelson, 'D. H. Robertson', *QJE*, LXXVII (1963) 528–36.
109. The quotation is from 'Wage Inflation' – an unpublished paper in private possession but it expresses Robertson's general view in the 1950s.
110. *SIF* (1948), pt. II, ch. IV.
111. *Macmillan* (n 56 above); evidence of 8 and 9 May 1930, pp. 321–47.
112. Ibid., Section 13.
113. Memorandum submitted to the Canadian Royal Commission on Banking and Finance, 1962 (repr. in *Essays in International Finance*, no. 42, May 1963, Princeton University).
114. *Utility and All That* (London: Allen & Unwin, 1952) [hereafter cited as *UAT*], p. 93.
115. Comment on 'The Douglas Credit Scheme', *The Listener*, IX, 28 June 1933, no. 233.
116. *Macmillan*, op. cit., paras 4928–30.
117. Oral evidence to the Canadian Royal Commission on Banking and Finance, 1962, loc. cit., pp. 5125–6.
118. Memorandum to the Canadian Royal Commission, loc. cit., p. 17.
119. For a more thorough discussion see J. R. Presley, op. cit., pt. III.
120. A phrase used by Robertson in an address to the Marshall Society in Cambridge, 19 October 1961, called 'Mr. Lloyd's Fireworks' – not published but text in private possession.
121. *UAT*, p. 91.
122. Council on Prices, Productivity and Incomes, *First Report* (London: HMSO, 1958) appendix VIII, p. 71.
123. *UAT*, p. 94.
124. Oral evidence to the Canadian Royal Commission, op. cit., pp. 5183–4.
125. *LEP*, pp. 442–6.

7 R. G. Hawtrey, 1879–1975

E. G. DAVIS

Introduction – biographia

The career of Ralph George Hawtrey spanned the first three-quarters of this century. He came to public attention in 1897 when his article in the *Fortnightly Review* attacked British naval procedures and brought his father the congratulations of Gladstone.[1] He remained active on the public scene through 1970 when a final letter to *The Times* criticised the conduct of monetary policy and reiterated arguments from his last book, *Incomes and Money*, published but three years before. During the many years between, Hawtrey combined the career of a senior civil servant in the Treasury with that of an important theorist in monetary economics.[2]

He was born in Slough on 22 November 1879, the first son and third child of George Procter Hawtrey and Eda Strahan. His grandfather had established St Michael's, a preparatory school there, and his father was assistant master. From this beginning he travelled the common path for the elite of his day which led to Eton and on to a position of prominence. He was, however, raised in straitened circumstances. His father left teaching to follow a famous brother, Charles Hawtrey, to the stage. He then failed in this attempt to earn a living as an actor. This experience shaped Hawtrey's life. He decided, while at Eton, to sit for the Civil Service examinations when he learned one could earn a thousand pounds a year by the age of 40, and receive a pension besides.[3]

From Eton Hawtrey went up to Trinity College, Cambridge in 1898. There he read mathematics but his achievements, while creditable (he was Nineteenth Wrangler) were not outstanding. But his interests broadened as he came under the influence of the philosopher G. E. Moore, whose ethics made a profound and lasting impact on Hawtrey's thinking. He was selected for

203

membership of the Apostles, an exclusive society of intellectuals united at that time by their association with Moore. When after Trinity Hawtrey moved on to London, these connections drew him into the Bloomsbury Group, and his name is often mentioned in the literature on that subject. This part of Hawtrey's life resembled the path followed by Keynes four years later. Both read mathematics at Cambridge, and through insufficient application, finished down the list of Wranglers. Their social lives paralleled too for each joined the Apostles. Hawtrey helped to select Keynes for membership in the society. Thus began a lifelong friendship between the two men, cemented by their common interest in economics, and their participation in the social gatherings of the Apostles and Bloomsbury.

In 1903 Hawtrey started his Civil Service career in the Admiralty, a natural choice in view of his early interest in naval matters. However, a year later he transferred to the Treasury, where he remained until his retirement in 1947.[4] In his biography of Keynes, Harrod speculates about how different things might have been for Britain had Keynes become a permanent civil servant in the Treasury instead of an academic.[5] Instead it was Hawtrey who filled this role. In 1919 he was appointed Director of Financial Enquiries, whose duties were to offer advice on all aspects of economic policy. His views were an important ingredient in the shaping of Treasury policies during the inter-war period.

Despite his lack of formal training in economics at Cambridge, Hawtrey began to shift in that direction upon joining government service. He gained recognition with the publication of his first book, *Good and Bad Trade*, in 1913, and established his name six years later when he wrote *Currency and Credit*. This book became a much-used text, and was the standard work on monetary theory during the 1920s for the Cambridge Tripos. It remained popular, for its final edition appeared 30 years after the book was first published. Hawtrey became a prolific writer with many books and journal articles to his credit.[6]

After his retirement from the Treasury, Hawtrey continued his career as an economist. He served as President of the Royal Economic Society from 1946 to 1948. In 1947 he was elected Henry Price Professor of International Economics at the Royal Institute of International Affairs, a position he occupied until 1952. Although he held no further formal post, he continued with unfailing energy to produce articles and books virtually until his death in 1975 at the age of 95.

For this distinguished career Hawtrey was the recipient of many honours: Fellow of the British Academy; honorary DSc (Econ.) of London University; honorary Fellow of Trinity College, Cambridge. He was awarded the CB in 1941 and knighted in 1956.

The dual nature of Hawtrey's career suggests that his thinking be discussed along the dimensions of theory and policy. The theoretical part of this chapter is divided into five sections. The first indicates some early influences on his intellectual development. Next comes a discussion of his ideas on Bank Rate policy. The third section presents his thoughts on the Business Cycle and stabilisation policy while the following two parts analyse the remainder of his monetary theory. With respect to policy three topics are examined. Hawtrey's views on bond-financed public works are detailed first. Then his interpretations of the events of the inter-war period are presented. Finally, there is a section on his thoughts about the world after Bretton Woods.

Economic theory

(i) *The formative years*

Hawtrey came to economics on his own. At Cambridge his exposure to the subject had been limited to a few lectures taken in preparation for the Civil Service entrance examination.[7] His attention shifted to economics after university as a result of his interest in current events and his experiences in government. It is worthwhile discussing these influences first as a backdrop for his economics. It is often true that those who learn a subject without benefit of formal instruction are particularly sensitive to outside forces which influence their thinking. This appears to have been the case with Hawtrey.

His initial concern for economics was kindled by a political controversy. Hawtrey took considerable interest in Joseph Chamberlain's efforts to implement tariff reform which dominated the political stage in Britain from 1903 until the election of 1905.[8] There was much discussion of trade statistics in the course of the debate. Hawtrey realised that in comparing different years it was important to recognise that the general level of prices changed as well. As a result he was led to consider the forces which determine prices and became committed to the study of economics, with a particular focus on monetary theory.[9]

One factor in Hawtrey's early development was the state of the British economy during this formative period in his thinking.[10] The year 1904 was the bottom of a mild depression. The Bank of England responded with an extended period of low interest rates, and the economy started to revive. Prosperity returned by 1906 but in the autumn of the year the Bank Rate was raised when gold began to flow to the US. By the spring business had begun to slacken. The trend was accelerated by Bank Rate increases in the autumn of 1907 as the American situation developed into a major financial crisis. This episode triggered complaints from the business community that domestic activity was being adversely affected and, consequently, the Bank of England instituted an inquiry into the internal effects of its policy. As the crisis eased the Bank Rate was lowered in the spring of 1908. An extensive and long-lasting recovery soon began, which was popularly attributed to the return of 'cheap money'. Since this was the period during which Hawtrey shaped his views on economics, it is perhaps not surprising that a belief in the power of changes in Bank Rate to affect economic activity became an important component of his thinking.

The working environment Hawtrey experienced at the Treasury must have been another important influence on his economics.[11] The two main tasks of the Treasury were to ensure a balance between government revenues and expenditures, and manage the public debt. It aimed at reducing the debt as quickly as possible while refinancing at lower interest rates whenever an opportunity appeared.[12] Such an undertaking required a close understanding of the workings of financial markets. Hawtrey always remained faithful to the traditional canons of government finance, and paid careful attention to the fashion in which markets actually functioned.

(ii) Bank Rate policy

Hawtrey became the foremost modern exponent of the virtues of Bank Rate[13] which he considered to be a useful and efficient weapon of monetary policy. The half-century ended by the First World War was, as Hawtrey put it, 'the Antonine age of Bank Rate'[14] after the Roman Emperor whose reign was known for a feeling of well-being which pervaded the empire. It was a period when the Bank of England gained considerable power with respect to the money markets, and faith in the efficacy of Bank Rate ran high. The Bank regarded itself as primarily responsible for its gold reserve, a task for which Bank Rate was felt to be an effective tool.

The original rationale for Bank Rate policy was rooted in the quantity theory. This view pictured Bank Rate as a regulator of the quantity of money. Any change altered the demand for discounts from the Bank. There was then an impact on the volume of bank lending and prices, in turn, were affected. Thus Bank Rate policy was seen as protecting the exchanges through its impact on the domestic economy. Subsequently it was also held that the Bank Rate worked by influencing foreign lending. An increase in interest rates was felt to have a favourable effect on the exchanges by preventing the departure of capital or encouraging an inflow.

Hawtrey went beyond the traditional ideas about the *modus operandi* of Bank Rate to focus on a precise route by which the domestic economy was affected. He stressed the importance of those who hold stocks with funds borrowed from the banking system.[15] It was his opinion that the buying and selling decisions of this group were significantly affected by changes in short-term interest rates, and that this effect was the cutting edge of Bank Rate policy. The importance of short-term interest rates in the determination of the desired holdings of stocks was a constant theme in all of his writing.

As a matter of economic rationality any change in the cost of financing alters the size of the optimal inventory given the other factors involved. But Hawtrey stressed that retail and wholesale dealers were particularly sensitive to changes in the cost of bank credit.[16] Compared with their own capital, which is usually quite small, they buy, hold and sell large amounts of goods. Besides, as long as stocks are held above some minimum level which is considered essential, the operations of such businesses are unaffected by changes in inventories. Yet when merchants reduce their purchases, the manufacturers receive fewer orders so that there can be a rapid effect on production when there is a change in the desired level of stocks.

Hawtrey's emphasis on the importance of the merchant class may have been the result of practical observation about the economy. At the end of the Edwardian Age, England was not far removed from the nation which in Napoleon's attributed retort was composed of shopkeepers. In modern times the significance of short-term interest rates on stocks held by dealers must have diminished greatly compared with nineteenth century conditions. With the increase in vertical integration and the decline of the mercantile sector business became less sensitive to bank lending rates.

Hawtrey's argument generalised to cover international trade for there too were merchants who held stocks which had to be financed.[17] Much of the world's foreign trade was financed with credit from Britain. Importers everywhere accepted bills payable in London, while, whatever the country of origin, exporters drew bills payable there. The commercial bills which arose from these transactions were a significant part of the assets of banks. When credit contracted in the UK the entire international system of trade and finance was affected. Hawtrey felt that international merchants became reluctant to buy and anxious to sell when the Bank Rate was raised in England, for all over the world the cost of carrying stocks increased. Thus he considered that the power of Bank Rate was due to London's position as an international financial centre.

These views of Hawtrey on Bank Rate policy triggered a famous debate with Keynes. Originally their positions were similar.[18] Schumpeter in fact commented that 'from the *Tract* to the *Treatise*, Keynes was a Hawtreyan'.[19] Then a sharp difference emerged as Keynes began to stress the term structure aspect. In the *Treatise* the argument was that Bank Rate influenced short-term interest rates, and these in turn affected long-term rates and fixed investment.[20] Academic opinion divided on the topic, and as late as 1939 Hicks wrote of 'the great debate about the working of monetary control – a debate which has made most English economists either Keynesians or Hawtreyans'.[21]

Hawtrey was very critical of Keynes's view of the transmission mechanism for Bank Rate policy. He considered history had demonstrated the effectiveness of changes in Bank Rate and doubted that the impact on long-term investment was sufficient explanation. As a matter of practical observation he thought the relationship between short- and long-term interest rates was not close, and furthermore, that fixed investment was not very responsive to interest rate changes. He provided a persuasive argument in support of this position.[22]

(iii) *Business cycles and stabilisation policy*

As trade, industry and finance expanded during the middle of the nineteenth century, the increasing interdependence of countries led to the emergence of the Business Cycle. There was a series of well-defined fluctuations in prices and economic activity which upset the world economy.[23] The pattern exhibited was sufficiently regular to make a considerable impression on economic thinking. No longer did the specifics of financial crisis, speculative excess and harvest failure appear to provide an adequate explanation. The study of this phenomenon became an extensive part of economic analysis called Business Cycle Theory.[24]

Within this subject Hawtrey was categorised as an advocate of the 'purely monetary' approach, but this identification requires elaboration.[25] Before the First World War the general tendency of English economists had been to downplay the role of money.[26] By contrast Hawtrey was a monetarist in the sense that his work emphasised the fundamental importance of money and the workings of the monetary system. However, unlike modern counterparts, he considered the monetary system to be inherently unstable. The idea that this instability was fundamental to the nature of the fluctuations, and the further proposition that the periodicity (the tendency towards a regular pattern) came from characteristics of the monetary system, constituted his theory of the business cycle.

He began with the notion that depression meant a slackening of the flow of spending on commodities, while an expansion was an augmentation of this demand. The flow of money (the demand for goods in terms of money) was seen to be an endless chain, as incomes generated spending, and spending created incomes. Hawtrey considered that any deviation from equilibrium would be magnified, for an expansion or contraction, once started, proceeded by its own momentum. This process he termed 'the vicious circle'. These cumulative disturbances went hand in hand with appropriate changes in credit.

Hawtrey emphasised the role of price changes and the expectations these arouse, and stressed the place of merchants. As prices increase dealers have an incentive to hold larger stocks. Their orders raise incomes and sales improve. Stocks are thus reduced so dealers order more, and expansion continues. When prices are falling dealers wish to hold smaller stocks. The reduction in orders leaves producers and their employees with less to spend. Sales drop off, as do orders, and deflation goes on. A further source of instability arose because there would normally be a proportional relationship between the desired level of stocks and sales. When sales change, and dealers began to adjust their stocks to the new level of demand, there would be a more than proportional change in orders. In the case of a drop in demand faced by dealers, they would reduce orders by a greater proportion to reflect lowered demand, and vice versa.[27] Thus in Hawtrey's view the instability of the system came as a result of the rational behaviour of economic agents as they responded to changed circumstances. In this sense it was an ordered instability.[28]

Hawtrey did not claim all disturbances were caused by purely monetary factors; these, however, provided the explanation for the periodicity of the cycle. He felt this regularity had been due to the workings of the monetary system under the conditions of the pre-war gold standard. As a result of the changes in the system after the First World War he thought the cycle in this form no longer existed.

His explanation highlighted the need of the economy for currency. In the England of that day gold circulated internally and was used for wages and retail transactions. When the earnings of the working class increased, they absorbed cash. Their money balances were held in legal-tender form, rather than in bank balances which were held by those better off. As a result the reserves of the banking system were weakened. In the opposite case when working class earnings diminished, currency returned from circulation to the banking system and bank reserves increased. Hawtrey's account of the turning points was based on the drain of cash from the banks during expansion, and the reverse flow during the contraction phase of the cycle. This phenomenon of the internal drain was a well-known fact observed during the cycles of the pre-war period[29] and had been much discussed. Hawtrey, however, claimed this lag in the demand for hand-to-hand currency behind the expansion or contraction of credit was the reason for the periodicity of the fluctuations.

Hawtrey thought problems arose because the banking system was regulated with respect to the reserve proportion. Since wages lag behind changes in prices, the rise of prices preceded the drain of legal tender money into circulation, and vice versa. As a guide for banking policy currency flows came too late. Since the drain of cash continued after the credit expansion had ended, banks, focusing on the current level of their reserves, did not realise that these would continue to shrink even after credit had ceased to expand. Restrictive measures were usually taken after the point which was ultimately consistent with available reserves, so banks were likely to over-expand. Similarly when banks decided whether to cease contraction based on the state of their reserves they did not recognise that the inflow of cash would continue. The contraction of credit then would also go on too long. Hawtrey felt that this process was the fundamental cause of the pre-war cycle. It appears that this explanation posits myopic behaviour on behalf of the banks for one would think they could learn from experience.

Hawtrey drew the implication that if central banks looked beyond the reserve position to the actual state of the economy, the Business Cycle could be prevented by timely intervention. It was essential that central bank actions be prompt, for otherwise the disturbance could develop sufficient force that it would be difficult to reverse. He held that depressions were usually the result of timing errors in central bank policy.

This view led Hawtrey to be among the first to emphasise that the economy was not automatically self-regulating for he considered that there was a need for discretionary stabilisation policy. Moreover he was an optimist about the possibilities for stabilisation.[30] Since expansions and contractions were cumulative, it was only necessary to start the appropriate movement ('break the vicious circle'). The situation could then be left to gather momentum on its own without further interference. He was confident that monetary policy, if applied quickly, could control the flow of spending and eliminate the cycle.

This century has witnessed a fundamental change in economic thinking as the State has taken up responsibility for regulating the performance of the economy. Hawtrey's importance in the popularisation of these ideas was considerable: Hicks held that the publication of *Currency and Credit* in 1919 began the era of stabilisation policy,[31] while Schumpeter gave Hawtrey credit for influencing American thinking on the subject.[32]

(iv) *Monetary theory*[33]

Hawtrey took the proportion of wealth or income which people choose to hold in the form of money as the centre-piece of his economics. He started, then, from the work of Marshall and Walras by emphasising the importance of the cash-balance version of the quantity theory. One of his main contributions was an original development of the cash-balance approach.[34]

In Hawtrey's terminology the expression 'unspent margin' meant the total amount of bank credit outstanding plus currency in circulation.[35] According to his version of the quantity theory, the unspent margin was equated to the command over resources which people hold in reserve. The price level or wealth value of the monetary unit was determined accordingly. Hawtrey stressed that each economic unit held balances of bank credit and cash, in an amount related to income or wealth for an individual, and turnover in the case of a business.[36] Banks determine the amount of the unspent margin,[37] while people choose what portion they wish to hold in currency. Credit and currency were related because banks must have sufficient cash reserves to satisfy the currency needs of customers. Furthermore, there were legal regulations governing the issue of coins and legal tender paper.

It was characteristic of Hawtrey to mix traditional ideas with new approaches. In addition to being an exponent of the cash-balance analysis, he was the most eminent early sponsor of the income approach.[38] This had its roots in Tooke's suggestion that an explanation of prices should start from consumers' income rather than the quantity of money. Hawtrey insisted that this income approach was compatible with the quantity theory of money, and attempted to use both forms of analysis in a consistent fashion. He differentiated consumers' income (total income expressed in terms of money) from consumers' outlay (spending on goods and securities out of incomes).[39] A difference between them represented a change in money balances. Hawtrey felt that any such difference was an important factor governing the behaviour of prices. In essence he completed his economics by emphasising that money balances for all economic agents alter to the extent of a difference between expenditures and receipts.

Hawtrey was responsible for introducing the income approach to international trade theory.[40] He considered that any increase in consumers' outlay was likely to involve a proportional increase in the consumption of imports. As a result the balance of payments worsened. Thus he associated changes in income and the state of the balance of payments, with expansion making the exchanges unfavourable and vice versa.

Hawtrey's basic model followed the style of the quantity theory. If an unchanged stream of money flowed through consumers' income to demand, and back in turn to incomes, activity would be maintained. If part of the stream was absorbed, activity diminished; if money were released, the stream was enlarged and an increase in activity resulted. An absorption of cash meant that for some group receipts exceeded disbursements,[41] which created a shortage of demand and compressed consumers' income, while a release of cash did the opposite.[42] He pictured consumers' outlay as a stream of spending while the cash balances of the traders were seen as reservoirs of money. The cash position of the dealers provided a balancing item for if they released or absorbed cash they added to or subtracted from the demand given by the consumers' outlay.[43]

This theoretical view was a logical extension of the cash-balance approach. It survives to some extent today in arguments that highlight differences between actual and desired holdings of money. However, this form of disequilibrium can be quickly eliminated by each individual economic agent although the macroeconomic consequences may well continue, and in Hawtrey's view could easily gather momentum. His theory, then, was set in the time frame of the very short run as economic agents brought their money balances to equilibrium.

Hawtrey's stress on the importance of market intermediaries who hold inventories combined with this short time horizon led him in a novel direction towards a world where quantities rather than prices adjust. Prices are not now, nor where they then, flexible in the very short run. His focus on the distributional system provided a further impetus: the first response of a retailer to, say, a decrease in demand would not be to lower prices but to order less from the wholesaler. Ultimately prices would be cut by the producers in the face of excess capacity, but the initial stage of a disturbance involved the adjustment of inventories.

Hawtrey's time frame and general orientation led him in a direction which was to become fashionable. But one can argue that his view was distorted by a preoccupation with very short run phenomena. Indeed, Keynes, whose name is often associated with the short run, criticised Hawtrey on this point in their correspondence after the *General Theory*.[44]

(v) *Savings–investment analysis*

This century has seen substantial progress in macroeconomics. It was left to the generation after Marshall to construct theory capable of dealing adequately with fluctuations in economic activity. Classical thinking failed in an attempt to use long run analysis to study cyclical phenomena for the implications of changes in income were obscured. This occurred partly through the implicit assumption of full employment, and partly due to a preoccupation with the question of distribution among the factors of production. There were, in addition, ways in which the quantity theory complicated matters. Major advances in theory have taken place since, as the economics of the short run was greatly improved. In this endeavour the development of savings-investment techniques was an intellectual breakthrough.

In this achievement Hawtrey took a significant part and made important contributions. Yet his role in the story is complicated for in characteristic fashion, he was also an adherent of older traditions of thinking. Classical analysis pictured savings flowing smoothly into the stream of spending. Savings and investment were considered to be equated by variation in the rate of interest while the effects of changes in income were missed. It was an important step for economics to drive a wedge between savings and investment. Hawtrey participated in this task but also affirmed earlier thinking that savings were not a cause of difficulty for the economy: in his monetary theory money spent on securities was routinely channelled into expenditures for investment.[45]

Hawtrey brought his emphasis on market intermediaries to his depiction of the workings of the long term capital market. His analysis ran in terms of what he called the 'investment market' composed of all dealers in securities.[46] This group made the market in financial assets with a stock of securities held with bank financing. This was a conception analogous to his treatment of commodity markets.

He regarded the investment market as an intermediary between those with savings to invest and producers needing finance for capital formation. The balances of financial assets held by these dealers provided a reservoir between the streams of savings and spending on fixed capital. In his view the investment market did an efficient job of equalising these flows, as dealers took steps to eliminate any undesired change in their stocks of securities. If the dealers in the investment market found that their inventories changed in a fashion they did not wish, the rate of interest could be altered. Hawtrey, however, was prone to emphasise the direct techniques by which issuing houses control the placement of new issues. He saw the long term investment market as imperfect, with an unsatisfied fringe of would-be borrowers. In normal circumstances new fixed investment would be found to use up whatever resources new savers had deposited with the market. If, however, the investment market found its stock of securities building up, dealers might flatly refuse a new issue. Here, then, was a form of quantity adjustment. In short, he felt that the investment market adjusted new issues to equal the savings available.[47] Thus he considered that money invested in financial assets became spending on new capital goods for savings used to purchase securities came to rest ultimately in a new issue.[48]

It should be noted that Hawtrey regarded the exchange of financial assets after the initial sale as of lesser interest, for his analysis highlighted the flow of new savings. Thus the significance of the 'second-hand' market in securities was played down. Keynes was, of course, largely responsible for drawing attention to the importance of the pool of previously saved money. Now it is common knowledge that the stock-flow nature of financial markets must be recognised, for in such a market expectations matter a great deal.

This theory led Hawtrey to err in another direction: he overlooked the importance of changes in the desire of firms to acquire fixed capital. His emphasis was directed to the fact that as income changes, savings alter, which has implications for the investment market and new issues.[49] Fluctuations in the capital-goods industries were seen as a consequence, not a cause, of disturbances. He realised that during depression, both savings and the desire to invest fell off, but considered the main cause of diminished spending on capital goods was the decline of savings.

Hawtrey had, however, crafted a model within which differences between savings and fixed investment could be discussed. They would show up as undesired changes in dealers' stocks of securities with a corresponding change in their position with respect to the banks. If, say, the rate of interest was too high, so savings exceeded investment, dealers would sell more securities than they bought and take in more money than they paid out. Hawtrey regarded this as an absorption of cash by the investment market and was well aware of the deflationary consequences.[50]

Hawtrey's involvement did not cease at this stage, for he participated in further developments of this style of analysis. There was a growing body of opinion which pictured savings as contributing to Britain's problems. The matter first came to public attention through the underconsumptionists led by J. A. Hobson. He took as his central proposition that because of the unequal distribution of income the savings of the nation were excessive, and the purchasing power of workers was insufficient. Keynes contributed to this thinking for he made the difference between savings and investment the centre-piece of his economics. By contrast, in Hawtrey's analysis, as has been seen, these flows were kept equal by the workings of the investment market.

The main point of the *Treatise* was that differences between savings and investment caused changes in the price level. These, in turn, generated profits or losses, followed by changes in business activity. Hawtrey was always a fair and careful critic of the work of his contemporaries who tried hard to be constructive. He had not given differences between savings and investment much stress in his work, but an examination of the *Treatise* led him to give the matter more thought. As a result he made an important advance in theory.

The principal error of the analysis in the *Treatise* was that Keynes did not deal adequately with the implications of changes in output. Differences between savings and investment generated price changes, but the effect of changes in economic activity, and the impact on savings were omitted. These mistakes dovetailed neatly with Hawtrey's economics for his strengths corresponded to the weaknesses of the *Treatise*. Hawtrey's time frame caused him to highlight changes in inventories, and the adjustment of quantities rather than prices. Furthermore, the relationship between savings and economic activity was a basic part of his monetary theory. In his criticism Hawtrey stressed the importance of changes in output, and made the link with savings explicit.[51]

In this way Hawtrey was led to an important theoretical leap. He created a model where savings varied with output, while investment was a parameter. A difference betwen savings and investment showed up as an undesired change in unsold goods. The model identified quasi-equilibrium positions where output, and hence savings, had adjusted sufficiently that inventories were returned to equilibrium. In the argument presented, if investment increases, income is augmented, and part of the change will be spent and part saved. Output and income will continue to change, with prices constant, until savings and investment are again brought to equality. The situation when there is a deflationary change in investment is handled similarly. Moreover, a version of the multiplier emerges. The change in output resulting from a change in investment was related to the savings proportion in the familiar fashion.[52] This analysis was done in the form of numerical examples in a working paper of the Macmillan Committee dated January 1931.[53]

At this early date Hawtrey was able to construct a very advanced macro model which contained modern elements.[54] It would seem that this material necessitates some revision in the existing accounts of the coming of the *General Theory*.[55] In general, published discussions of Keynes's intellectual progress after the *Treatise* have paid little attention to Hawtrey, although Keynes made a direct admission of the value of this work.[56]

This material also requires that certain interpretations of the distinctive features of Keynes's economics be modified. Consider, for example, the view of Patinkin that 'the really distinguishing mark of the *General Theory*' is 'the crucial role of changes in output as an *equilibrating force* with respect to aggregate demand and supply – or equivalently, with respect to saving and investment'.[57] It is true that this statement is an accurate account of a major difference between the *Treatise* and the *General Theory*. However, it does not present a true picture of Keynes's contribution to theory. Five years before the *General Theory* Hawtrey was able to construct a sophisticated model where output changes brought savings and investment to equilibrium. It was Hawtrey, not Keynes, who first introduced output changes in an equilibrating role, and the concomitant identification of quasi-equilibrium positions, to economic theory.

Economic policy

(i) *Bond-financed government spending*

The Minority Report of the Commission on the Poor Laws suggested in 1909 that the government could ameliorate the conditions of a depression by the appropriate use of public works financed by bond sales. In 1924 this policy gained its most important advocate when Keynes declared his support. However, during the twenties and early thirties the British government was firmly against such an undertaking.

This official opposition continued an historical tradition on government spending. It was accepted by successive Chancellors of the Exchequer that their aim should be to maintain a balanced budget of minimum size which included, hopefully, some funds for debt-redemption. This creed took on particular importance at a time when the First World War expenditures had increased the government debt by a substantial amount. The government received support in its opposition to public works from the famous 'Treasury View': it was the opinion of the Treasury that little additional employment could be created by a policy of State borrowing and expenditure.

Here was a case where Hawtrey's economic theory made him a

defender of Treasury orthodoxy. His view of the workings of the investment market caused him to oppose the use of bond-financed government spending as a counter-cyclical device.[58] It was an implication of his theory that such a policy could do little good, for the supply of savings was determined by income and constrained total spending on fixed capital. The sale of government bonds would only displace private securities. The dealers of the investment market, finding they were selling too few bonds relative to the supply, would return their inventories to equilibrium levels by curtailing new issues.

Hawtrey did consider the policy expansionary if people were induced to shift out of money balances into securities. He thought, however, that the increase in idle balances during a depression represented unemployed circulating capital.[59] With output curtailed firms would hold in liquid form funds which normally finance their operations. Hawtrey felt such enterprises had a need for liquidity and would be unlikely to hold bonds. They would want to be ready to expand production when required, and would be slow to acquire assets whose value might decrease as the return of prosperity brought an increase in interest rates.[60]

He considered the argument that the public works could be financed out of the savings that result from the policy: there would be lower expenditures on unemployment insurance, and the resources received by the investment market would increase as activity improved.[61] Hawtrey, however, regarded this answer as begging the question. If the policy did not succeed in increasing employment there would be no additional funds available for what he thought was an exercise in unsound government finance.

He also articulated practical objections to public works. There were the questions of the magnitude, and the preparatory interval required. He thought that the policy was a slow and high-cost method of creating jobs, and the projects themselves might not be worthwhile. These difficulties were commonly discussed. He preferred that the government run deficits from a remission of taxation which could be financed by the creation of bank credit.[62]

During the interwar period Hawtrey prepared a stream of memoranda attacking the policy of bond-financed public works. This theoretical support was influential in keeping the Treasury on an orthodox path.[63] Ultimately his superiors in the government, Sir Richard Hopkins and Sir Frederick Phillips, became converted by the Keynesian arguments and the Treasury View passed into history.[64]

(ii) *The interwar period*

In September 1919 Hawtrey was appointed Director of Financial Enquiries at the Treasury, and his duties were to comment on all aspects of economic policy. In the same month he gave a speech before the British Association entitled 'The Gold Standard'.[65] This address detailed a proposal for the organisation of the international monetary system which came to fruition at the International Financial Conference at Genoa in 1922. This episode, generally considered a high point of Hawtrey's official career, provides a logical beginning for his views on the interwar period. Characteristically, Hawtrey's proposals were a middle ground position, which retained orthodox features of the Gold Standard combined with sufficient flexibility to allow the system to be managed.[66]

There had been concern in official circles that a return to the Gold Standard would be inhibited by a shortage of gold. Prices were much higher than before the war, and thus if there was a general return to the old parities there might be insufficient gold. The Gold Exchange Standard used before the war in various countries, notably India, was receiving attention from those concerned about the adequacy of gold supplies. Hawtrey picked upon the idea that the Gold Exchange Standard could be widely introduced to economise on the use of gold for monetary purposes. Since countries would hold foreign exchange, much presumably in sterling balances as a substitute for gold, there was a special advantage for Britain: the demand for the pound would be increased at the same time the demand for gold lessened.

Hawtrey felt it was vital to the survival of the Gold Standard system in the post-war world that there be some mechanism to prevent fluctuations in the demand for gold for monetary purposes.[67] He suggested there should be international cooperation concerning the relationship between gold reserves and the structure of credit in various countries, so that the purchasing power of gold would be stabilised. To aid in this task he proposed the use of an index number of world prices.[68] His intention was to introduce enough flexibility to prevent the world economy from being upset by monetary disturbances relating to the demand and supply of gold. However, he sought to combine this scheme with the traditional legislative limit on the note issue to prevent inflationary excesses.

These suggestions of Hawtrey played an important role at Genoa.[69] He prepared the draft resolutions which the Treasury presented at the preliminary meeting of experts in London. The proposals concerning stabilisation were dropped initially but reintroduced[70] so that the currency resolutions passed by the conference followed Hawtrey's draft.[71]

There was supposed to be a follow-up meeting of central bankers after Genoa, but it was never held.[72] Montagu Norman told the Macmillan Committee that other central banks were unwilling to cooperate and would not come to such a conference. It is likely this negative result was due to Benjamin Strong, the Governor of the Federal Reserve System of New York. He was dubious of the danger of a shortage of gold, and much preferred informal discussion to well-publicised conferences.[73] Thus the idea that central bank cooperation could stabilise the world economy by preventing gold from causing trouble passed from the scene although the Genoa resolutions on currency were famous long afterwards.[74]

After Genoa it was respectable for countries to return to gold at parities which devalued their currencies with respect to pre-war values. But as the centre of the international system, Britain was another story. Hawtrey accepted in principle that the old parity was not an automatic choice but found the practical arguments in favour of its return convincing. He felt it was desirable to have a parity which was not only fixed but was expected to remain so.[75] The chief advantage of the old parity was that it commanded confidence in a way that no other could for it had existed for two centuries. Besides if a legal standard could be altered once, it could be changed again.

Despite his opinion that the old parity was the correct choice, Hawtrey was unwilling to sacrifice the well-being of the domestic economy. He was concerned about the high Bank Rate maintained in preparation for the return to gold. It was his contention that high short-term interest rates interrupted the progress of the world economy for the London money market had considerable impact on world trade, while the British economy was correspondingly affected.

Hawtrey was instrumental in a fanciful alternative policy, which he hoped would reconcile the external objective with domestic conditions and allow the Bank Rate to come down. He favoured a large export of gold to the United States,[76] which he thought would stimulate the US economy sufficiently to allow Britain to return easily to the old parity without further deflation. Hawtrey believed, circa 1923, that the Federal Reserve Board would not persist in the sterilisation of gold. However, in reality a definite decision had been made to prevent such gold from causing inflation. Hawtrey was so informed by Benjamin Strong during a face to face encounter in London.[77] Thus a second policy initiative of Hawtrey was blocked by Strong's opposition.

Hawtrey considered that it was a disastrous mistake to maintain Bank Rate at 5 per cent after the return to the Gold Standard for he thought this a very high rate at a time of considerable unemployment. He preferred lower interest rates and would have let gold be exported to satisfy the demand. If necessary he would have suspended the legislative limit on the fiduciary issue, or had the pound go to a discount rather than embark on further credit restriction.[78] In the discussions which led to the Currency and Bank Notes Act of 1928 Hawtrey followed through on this argument by advising that Britain cease the legal regulation of gold reserves. In his view a gold reserve law was irrational, for it immobilised without purpose part of the gold stock. He felt the only necessity was to legislate the requirement of conversion into gold. This would free the entire stock of gold to defend the pound.[79]

In 1929 Hawtrey had more success with another suggestion based on his theoretical view of the financial markets. He wanted to raise a large long-term government loan, with the proceeds used to reduce floating debt. Such a procedure was desirable from the point of view of orthodox Treasury thinking. It was also favoured by the Bank of England as a help in regaining control over the money markets. From his monetary theory, Hawtrey thought the policy would support the pound and stimulate the domestic economy. The long-term loan diverted resources from external investment and thus improved the Balance of Payments. His theory, unlike that of Keynes, did not attribute much deflationary influence to whatever increase in long-term rates might occur. As Treasury bills were reduced, bank lending would be stimulated, as holdings of commercial bills and advances were increased as a substitute. When banks have idle money, they either induce customers to borrow and spend, or they buy long-term securities which leads the investment market to accept more new issues. Hopkins's testimony before the Macmillan Committee indicated that Hawtrey's analysis provided the rationale for the Conversion Loans of 1929 and 1930.[80]

When the Depression broke over the world Hawtrey laid the blame on a conjunction of deflationary factors. Throughout the twenties he had been critical of the Bank of England which kept the

Bank Rate high in an effort to protect the pound. In 1928 the Federal Reserve System initiated a policy of credit restriction which reinforced the effect of high interest rates in the London market, and further weakened the world economy. Then France began to import large amounts of gold. Hawtrey considered the French absorption of gold was one of the most important causes of the depression for it contributed to restrictive monetary policy in other countries.[81]

Hawtrey's explanation of the gold imports highlighted the need for currency in France. In this episode he perceived the situation which the Genoa Conference attempted to avoid – a demand for gold for monetary purposes which destabilised the international system.[82] He considered that after France returned to the Gold Standard, its money supply was insufficient for the requirements of the country.[83] The French government withdrew funds from circulation, and created a vacuum in the stock of currency, by paying off its advances from the Bank of France. As a result the commercial banking system needed to replenish their reserves, and did so by selling gold and foreign exchange to the Bank of France.[84]

This account of the reasons behind the absorption of gold drew attention to the institutional characteristics of the French monetary system. The Bank of France could not use open market operations to satisfy the need for additional cash for it was forbidden by legislative statute from purchasing securities in the open market.[85] In addition, there was a limited supply of bills eligible for discount at the Bank of France. Thus, an expansion of the note issue could only be effected by the banking system drawing on its holdings of foreign exchange. The official British view of these gold flows was strongly influenced by Hawtrey's position, which conveniently placed the blame on the rigidity of foreign institutions.[86]

After the onslaught of the Depression Hawtrey felt the transition to lower levels for Bank Rate was too slow on both sides of the Atlantic. He agitated in support of lower rates for he considered the policy of the Bank of England was too cautious. It was his view that this delay allowed deflation to get such a powerful hold over the world economy that when low discount rates were established by the spring of 1930 they were ineffective. In his terminology a credit deadlock had occurred so that cheap money could not bring recovery. He thought however that a lavish policy of open market purchases might have been sufficient, but such measures were not tried. Thus the depression continued to gather momentum.

After Britain suspended the Gold Standard in 1931 the Bank Rate was raised again. Hawtrey was optimistic about the devaluation, for he considered it could help the world economy break the credit deadlock which made monetary policy impotent. However, he thought the return of higher interest rates short-circuited the beneficial effects of the depreciation of the pound.

In the years that followed Hawtrey turned more and more to currency depreciation as the solution to the difficulties of the world economy. He saw this as a device for starting a rise in prices and a revival. Once this corner had been turned and recovery began, the process would gather momentum on its own as the expansion of demand spread. He realised that the effects of devaluation would be nugatory if tried by all countries at the same time but did not consider this a serious problem. There was bound to be some interval between the times at which the measure was taken in different countries. Thus, revival could start in the first country to devalue and gain momentum before the off-setting effects of subsequent devaluations appeared. He drew the analogy that Britain, France and the US were like three people trapped in a pit who could not all climb out at once. However, anyone could escape using the shoulders of the other two, and the first out would help the next.[87]

(iii) After Bretton Woods

Hawtrey was sharply critical of Bretton Woods and the International Monetary Fund as the basis for a permanent system. He was concerned about the lack of commitment to stabilisation of the monetary unit. Without a safeguard of this type there was the danger that the real value of the world's currencies would alter in concert. Since the US gold stock was immense the dollar could change in real value, and take gold along. Thus, although the dollar was the equivalent of gold, it was potentially an unstable unit. Under this system the US could export inflation protected by its vast gold reserves. This echoed Hawtrey's warning in 1919, that under the Gold Exchange Standard, the danger was an indefinite expansion of money on a fixed base of gold.[88]

He considered that under fixed exchange rates, economic factors were brought into play to adjust the wage level to the exchange rate. Thus wages in any country under the Bretton Woods system would depend on US monetary policy. He attacked the thinking which linked the pound to the dollar and then attempted by an apparatus of controls to prevent the pound from sinking with the dollar to lower real values. He argued that successive British Governments failed to appreciate that an exchange rate decision was in fact an incomes policy, for costs and incomes in the UK must adjust to the level chosen.[89]

Furthermore, Hawtrey was concerned that a serious mistake had been made in Britain's choice of an exchange rate. After a decade at $4.03 with the help of exchange control, the pound was fixed in 1949 at $2.80, a value far-removed from the famous $4.86 level of the pre-1931 Gold Standard. Hawtrey argued against this decision, for his purchasing-power calculations indicated that the pound was under-valued.[90] He considered excess demand from abroad was the primary cause of the inflation after 1949, while increases in wages and prices were a secondary phenomenon, occurring as a consequence of the undervaluation.

The primary evidence for the undervaluation of the pound Hawtrey took to be the intense demand for labour. Despite persistent increases in wages, there were indications of excess demand: unemployment was abnormally low,[91] and considerable overtime was worked. Governments warned repeatedly that rising wages would price British manufacturers out of the export markets, yet industry continued to expand. He thought the persistent mistake had been to misread the adverse balance of payments as due to excess costs, when in reality it was the result of an excess demand inflation. Monetary policy, not devaluation, was the appropriate response.

In the early 1960s Hawtrey stressed that a devaluation of the dollar was required for it was over-valued not just in relation to the pound but especially with respect to the mark and the yen.[92] The British devaluation to $2.40 in 1967 was, he thought, a further blunder. Ultimately, he became an advocate of flexible exchange rates to free Britain from world inflation.[93]

It is a little inappropriate to discuss controversial matters of recent economic policy in a volume concerned with the history of thought but this is unavoidable given the longevity of Hawtrey's career. It is impossible at this juncture to be definitive so that some future economic historian will have the final word on this aspect of Hawtrey's writing. Even so some assessment seems in order.

At the time Hawtrey's view on the 1949 devaluation was very

much contrary to prevailing opinion. Similarly the proposition that the UK was suffering from over-employment during the post-war period had few supporters. Yet with the passing years interpretations of the period and the mechanisms at work have moved much closer to Hawtrey's analysis (with the exception of the attention he paid to Bank Rate and the holders of stocks).

There is now a growing number who agree that an under-valued pound was part of the problem.[94] The possibility of over-employment in Britain during that period has since gained respectability as well.[95] Finally a monetary approach to the Balance of Payments is much more fashionable now than then. In summary it would be hard to deny that in this final stage of his career Hawtrey remained a source of wisdom which, like the pound, may have been under-valued.

Conclusion

Every economist requires what Schumpeter called an 'ideology': a vision of the world which he believes to be true.[96] The social sciences cannot avoid ambiguity, for it is impossible to prove or refute most hypotheses. In a world where it is impossible to be certain of the truth of one's convictions, a jump into faith becomes necessary. Hawtrey was very aware of this problem: indeed his Presidential address before the Royal Economic Society was entitled 'The Need for Faith'.[97] He was himself an ideologue for he developed his fundamental ideas at the beginning of his career and his thinking did not deviate from this initial vision.[98] His faith in the correctness of these views was never shaken. He retained an unwavering belief in the importance of short-term interest rates and the critical role of those who hold stocks. He felt strongly that economists should be quick to revise their thinking in the light of criticism,[99] but simply defended his ideas against all comers and never found opposing positions convincing.

This fact made him appear to be an extremist. He was apt to be regarded as someone who took an outlying position at the beginning and refused to modify his thinking. This opinion about Hawtrey does not do him justice for he made strenuous efforts to subject the writings of his contemporaries to fair and constructive criticism. One can endorse the fashion in which Hawtrey conducted his intellectual inquiries even if one cannot accept the content of some of his doctrines.

The orientation of Hawtrey's economics led in fruitful directions for he studied the functioning of the economy in the short run. His theory pointed to a world where quantities rather than prices adjust, and markets equilibrate through inventory adjustment. This was a major step forward. He made important innovations for savings linked to output, and models which identify quasi-equilibrium positions occur first in his work. Yet his economics caused him to err as well. Hawtrey did not realise that the desire to acquire fixed investment was a crucial factor in the behaviour of the economy. He failed to appreciate that public works were an important means of expanding the flow of spending. Short-term interest rates were not as critical a factor, nor the inventory decisions of dealers as significant, as he made them out to be.

Hawtrey's work combined new elements with an endorsement of traditional perceptions about economics. This style caused him to be under-appreciated. Those who explore and innovate in a neighbourhood of familiar paths appear more dated; the refinement of accepted doctrines is less exciting than the ideas of those who break new ground in a radical direction. Now the wheel has turned full circle and economics has rediscovered pre-Keynesian ideas. Money has been returned to a position of prominence in open- and closed-economy macrotheory. Savings has again begun to be seen as a virtue. An extensive literature about Crowding-Out has appeared, and concern with the canons of sound government finance has emerged. Ideas which Hawtrey supported throughout his career have regained popularity.

NOTES

1. R. D. C. Black, 'Ralph George Hawtrey, 1879–1975', *Proceedings of the British Academy*, LXIII (1977) 363–97, at p. 364.
2. He had in addition serious interests in mathematics and philosophy. In 1908 he corresponded with Bertrand Russell about the proofs of various theorems during the writing of *Principia Mathematica*. In the 1960s he had two manuscripts on ethics rejected by major publishers as lacking, despite their competence, the sustained originality to justify publication in such a specialised field.
3. Black, 'Hawtrey', p. 366.
4. He retired on his 65th birthday in 1944 but was re-employed on special duties until 1947. His only period outside the Treasury was the 1928–9 academic year which he spent as a visiting professor at Harvard University.

5. R. F. Harrod, *The Life of John Maynard Keynes* (London: Macmillan, 1963) pp. 120–1.
6. In addition he prepared innumerable papers on a great variety of economic subjects which provide a record of his years in the Treasury.
7. These were given largely by G. P. Moriarty, Director of Studies for the Examinations, although he did attend some lectures by Sir John Clapham. Marshall, however, played no part in his education.
8. A. W. Coats, 'Political Economy and The Tariff Reform Campaign of 1903', *Journal of Law and Economics*, XI (1968) 181–229, at p. 181.
9. F. J. Spreng, 'Conversations with Sir Ralph Hawtrey', mimeo 1976 (see note 33 below) pp. 1–6.
10. See Hawtrey's own account of the events of 1904–8: R. G. Hawtrey, *A Century of Bank Rate* (London: Longmans, 1938) [hereafter cited as *CBR*], pp. 115–18.
11. Lord Bradbury, then Principal Clerk of the Finance Division and later Permanent Secretary, took a particular interest in Hawtrey and became his mentor.
12. In his memoirs Sir Frederick Leith-Ross recalled that the first book he encountered when he joined the Treasury in 1909 was entitled *Conversion and Redemption*. He assumed it was of religious significance (and apparently it had been sold as such by some booksellers) but in reality it dealt with Gladstone's successful conversion of 3 per cent consols. F. Leith-Ross, *Money Talks: Fifty Years of International Finance* (London: Hutchinson, 1968) p. 22.
13. The Bank Rate was the rate of discount at which the Bank of England bought highest-quality commercial bills from the discount market. However, the practice developed of linking the rate on Bank loans (and overdrafts) to the Bank Rate, but 0.5 or 1 per cent higher.
14. Hawtrey, *CBR*, Preface.
    Antonius Pius, the adopted son of Hadrian, was Emperor of Rome from AD 138 to 161. His regime was known for its careful financial management. He is also remembered for the Antonine Wall across southern Scotland.
15. Historically, there were precedents for this opinion and Hawtrey attempted to present his ideas as the continuation of earlier views. His purpose in *CBR* was to discuss the origins of Bank Rate tradition. He demonstrated that the early protagonists looked to Bank Rate to exercise its effect mainly by modifying domestic activity. To what extent they can be said to have endorsed his transmission mechanism with its emphasis on changes in the desired holdings of inventories is a debatable point. Cramp has provided a careful and critical examination of Hawtrey's analysis of the early years of Bank Rate policy. He found confirmation for the thesis that Bank Rate increases checked the accumulation of stocks of commodities. However, he felt this was not due to Hawtrey's explanation (that the merchants lower their demand for credit), but because merchants expected, based on previous experience, that the supply of credit was likely to be curtailed, i.e. that there was a liquidity rather than an incentive effect to changes in Bank Rate. See A. B. Cramp, *Opinion on Bank Rate, 1822–60* (London: Bell, 1962) pp. 98–9.

16. Certainly merchants are the class of trader which is most sensitive to credit conditions. For the producer, the amount of working capital is rather more closely geared to the level of output.
17. Hawtrey did not stress the effect of interest rates on international flows of capital. He felt the advantage of such flows was limited. Once the funds ceased moving, they became a source of weakness for they were liable to be withdrawn at times of crisis.
18. D. E. Moggridge and S. Howson, 'Keynes on Monetary Policy, 1910–1946', *Oxford Economic Papers*, XXVI (1974) 226–47, at p. 232.
19. J. A. Schumpeter, 'John Maynard Keynes 1883–1946', *American Economic Review* [hereafter cited as *AER*], XXXVI (1946) 495–518, at p. 509.
20. Keynes's discussion of the workings of Bank Rate policy can be found in *Treatise on Money* (London: Macmillan, 1930) ch. 13.
21. J. R. Hicks, 'Mr. Hawtrey on Bank Rate and the Long-Term Rate of Interest', *Manchester School*, X (1939) 21–37, at p. 21.
22. On the basis of Hawtrey's evidence in *CBR*, Hicks found Keynes's hypothesis that monetary policy had operated through long-term interest rates 'very hard to believe', ibid., p. 23
23. There were at least four such cycles dated (peak to peak) as 1825–37, 1837–47, 1847–57, 1857–67. This was the pattern Schumpeter called the 'ten-year Juglar cycle'.
24. G. Haberler's classic summary *Prosperity and Depression* (Geneva: League of Nations, 1937) still provides the best introduction to this body of knowledge.
25. Ibid., pp. 14–28.
26. E. Eshag, *From Marshall to Keynes: An Essay on the Monetary Theory of the Cambridge School* (Oxford: Blackwell, 1963) [hereafter cited as Eshag], p. 97.
27. R. G. Hawtrey, *The Art of Central Banking* (London: Longmans, 1932) [hereafter cited as *ACB*], p. 161.
28. Keynes, by contrast, came to see the source of instability as the fundamental unknowability of the future. This point was made in R. V. Brown, 'Aspects of Hawtrey's Monetary Thought', mimeo 1978, p. 18.
29. It occurred, for example, in the period when Hawtrey was moving toward economics. During the expansion of 1905 there was a significant drain of gold from the Bank into circulation, which to some extent continued until the war.
30. Despite his optimism about stabilisation policy, Hawtrey was not oblivious to the difficulties which might be involved in remedying disturbances through Bank Rate policy. Once a dealer had been led by low short-term rates to hold stocks at a level which provided maximum convenience, nothing further could be done. Hawtrey used the term 'credit deadlock' for this situation where further reductions in interest rates accomplished nothing. However, he considered this possibility a rare occurrence which only arose after 1930. There were also limits to Bank Rate policy in inflationary situations, for, once stocks were reduced to the lowest possible level, the effect of the credit measures was exhausted. He drew the lesson that it was important for policy to be quick and decisive to stop disturbances from developing the

momentum to move into these difficult zones. However, even in these situations when Bank Rate policy was impotent, Hawtrey retained faith in the power of open-market operations.

31. J. R. Hicks, 'Automatists, Hawtreyans and Keynesians', *Journal of Money, Credit and Banking,* I (1969) 307–17, at pp. 307–8.

32. Schumpeter wrote that: 'Throughout the twenties, Hawtrey's theory enjoyed a considerable vogue. In the United States, especially, it was the outstanding rationalization of the uncritical belief in the unlimited efficacy of the open-market operations of the Federal Reserve System that prevailed then.' *History of Economic Analysis* (London: Allen & Unwin, 1954) p. 1121.

33. Contemporary comment on his economics ceased at the end of the 1930s with the writings of Hicks (see note 21 above), Kaldor and Saulnier. See N. Kaldor, 'Mr. Hawtrey on Short and Long Term Investment', *Economica*, n.s., V (1938) 461–7; R. J. Saulnier, *Contemporary Monetary Theory* (New York: Columbia University Press, 1938). However, Hawtrey has recently been subject to re-examination. See Black (see note 1); Brown (see note 28); E. G. Davis, 'The Correspondence between R. G. Hawtrey and J. M. Keynes on the *Treatise*: The Genesis of Output Adjustment Models', mimeo 1978; S. Howson, 'Monetary Theory and Policy in the 20th Century: The Career of R. G. Hawtrey', *Proceedings of the Greater International Economic History Congress* (Edinburgh: Edinburgh University Press, 1977); and F. J. Spreng 'The Macroeconomics of Sir Ralph Hawtrey: A Mirror Image of British Economic Doctrine', Ph.D. thesis, University of Pittsburgh (1976).

34. His analysis was put in nominal terms so that he was an exponent of the money-balance as opposed to the real-balance version; see Eshag, p. 21.

35. Hawtrey, *Currency and Credit* (London: Longmans, 1919, 1950) [hereafter cited as *C&C*], pp. 34–5.

36. Ibid., p. 37.

37. Hawtrey recognised that if there were changes in the cash reserves of the banking system, it was up to the banks to decide whether they would alter their other assets and liabilities, so that changes in the unspent margin depended on the actions of the banks in creating more or less credit.

38. Schumpeter, *History*, p. 1109.

39. *C&C*, p. 41.

40. Eshag, p. 41.

41. He realised that a net release or absorption of cash for the community as a whole could only be effected by the banking system. The absorption of cash was different from hoarding for it included the repayment of bank advances, as well as the accumulation of money balances.

42. *CBR*, p. 38.

43. Consumers' outlay did not include the expenditures of traders for this spending arose, not out of income, but out of the gross receipts of the business.

44. See *The Collected Writings of John Maynard Keynes*, vol. XIV (London:

Macmillan for the Royal Economic Society, 1973) [hereafter cited as *CW*], p. 27.

45. His terminology did not clearly distinguish spending on goods from that on securities for each was part of 'consumer's outlay'. Ultimately he admitted this mistake: 'In the previous editions I took for granted too readily that money saved would be invested and that money invested would be spent . . . [although] I devoted some discussion to the causes affecting the accumulation of idle money', *C&C*, p. vi. Here Hawtrey used the word 'invest' to mean the purchase of securities.

46. This concept was part of his analysis from 1913 on. See his *Good and Bad Trade* (London: Constable, 1913) [hereafter cited as *G&BT*], p. 208.

47. In normal times Hawtrey considered that the investment market would succeed in placing into capital outlay all the resources it received. However, the realities of the 1930s caused him to contribute to capital theory the concepts of capital widening and deepening. The former meant the extension of existing enterprises without a change in the ratio of capital to output and was based on the prospect of additional demand. Capital deepening involved the substitution of capital for labour, and was stimulated by reductions in the long-term rate of interest. Hawtrey relied on the deepening process to adjust capital outlay to savings, though he recognised that during a severe depression difficulties could arise. He used the term 'glut of capital' to describe the situation when the shrinkage of demand had so reduced capital widening that the deepening process was unable to employ the remaining saving, which at such times was augmented by funds from the liquidation of working capital.

48. Hawtrey's picture of the market for long-term investment contributed to his optimism about the efficacy of open-market operations. When banks found it difficult to employ excess reserves in the normal channel of short-term lending, they commonly resorted to the purchase of securities to add an earning asset to their portfolio.

The resources of the investment market would be augmented and dealers, finding their stock of securities drawn down, would encourage new issues. Indirectly, the idle reserves of the banks would be added to the spending stream. Hawtrey recognised that the investment market might simply pay off its advances to the banking system so the banks would again be left with excess reserves, but underestimated this difficulty.

49. This is mentioned in his first book *G&BT*, pp. 205–6. See also *C&C* (1919 edn.) p. 142.

50. *ACB*, p. 361.

51. *CW*, XIII, pp. 152–3.

52. Hawtrey considered an increase in investment of £5 million. He postulated when income increased, three-fifths would be spent on consumption and two-fifths on savings. The dynamic process would continue until savings and investment balanced again at an output which was £12.5 million higher. The same argument applied in reverse to a deflationary disturbance.

53. In Hawtrey's papers there are two handwritten drafts (HTRY 11/4) and a final version of the working paper (HTRY 11/3). In the Public Records Office there is an identical typed version dated January 1931 (PRO T208/153). Thanks are due to the Controller of Her Majesty's Stationery Office and the Archivist of Churchill College, Cambridge, for permission to use these sources.

54. Hawtrey presented a more elaborate version in *ACB*, pp. 350–8.

55. A start has been made in this direction – see Davis 'Correspondence' (note 33 above).

56. In a letter dated 16 February 1931, Keynes wrote to Hawtrey that he 'felt enormously honoured by the final version of your *opus* on me and the trouble you had taken. It is very seldom indeed that an author can expect to get as a criticism anything so tremendously useful to himself (HTRY 11/3). Both Moggridge and Patinkin minimised Hawtrey's role in their accounts: D. E. Moggridge, 'From the Treatise to the General Theory: An Exercise in Chronology', *History of Political Economy*, V (1973) 72–88, esp. p. 75; D. Patinkin, *Keynes' Monetary Thought: A Study of Its Development* (Durham, NC: Duke University Press, 1976) esp. pp. 54, 57, 65. Recently, each gave Hawtrey slightly more prominence. See D. Patinkin and J. C. Leith, *Keynes, Cambridge and 'The General Theory'* (Toronto: Toronto University Press, 1978) pp. 6, 66.

57. Patinkin, *Keynes' Monetary Thought*, p. 65.

58. He addressed this topic many times. Extended treatments can be found in 'Public Expenditure and the Demand for Labour', *Economica*, V (1925) 38–48; 'Public Expenditure and Trade Depression', *Journal of the Royal Statistical Society* [hereafter cited as *JRSS*], XCVI (1933) 438–77.

59. *Economica*, V (1925) pp. 38–42.

60. By contrast, Keynes's explanation of idle balances ultimately involved liquidity preference so that an increase in interest rates stimulated speculators to add to their portfolio of bonds.

61. Hawtrey, *Trade and Credit* (London: Longmans, 1928) [hereafter cited as *T&C*], p. 112.

62. *JRSS*, XCVI (1933) 452; *T&C*, p. 138.

63. S. Howson and D. Winch, *The Economic Advisory Council 1930–1939* (Cambridge: Cambridge University Press, 1977) p. 27.

64. Ibid., pp. 130, 150, 152.

65. This speech was subsequently published; see R. G. Hawtrey, 'The Gold Standard', *Economic Journal* [hereafter cited as *EJ*], XXIX (1919) 428–42.

66. Keynes favoured a widening of the gold points with a 'crawling peg' approach to parity adjustment – *Tract on Monetary Reform* (London: Macmillan, 1923) pp. 186–91.

67. In his opinion there were historic precedents for a depression caused by the competition for metallic reserves – he cited the depression from 1873–96 during the spread of the Gold Standard. See 'The Genoa Resolutions on Currency', *EJ*, XXXII (1922) 290–304, at p. 293.

68. *EJ*, XXIX (1919) 440. The notion that an inconvertible currency could be

regulated by an index number of prices can be found in earlier writers – see *ACB*, p. 191. In 1911 Fisher made an explicit proposal to link such a 'tabular standard' with the Gold Exchange Standard. See I. Fisher, *The Purchasing Power of Money* (New York: Macmillan, 1911) pp. 332–46. This book is referenced in *G&BT*.

69. Hawtrey had extended discussions with Montagu Norman during the preparations for Genoa. See H. Clay, *Lord Norman* (London: Macmillan, 1957) pp. 137–8; and R. S. Sayers, *The Bank of England, 1891–1944*, vol. I (Cambridge: Cambridge University Press, 1976) p. 156.

70. Spreng, 'Conversations', pp. 2–7.

71. In particular Resolution 11(7) stated that 'credit will be regulated, not only with a view to maintaining the currencies at par with one another, but also with a view to preventing undue fluctuations in the purchasing power of gold'. Thus stabilisation was legitimised as an official objective for the first time. The Brussels Conference in 1920 had specifically rejected a policy of stabilising the value of gold; see Clay, *Lord Norman*, p. 136.

72. There was a project for reviving the Genoa Conference plan before the World Economic Conference of 1933 but it died in committee. See R. G. Hawtrey, 'Light on Montagu Norman's Policy', *Bankers' Magazine*, CLXXXIII (1957) 505–9, at p. 509.

73. The US had not been represented at Genoa for the Conference was to discuss the reconstruction of the economy of Europe. See Hawtrey's analysis of the failure of the Genoa Conference in ibid., p. 508.

74. The establishment of the Bank for International Settlements in 1929, and the widespread adoption of the Gold Exchange Standard can be seen as the legacy of Genoa.

75. R. G. Hawtrey, 'The Return to Gold in 1925', *Bankers' Magazine*, CCVIII (1969) 61–7, at p. 65.

76. See Sayers, *Bank of England*, vol. I, pp. 127, 133; and Howson, 'Monetary Theory' (note 33 above) p. 508. Keynes also favoured gold exports to the US. See his *The Economic Consequences of Mr. Churchill* (London: Hogarth Press, 1925) pp. 27–8.

77. Hawtrey, 'Return to Gold', p. 66.

78. See D. E. Moggridge, *British Monetary Policy 1924–1932: The Norman Conquest of $4.86* (Cambridge: Cambridge University Press, 1972) [hereafter cited as *BMP*], p. 73.

79. Sayers deemed this approach 'brilliant but untimely' but it was written off as impractical and dangerous at the time. See *Bank of England*, vol. I, p. 289.

80. Howson, 'Monetary Theory', p. 509; and ibid., *Domestic Monetary Management in Britain 1919–38* (Cambridge: Cambridge University Press, 1975) pp. 40–1.

81. *ACB*, p. 38.

82. Hawtrey, *Bankers' Magazine*, CCVIII (1969) p. 508.

83. *ACB*, pp. 14–18.

84. For Hawtrey's views of the flows of funds involved, see *ACB*. Other observers reached similar conclusions. See W. H. Wynne, 'The French

Franc, June, 1928–February, 1937', *Journal of Political Economy*, XLV (1937) 484–516, at p. 490.

85. At the time the French believed that it was contrary to sound banking principles to hold Government securities against the note issue. Open-market operations were regarded as an Anglo-Saxon vice – indeed there was no French term for the policy.

86. *BMP*, p. 240.

87. 'Devaluation in the United States', HTRY 11/7.

88. Hawtrey, *EJ* (1919) p. 437.

89. R. G. Hawtrey, *Incomes and Money* (London: Longmans, 1967) p. 27.

90. Hawtrey, letter to the editor, *The Economist*, 23 August 1947; letter to the editor, *Financial Times*, 13 January 1958; and *An Incomes Policy*, Woolwich Economic Papers, IV (1965) p. 12.

91. In 1944 Beveridge concluded that the irreducible minimum for unemployment in England was 3 per cent, yet from 1948 to 1966 unemployment averaged only 2 per cent. Hawtrey used this as conclusive evidence that Britain was suffering from over-employment. See *Incomes and Money*, p. 26.

92. Hawtrey, *Incomes Policy*, p. 17.

93. Hawtrey, letter to the editor, *The Times*, 16 November 1970.

94. A. R. Conan, *The Problem of Sterling* (London: Macmillan, 1966) pp. 41–51. See also R. J. Ball and T. Burns, 'The Inflationary Mechanism in the UK Economy', *AER*, LXVI (1976) 467–84 (at p. 475), who described the 1949 devaluation as excessive. The undervaluation of the pound plays a significant role in their discussion.

95. Recently T. W. Hutchison, in *Keynes v. the 'Keynesians'* (London: IEA, 1977) pp. 11–15, 27, 62–3, presented compelling evidence to the effect that Keynes would have considered the British economy over-employed in the post-war period. D. Laidler in 'Inflation in Britain: A Monetarist Perspective', *AER*, LXVI (1976) 485–500, has expressed the view that the basic error was to neglect the control of the money supply while pursuing an unrealistically low unemployment target (p. 485).

96. J. A. Schumpeter, 'Science and Ideology', *AER*, XXXIX (1949) 345–82, at p. 349.

97. R. G. Hawtrey, 'The Need for Faith', *EJ*, LVI (1946) 351–65.

98. Hawtrey struck this note in the final lines of the published correspondence with Keynes after the *General Theory*:

> I have adhered consistently to my fundamental ideas since 1913, and in so far as they have developed and grown the process has been continuous since then. There has not been a departure followed by a relapse. I do not think this conservatism is a merit: indeed I should rather like to go in for something novel and extravagant if I could be convinced of it. *CW*, XIV, p. 55.

99. *EJ*, LVI (1946) p. 351.

8 F. A. Hayek, 1899–

G. L. S. SHACKLE

Introduction – biographia

Aristocratic in temper and origins; physically, morally and intellectually fearless; clear and incisive in thought; the embodied principle itself of following the logic where it leads; the soul of scholarly generosity; Friedrich August Hayek is one of the outstanding sculptors of this age's thought. He was born on the 8 May 1899 into a family academically distinguished on both sides. At the University of Vienna he gained two doctorates, becoming Dr. jur. in 1921 and Dr. rer. pol. in 1923. From 1927 till 1931 he was Director of the Austrian Institute for Economic Research. In 1931 as visiting lecturer at the London School of Economics he gave the lectures which were published in that year as *Prices and Production*[1] and which gained for him, in those days of baffled debate about the causes of the great depression which had struck the industrialised world like a plague, his first sensational prominence. In that year he was appointed Tooke Professor of Economic Science and Statistics in the University of London. He held this Chair until, in 1950, he moved to Chicago. In 1962 he was appointed Professor of Economic Policy at the University of Freiburg, and in 1974 he was made honorary professor at the University of Salzburg. In 1944 he had been given an honorary Doctorate of Science by the University of London, and in that year also he was elected a Fellow of the British Academy. In 1974 he was awarded the Nobel Prize in Economic Science.

At a meeting in 1976 with a Spanish editor of penetrating and sympathetic insight, Hayek answered a question by quoting a fragment from the poet Archilochus, which is well-known through its earlier use by Sir Isaiah Berlin: 'the fox knows many things, but the hedgehog knows one big thing'. Hayek was then referring to his half-century of effort to explain to scholars, politicians and people the nature and detailed working of the disastrous, multifarious and recently almost universal monetary debasement of our times. This message was, he told us, the 'one big thing' to which his scholarly life had been devoted. I think it may be permissible to elaborate that statement in two respects. In the first place, though the theme of monetary profligacy and of the imperative need to eschew it is an essential unity, it is also a many-stranded skein of utmost subtlety and complexity. Secondly, there is unquestionably another 'big thing' which Hayek in later decades has pursued with a burning zeal, the idea of freedom. And I think even a third quarry has led his tireless tracking of ideas, of truth itself. This third trail is the question of the method by which human affairs can be effectively analysed and understood.

Our age lives in the glare of natural science, and the supposed methods of natural science have soaked into the fibre of our thought as economists. Yet if we looked at some of the still-central concerns and professions of mankind, we should see the law, based on classification and precedent; and medicine, with its recognition of the deep mysteries of the human psychosomatic personality, *The Self and Its Brain*.[2] Economists would do well to ponder the diversity of Hayek's intellectual horizons. The participant in economic life is a human being. The study of human nature and institutions is not alien to the work of the economist, but fundamental to it. To attempt, however, in the space of some twelve thousand words, to give insight into all of Hayek's interests is impossible. I have confined this chapter to a study of two books and a few articles which seem to me to present the core of his more strictly economic thought. The mountain of his work on *The Constitution of Liberty*[3] and *Law, Legislation and Liberty*[4] I must leave for others to scale elsewhere. The sections of this chapter are labelled with the titles of those books and articles.

Prices and production

Hayek's fame sprang at first from a highly individual account of the nature of the trade cycle. This conception was first presented in English in 1931 in lectures delivered at the London School of Economics and printed as *Prices and Production*.[5] A new version, considerably revised from the former, appeared as a long essay in the volume called *Profits, Interest and Investment*[6] in 1939. *Prices and Production* fascinated many minds, not only at LSE, partly, I believe, because of its arcane and obscure suggestion of a radical telescoping together of ideas into some new incisive simplicity. Two of the ideas that were thus treated as one, however, were those that we should now call the rate of profit and the rate of interest, and this conflation was recognised by Hayek in *Profits, Interest and Investment* to have been a mistaken policy. It sprang very naturally from Böhm-Bawerk's view of the nature of interest as that variable (let us define it in the abstract as the proportion of itself by which a capital sum increases per unit of time) which brings to equality the irksomeness of marginal consumptions foregone and the pleasure of gains hoped for from marginal augmentations of equipment financed by those savings. Wicksell in his *Geldzins und Güterpreise*[7] of 1898, and in his *Lectures on Political Economy*[8] published in English in 1934, had based a theory of the phenomenon of a progressive general rise of prices on the relation of the rate of interest charged by the banking system on loans of money, to the rate of profit which could be earned by the use of this money in industry and commerce. In *Prices and Production* Hayek used the term 'rate of interest' as a substitute for 'rate of profit'. One of his chief concerns in *Profits, Interest and Investment* was to dissolve this confusion. This was very necessary, for Hayek's argument ascribes the trade cycle as a whole, partly on Wicksellian lines, to the natural action of the banking system.

The theme itself to be found in these two books is inherently elusive, involving a complex evolution of outputs, prices and profit-rates through subtly merging phases. Hayek's statement of it has the vitality and excitement of a work of art seen almost in process of composition. In another mood we might say that successive attacks from various directions (thoughts of Hayek's own, the fruit of an implacable self-criticism) are despatched or fended off by a lithe play of resource. To make such a work intelligible without doing violence to its intricacy and subtlety is a daunting task. I shall first set out in brief the central strand of Hayek's theme, distinguishing between the version of *Prices and Production* and that of *Profits, Interest and Investment*.

The services of men and nature applied in production yield a consumable result only after a lapse of time. The longer the time that can be allowed, over the variously dated applications of human and natural forces as a whole, before their consumable product emerges at some one date, the greater this product can be for given amounts of such forces. This is because such forces, applied long enough in advance, can be used for making tools to make further tools, etc., in a sequence which goes far in substituting equipment for men and nature. The building-up of the material means of such a system, as distinct from its continued operation once built, requires a lengthening of the pause between effort and consumption, on the whole, as compared with the continued use of a less complex, subtle or powerful system. If for some reason, in the course of building, this endeavour is interrupted before an output of consumable goods from it begins, the part which has been built will stand to be abandoned while all gatherable efforts of men and nature are concentrated at the near-consumption stages of a shorter system. If those who are working at the 'early' and now-abandoned stages are highly specialised to the work of those stages, they will be disemployed by this retreat. Thus we have the seeds of depression. The question now is, what can be the source of an interruption of the building-up of a new, more time-taking, more labour-and-land economical system of production? If the only source of funds to pay for the services of men and nature engaged in the building process during the time when it is not turning out any consumables which can be sold, is the saving done by people at large out of their incomes, it may be reasonable to suppose that the conditions on which these funds are lent and borrowed will in some degree serve to constrain the time-length of the new system to what the savers are prepared to finance out of their abstention from current consumption. If so, there is nothing which need evidently frustrate the achievement of the more efficient system. But if there is a banking system, extra funds, beyond those savings which correspond to non-consumed income earned in production, may be provided to the entrepreneurs seeking to build the new system. This money will be paid, in wages, rent and profits, to those who are building the new system. They will not save all of it. Some will be added to the monetary demand for consumers' goods, which however are not yet being produced in greater daily or annual quantity than before. Prices of consumers' goods will rise and profits for those business men directly concerned in making consumables will increase. These business men will seek by all means to increase their output quickly, and the only way in which they can do so is by adopting shorter, rather than longer, systems of production, drawing the services of men and nature for this purpose away from those who are seeking to build longer systems. At the furthest extreme from the direct production of consumables, there will thus be firms making equipment for the new longer systems, who will be starved of orders and unable to pay their employees. Thus business depression will set in.

The foregoing passage broadly presents, I believe, the theme of both the two books we are discussing. The differences between those two accounts arise from Hayek's recognition of vulnerable features in *Prices and Production*. Even in the later essay he did not, perhaps, fully come to terms with all of them. His theme appeals essentially to the intimate dependence of elaborate tool-using methods of production on the willingness of people to allow a considerable time to elapse between effort and result. Tools must be made, *then* used. Tools are needed in order to make tools. But there is, I think, a distinction to be made, important in practice though not evidently basic in principle, between the fact that in building up a more elaborate system of equipment-using production, things must be done one after the other, and the fact that when such a system has been established, there will be a difference of date between the rendering of some productive service by men or nature, and the emergence of the identified quanta of consumables to which this service has contributed. For if the postponement of consumption during the building process becomes intolerable, that process can be stopped, and other methods of production reverted to. But when the new system is fully in business, the elimination of its inherent time-lapses would involve its dismantling, that is, its reduction to scrap, in a suicidal vulturine scramble for its flesh. Even in the later essay, Hayek does not seem to keep this distinction always in focus. The necessity and effects of time-lapse in production is one perspective of the use of equipment, that is, of tools in a very general sense, in production. This perspective is the basis of the 'Austrian theory of capital', due chiefly to Eugen von Böhm-Bawerk, whose principal purpose is to explain why the providing of the services of equipment generates and justifies an income, a share in the total product. But the connection between time-lapse and the use of an elaborate division of labour is complex, subtle and elusive to the last degree, and Hayek became aware that his representation of it, or his neglect of its problems, in *Prices and Production* placed the argument of that book at a serious disadvantage. In *Prices and Production* Hayek speaks as though every productive operation and hence every tool used and every person engaged in that operation could be located, in relation to every other operation contributing to the output of a specific kind of consumable at a named date, as either nearer to or further from the final operation from which that consumable directly emerged. Evidently examples of such a 'linear' sequence can easily be thought of. Ploughing the field and rolling it, drilling in the seed, hoeing, reaping, threshing and milling the grain, baking the bread, compose such a process. Even here, however, there are tributary streams of operations: those concerned with the making of implements, the breeding and feeding of horses or the supply of fuel and chemical fertiliser. Hayek envisages such converging lines, but this idea hardly touches the problem. Production in an advanced industrial society needs for its description a Leontief table of input coefficients, where in principle, and in algebraic practice so far as computation allows, every operation or every industry or sector is deemed actually or potentially to contribute means of some kind to every other, both directly and indirectly. Such sectors as transportation, the telephone system and the electric power industry plainly have a hand to some degree in everything that is done by anybody anywhere, even though it may represent only a small part of the cost of a particular item of consumption. But there is more. The web of inter-contributory operations or sectors, though its individual parts may have technically constant kinds of output, can direct these in variable proportions to other sectors. It can change those proportions. The dedication of any sector to the making of a particular kind of machine or material, the *specificity* of the product of each sector, is as we might say a micro-specificity. It does not render impossible a re-orientation of the web of production as a whole to an altered bill of goods for consumption. These considerations by no means destroy Hayek's theme, but that conception needs to be seen in their light.

In seeking greater force of persuasion for his theme, Hayek characteristically went to the foundations. These rested on the Böhm-Bawerkian theory of capital. With an inexhaustible energy, Hayek undertook its re-working and re-expression. I shall attempt below to explain and assess the conception he achieved. Meanwhile I must try to show what those inherent problems of the Austrian theory of capital are, which make it so intractable for Hayek's purpose.

Lapse of time between the input of productive service and the output of a consumable product can be due to different kinds of circumstance. In *Prices and Production* Hayek's dominant assumption was that time-lapse occurs because a piece of material, having an identity which it retains throughout all operations on it, requires to be extracted, shaped, fabricated and finished by operations which individually take time and have to be performed successively, each having an effect which, from the moment of its performance until the object is sold for consumption, remains as it were embodied in the object and adds something to its accumulating value. In the case of the building of a house, time-lapses from this source may be a matter of weeks or months. But what are such intervals compared with those involved in the use of the house? The greatest source of time-lapse in production must surely be durability. A house whose foundations are begun today may be lived in for a hundred years. Even ships and locomotives may be in use for decades. Tools and machines may be in use, after many years of their life, to make other tools. Durability of tools and of products has two consequences for Hayek's theory. It renders extremely difficult and elusive the task of linking the application of measurable productive service by men and nature on one date with the emergence of a measurable consumable product at another date. And durability is a chief vessel of the governance of the present by the past. An existing piece of equipment may cost more to operate per unit of product than one which could now be designed. But unless the savings of operating cost expected from a new design, as compared with the existing tool, have a total discounted value not less than its construction-cost, it will not be ordered. Hayek's argument, viewing 'capital goods' as materials which only retain their physical identity through a process of fabrication into consumable form, overlooks the grip that durability has in constraining the business man's choice of productive methods. The span of the nine-year business cycle, to which his theory was meant to apply, is not long enough for a wholesale discarding of existing equipment during the latter half of its upward phase, say two or three years.

In referring just now to a test of worthwhileness of replacing obsolescent machines by new designs, we spoke of the savings *expected* to be made. This word reflects the most fundamental of all the difficulties which economic analysis faces. Time-to-come is not open to inspection, there can be no eye-witnesses of its history. That history (unless we are fatalists who abnegate the reality of choice) will be created by the decisions which flow from our conjectures as to what it can be made to yield. Time-to-come is the void, waiting to be filled by enterprise, by action which manifests originative acts of mind. *Expectation* names almost the whole business of pragmatic thought. In *Prices and Production*, however, there is no mention of expectation. Even in *Profits, Interest and*

Investment this lack is only formally recognised. Yet in a brilliant article in 1937[9] Hayek had asked what the economic choice-maker can know and how he can know it.

A question which, perhaps, even natural science has not attempted to answer, is why things that take place *take time to do so.* Why do events take time? The question perhaps belongs to that region of the inconceivable, which J. B. S. Haldane conjectured in saying that the universe is queerer than we *can* imagine. In natural science, however, we can at least know how much time definable changes will take under this condition or that. To make the same supposition in matters of human action is surely exceedingly dangerous. In seeking to describe and account for trains of economic events, economists have tended to assume that the economic system or organism of society works like a machine, or perhaps like a hydraulic system. Is there not a fluid which flows around the system, encountering goods at each movement and thus registering prices? It has been assumed, implicitly, by many theorists that money needs to arrive and be present in order to have an effect, just as the tide needs to arrive and be present in order to float a ship off the mud. But what we need to ask is, not what will float the ship off the mud, but what will cause the captain to make preparations for the moment when he can cast off and sail away. And what inspires the captain's activity is his *knowledge* of the tide. Money can exert a force upon events by merely being *thought of.* We must go further. Some philosophers in discussing the mind-body problem have spoken derisively of 'the ghost in the machine'. But this phrase fits the nature of the economic system remarkably well. It is a *system of thoughts* before it is a system of actions. One mind can act upon another, in an economic context, without moving money from one account to another or one holder to another. The picture which his words conjure in another mind can be the source of action. When he wrote *Prices and Production* Hayek treated the economic system as hydraulic, as a body whose muscles needed, as it were, a supply of blood, and were determined in their actions by the flows of blood. But the muscles, in a more interesting sense, are actuated by the neuronal system, by the messages which, as we must express it, come from thoughts. The phases of the trade cycle are depicted in *Prices and Production* as due to the flows or constrictions of money. Undoubtedly the muscles need blood, but they work because of thoughts. Hayek later wrote on questions of psychology, and, we are told, was at one time undecided whether to become an economist or a psychologist. Does not the psychologist need a field of real human action from which to draw suggestions? Economics should surely provide it. Like Adam Smith, Hayek was by instinct a moral scientist in the round.

Profits, Interest and Investment in some essential respects moved far from *Prices and Production*. In the latter Hayek felt obliged to start his train of events from a supposed state of full employment. He did so because in the later 1920s and early 1930s it still seemed to most economists that 'equilibrium' had a powerful practical as well as analytical ascendancy, and that it made full employment the natural state of affairs from which deviations had to be explained. In the later essay he assumed 'an initial situation where considerable unemployment of material resources and labour exists'. Here also he distinguished the 'rate of profit' from the 'rate of interest' and spoke of 'the inadequate distinction [he] had formerly drawn between the movement of money wages and the movement of real wages'. *Profits, Interest and Investment* was meant to re-state the theme of *Prices and Production* in a less vulnerable form. But *Prices and Production* had a drive and vitality, however peculiar, which make it a classic, and which the later essay lacked.

The pure theory of capital

Hayek's theory of the trade cycle took for granted a particular view of the nature and consequences of tool using production, which it regarded as time-using production. Some of the objections raised against *Prices and Production* were due to the inadequacies of its presentation of the theory of capital which it pre-supposed. In order to satisfy his critics, himself chief amongst them, Hayek decided to re-work from its foundations this theory of 'capitalistic production'. As this work progressed through several drafts during the middle and later 1930s, he responded to its ever-freshly multiplying difficulties with an intense and sustained effort nothing short of heroic. *The Pure Theory of Capital*,[10] published in 1941, is as it were a final report on Böhm-Bawerk's proposal.

In the theory which Hayek develops, the word *capital* names an aspect of the technological organisation of production. It might be said in brief to reflect the fact that in order to obtain consumable goods we first make tools and other preparations, and then make use of them. This fact can be looked on in two ways. We can say either that production via elaborate preparatory stages *takes time*. Or we can say that the tools and materials which embody such preparatory work are the vehicles which convey the effect of such work through time and pile it up with an added yield at the date of the emergence of goods ready for consumption. On either view, time is essentially involved in the notion of capital. On the former view, time-lapse *allows* of a highly instrumented method of production, or, in a broad meaning of the term, a highly-perfected division of labour. On the second view, it is the intermediary materials and tools, the *capital goods,* which allow time-lapse to exert its virtue in making the forces of men and nature more efficacious. On either view, there is an intimate connection between time-lapse and the material stepping-stones to consumable goods. There is a temptation, with some excuse, to identify capital, or capital-goods, with the operation of time as in some sense a factor of production. The originators of the theory which Hayek has carried, perhaps, to its ultimate pitch of usefulness, had indeed proposed that the endlessly heterogeneous collection of tools and materials in use at any moment could be reduced to a scalar quantity in terms of an average lapse of time between productive activities and their consumable result. Hayek takes pains to show that this notion is fallacious. Instead, we must divide all the productive services of men and nature which are applied at any one moment, into fractions small enough to let us discriminate every different length of time-lapse which occurs between the use of such a fraction and the emergence of the consumable product which constitutes its fruit. The entire assemblage of such time-lapses is the *output function,* and this is one means of describing the *time-structure of production* which validly replaces the inadmissible notion of an average period of production. An alternative is the *input function,* which we obtain by dividing the consumable product emerging at any one moment into such fractions as are due to human and natural services rendered at different earlier dates. The set of fractions into which the input of any one moment is divided according to the lengths of time to its maturity as consumables is not the same set as that into which the consumable output of any one moment must be divided according to the lengths of time which have elapsed since their corresponding inputs. For equal inputs will yield different quantities of output if they remain invested for different lengths of time. This notion is itself one of the essential strands in Hayek's skein, and its meaning must be carefully considered.

What governs the form of the output function? This question comprises several others. Is the form a matter of choice? If so, of whose choice? In making the choice, what end is sought? What principle guides choice in pursuit of this end, or what test shows it to have been attained? Is the chooser perfectly free in choosing, or what constrains his choice? Let us take these in turn.

Economic theory is centrally, essentially concerned with choice. If the form of the output function is not subject to choice, the economist need not spend time on it. For Hayek, the effect and the attainability of this or that form, the governance of this attainability by the society's endowment of materials, tools and consumables at the moment when the form to be attempted is being chosen, and its governance by the desires of the individual members, is the central matter of capital theory. The society has before it a range of rival forms of the output function. Other conceivable forms are excluded by the combined effect of the society's endowment and its tastes. How are those tastes, and the consequent constraint imposed on the choice, to be known? Hayek seeks in the first place to isolate the essential effects of time-lapse in production. In order to pursue this question without distracting issues, he at first assigns authority over the whole business of production to a single individual. This controller is assumed first to decide what quantitative mix of consumable goods is to be produced, and then to organise the use of all the productive resources available to him so as to secure the largest output of this mix which can be maintained indefinitely from the moment when he takes charge of affairs. We ought to notice the ingenuity of this scheme. The constraint imposed upon choice of productive method by the need for immediate consumption from the word 'go' is not excluded from it. This need can be met at first by existing stocks of ready consumables, and during the time thus gained, time-taking preparation of tools and partly-processed materials can proceed. As the stocks come to an end, the new process will begin to yield consumable goods, and it will be doing so at the highest time-rate (output) attainable under the assumed condition of constant consumption per time-unit from the outset. By this scheme, whose complexity in detail is rather more formidable than I have suggested, Hayek introduces the ideas of building-up the apparatus of a time-taking productive method under the constraint of desired consumption mitigated by the possession of stocks of ready goods. He thus illustrates, in a scheme which at first sight may appear highly contrived, two of the essential elements of the economic role of time.

We have viewed in two ways the part played in production by lapse of time between input and output. On one view such time-lapse allows the forces of men and nature (the *original means of production*) to produce consumables through a series of preparatory stages where tools and materials are produced as the means to make further such means until a last stage is reached in which consumables emerge in much greater quantity per unit of time than if labour and nature had been applied more directly. What, if anything, is given up for the sake of this gain in efficacy? It is here that the distinction is vital, between the situation where a time-taking method of production has merely to be continued and maintained, and the situation where its material embodiment of fresh kinds of tools and materials has to be built up in successive stages. In the former, the only sacrifice entailed in continuing the method of production which has been established is the forgoing of such brief higher rate of consumption as could be got by dismantling the apparatus of that method, that is to say, by starving some existing machines of the energy and materials needed for their operation, and even reducing to scrap the machines themselves. By thus subjecting their own apparatus and stores to a process of pillage, the society could enjoy a brief, suicidal orgy. In the second situation, the sacrifice required of an already fully employed society, in order to make the transition to a more time-taking method of production whereby the given flows of input of services of the original means of production would yield a larger consumable output, is a period of lower consumption than they have been enjoying. For some services both of the original means and the existing produced means (tools, systems and inventories of materials) of production would have to be diverted from producing consumables by the method hitherto in use, to building up by necessarily successive stages the new apparatus whose more efficient use of the services of men and nature, once this new apparatus was complete, would provide a permanently larger flow of consumables.

Which, then, of these two situations is the relevant one? Hayek's purpose in *The Pure Theory of Capital* is to develop the most austere and stringent abstract model of the role of time-lapse within a productive technology. For this purpose, he abstracts from money and, with a curiously arbitrary fragmentation, from uncertainty. (How can time as a field of choice (time-to-come) be discussed in any meaningful abstraction from uncertainty? Hayek thus reduces his problem to one which can be treated demonstratively, that is, by rigorous logic. But logic needs its data, which time-to-come conceals.) These two exclusions, of money and uncertainty, would themselves, I think, ensure full employment, but Hayek makes this also an explicit assumption.

In order to build up by successive stages a productive apparatus not hitherto existing, a society whose productive means are fully employed must forgo during some time-interval some consumption which it could otherwise have enjoyed. What is the inducement to make this sacrifice? Evidently it is the permanently higher rate of consumption which can thus be secured. Out of this extra stream of consumable goods, obtained from an unchanged input of the services of men and nature, a continuing reward can be paid to those who went without some of the consumption they could have had during some time-interval. That permanent stream of reward for the definite total of forgone consumption can be called a rate of interest on the total of their saving, for it can be expressed as an annual quantity related to a quantity of capital, a capital sum. A ratio which is the same in form but conceptually distinct in referend is that of the extra stream of consumable goods yielded by the improved method of production. How much saving, how much forgoing of consumption, a sacrifice of what amount per time-unit for how many time-units, will the members of the society be willing to do? The most familiar notion in economic theory, that of the equalising, at the margin, of sacrifice and advantage, suggests that their saving will be pushed to the point where a little more would be so irksome as to cancel the attractiveness of the prospect of the little addition it would make to the increase of consumption that their saving will yield. However, the sacrifice of consumption involved in building-up by successive stages the apparatus of a technology not previously used (though known) will not be uniform and equal for the various stages, for these are successive. The use of some services of men and nature to build the first stage will mean the withdrawal of these identified (as we might say, proper-named) services for the whole length of time it will take to complete the new apparatus in all stages. Those who forgo consumption, of some specific amount, for this relatively long time will require a greater reward than those who forgo an equal amount merely in order to make possible the final stage. To take account of this aspect of the transition to a new technology is to consider the matter from the side of the *need* for a reward for sacrificing consumption. What, then, of the possibility of supplying that reward? The process of building the physical embodiment of the hitherto unused technology consists in first making tools and materials which are, as it were, the seed of the whole process. The next stage rests upon the shoulders of the first, and the first takes some credit for the efficacy of the second. And so on through the stages. If we accept this view, a greater share of the total gain of capacity to produce consumables must be ascribed to the early stages than to the later. In fact, the early stages will be so chosen that they can claim this extra share of credit for the gain. They will be the natural first stages. How can the two ideas, that early sacrifices of consumption claim a greater reward and that early inputs of productive services to the building of the new apparatus are the source of greater shares of the gain of capacity, be formalised so as to make possible the conception of an equalisation at the margin?

The formal conception of a rate of interest is that of a *speed of proportionate growth*. Growth of what? In the world of business as it proceeds in reality, what grows is a debt expressed in money terms. If the debt starts at 100, and the contract between lender and borrower stipulates that 110 shall be repaid after one year, the debt is set to grow at 10 per cent a year. If at the end of a year the lender agrees to a postponement of the settling of the debt for a year more on the same terms as prevailed for the first year, the lender is effectively lending, for the further year, the 110 he could have received at the beginning of this second year. If he again receives the initial debt, of 110, plus one-tenth, the repayment due at the end of the second year will be 121. And so on. This is, of course, the principle of compound interest, and it is the meaning of a rate of interest in the fundamental formal sense. A rate of interest is conventionally stated as such-and-such a fraction of the initial or of the accumulated debt per annum, but the calculation of the interest due to be added to the debt, and the actual addition of it, need by no means be done at yearly intervals, but can be stipulated to be done at any intervals, say quarterly or daily or *continuously*. The notion that packets of productive service contribute a greater share to the ultimate increase of capacity to produce consumables, if they are applied early rather than late in the process of building up the new system, can be conveniently formalised by supposing these packets to be notionally carried through the respective time-intervals between their application and the emergence of their first consumable products, in the form of entities growing exponentially, that is, by compound interest.

Let us now suppose that a packet of productive service is applied to the building-up of the new system a specified length of time before the system is to be completed, and that the contribution it will make to the system can be measured. Let us suppose that the relation between the value of this input, and the value of its contribution, we expressed in terms of exponential growth, or compound interest, at a certain rate. And let us suppose that the same can be done for another input, of equal value when applied, but applied a different length of time before the completion of the system. And suppose that the 'rate of interest' expressing the notional growth of value is different for the two inputs. Is this a satisfactory arrangement of the affair? If more input could be applied at the higher rate, and correspondingly less at the lower rate, the value of the completed system, its productive capacity, would be increased. On this principle we may say that the aim of those who design the process of building up the new apparatus, under the constraint of a limited willingness of those who finance the operation to forgo consumption for that purpose, will be to make the scheme of time-intervals such that the rates of exponential growth of differently-timed inputs are *equal*. This rate, common to the whole process, will be determined by technological possibilities on one hand, and by the amount of saving that the members of the society will do, on the other. For this rate will express alike the gain of efficacy and the reward for forgoing consumption. The idea of this equality between gain and sacrifice at the margin is the familiar one, in economic theory, of maximising a dependent variable by suitable choice of the arguments on which it depends.

In this second section of my chapter I have sought to give, in some two and a half thousand words, an account of a theory to which Hayek devoted some four hundred and forty pages. *The Pure Theory of Capital* emerged in its published form from several manuscript versions which I had the privilege of reading during its composition. The sustained intensity of thought which it cost its author, the astonishing degree to which he has imposed coherence on a mountainous body of reasoning concerning a theme which is perhaps unmatched in economics in its intricacy, show theory-making as a task not for intellect alone, but for high moral courage and implacable resolve. To write such a work, it is not enough to be able to pile brick on brick for year after year until the heap is high enough. In the end there must emerge a unified conception informed by some single principle. A critic would find it hard to show that, on its own terms, *The Pure Theory of Capital* does not attain success by this test. The questions which it must elicit from any reader would be ill-judged if they sought to deny its element of the heroic. None the less we are bound to consider them in their widely various bearings.

What can a theory do, for its author or his readers? It can, in its most elevated role, give his spirit the ultimate satisfaction of the contemplation of beauty. It is hard to say what we mean by beauty, in this or any other context. But intellectual beauty involves, perhaps, an element of surprising conviction. Beauty is felt in a proof or an explanation, when this conception seizes the mind in a single thought. Beauty is sudden and dramatic in impact, no matter how still and timeless its form. Next we may say, I think, that a theory sets thought at rest. It provides a faith. This surely is the effect we demand of a theory, even if we reserve the thought that other theories may displace it. A theory which commands our assent is a stroke of Alexander's sword, cutting through a tangle of confusions. It is thus a powerful classifying agent, revealing unity and an essential strand in common amongst ostensibly diverse and unrelated things. A problem, may we say, is an ostensibly incomplete presentation of elements. To solve a problem is to reveal a hidden completeness or completeability. It is for this that a theory can serve.

In reading *The Pure Theory of Capital* one is likely, I think, to conjecture that Hayek very early in his scholar's life gave his allegiance to Böhm-Bawerk and to Wicksell, that his mind was seized by an arresting idea, namely, that in investigating the nature of capital we are investigating an aspect of the nature of time. Such a conviction gives an immense impulse to intellectual effort, for it removes at one stroke any fear that the problem in hand may prove trivial or peripheral. In seeking to grasp some manifestation of time we are driving at the heart of things. Some such influence seems needed to explain the huge effort which Hayek devoted to refounding the Böhm-Bawerk–Wicksell theory of capital. That such an effort was needed, that Hayek encountered numberless and daunting troubles, that so long a book was required to contain the implications of an ostensibly incisive idea – capital is the working of time-lapse in production – suggests inevitably that too much was expected of a tool which had, at first sight, so brilliant a glow of promise. Which of the purposes of theory does Hayek's intricate and elusively subtle construction serve? He has pursued to the uttermost the possibilities of his theme, and the conceptions involved in it are often beautiful in themselves. But the very austerity and unappeasable thoroughness of his detection of difficulties and his determination to cope with them have had the opposite effect of the presumably intended one. In his prodigious effort at final vindication of the Jevons–Böhm-Bawerk–Wicksell idea, Hayek has disdained the principle of benign imprecision without which so much of economic theory cannot breathe. He explains in detail why the skein of different lengths of time elapsing between the input of original means of production at some one date and the emergence of the quanta of consumable goods respectively attributable to various fractions of that input cannot be reduced to an *average period of production.* Yet it seems inconceivable that any statistical or practical use can be made of the Austrian theory of capital unless it can be epitomised into some such form.

The reader of Hayek's *Pure Theory of Capital* will, I think, find some particular difficulties or objections in addition to its general extreme complexity. In specifying those which seem to me important I am saying nothing which casts any shadow on my recognition of a masterpiece. In this book, Hayek has nailed his colours to the mast and has pursued to the uttermost limits the logic where it led. The result is a remarkable contribution to knowledge which could have been attained in no other way, and, I will venture to say, assuredly by no other man.

At the outset of his account of the output function and the input function, Hayek simply assumes that 'each separate unit of available input is expected to make a definite and determinable contribution to the output stream of the future'. He expressly defers the question 'on what principle particular parts of the future output stream can be attributed to particular units of input'. The discussion of the input and output functions, their meaning, the influences that govern their form and the possibility of determining it (finding it out) is spread over many chapters, one of which deals with the special difficulty posed by durable goods. In order to decide whether the problems of attribution of particular dated quanta of output to particular dated quanta of input can be solved so far as the structure of inference resting on this attribution requires, the reader needs to be alert through these many chapters to note and consider each reference to the matter. Hayek has preferred to deal first with the problem of describing supposedly determinable output functions and input functions, by means of ingenious and beautiful three-dimensional diagrams, rather than confront in one chapter at the outset the essential question of whether and how far the attribution, and thus the determination of forms of the functions, is possible. Yet this question is fundamental to the whole edifice.

The problem of assigning particular dated quanta of output to particular dated quanta of input (or vice versa) is made immeasurably more difficult by a fact which Hayek seems quite to ignore. In *Prices and Production* it is taken for granted that when services of men and nature are applied in some productive operation, the direct product of that operation is unqualifiedly nearer to the ultimate consumable good than is the material on which they work in that operation, this latter being the product of an earlier operation, more remote from the consumable. Productive operations, it is thus assumed, fall naturally and distinctly into what we may call a linear sequence, each being merely a preparation for the next in the series. Hayek recognises that contributory streams of such operations may converge into the making of a consumable good. But this is not the essential matter. Production in a modern economy is a network of operations every one of which, in some large or small degree, helps to provide means of every other. At what stage in the production of the goods that lie on the grocer's shelves are we to locate the work of the Post Office, the railways, or the electricity supply industry? The universal inter-necessity of all types of productive operation is pictured (with unavoidable simplification and aggregation of widely different things) by the Leontief table of input coefficients, a square matrix where every sector is present in the list of suppliers of materials or tools to any randomly-chosen sector. Thus every sector is deemed to be in principle directly supplied by every other sector, and indirectly by every supplier of its direct suppliers, and so on, in a pattern which only algebra can completely and intelligibly describe. The notion of 'stages of production' is not essentially absent from the Leontief scheme, but it would require an inexpressibly complex and elaborate procedure to discern in the data of that scheme a Hayekian output function.

When he came to write *The Pure Theory of Capital* Hayek had come under suggestive influence from a number of writers whose relevant work had been published too late to affect *Prices and Production*. His attitude had noticeably softened towards Frank Knight, with whom he had earlier engaged in seemingly irresolvable debate. He refers several times to Keynes's *The General Theory of*

Employment, Interest and Money,[11] especially to its view of the interest-rate as reflecting the public's desire for liquidity in face of the policies of the banking system. That conception was not immediately relevant to Hayek's purpose because he had explicitly excluded money. But Hayek's most significant reference, perhaps, is to Gunnar Myrdal's suggestion of the need to distinguish between the *ex ante* and the *ex post* temporal viewpoints. Myrdal's theme appeared originally in Swedish in 1931. In 1933 it appeared as one of four long essays by different authors in a book edited by Hayek.[12] In *The Pure Theory of Capital* Hayek constantly emphasised the forward-looking view. In 1937, in his remarkable article called 'Economics and Knowledge',[13] Hayek had made explicit a conception of equilibrium far removed from the notions derived from physical mechanics. Equilibrium, he said, should be deemed to consist in the compatibility of plans. In *The Pure Theory of Capital* he made ingenious and effective use of this idea. He had recognised (though he did not fully adapt his text to the recognition) that time-lapse takes on its vital importance, not in a stationary society, but in a society attempting to make the transition to a superior technology by building-up (despite the existing full employment of its means of production) the necessary material apparatus. How, at the moment when the decision to make such an attempt was being taken, could the skein of time-lapses that it would involve be known? They could be known only if the plans of different individuals or firms were not only quite explicit in their minds and each of them single-tracked (that is, envisaging a path of action without variants) but if also they were seen to be mutually compatible and to form a coherent whole which contained no internal contradictions. The time-lapses could be known, that is to say, only in a Hayekian equilibrium, as the sole alternative to a stationary state whose presumed indefinite persistence would also make their measurement possible, but which in the nature of things was the negation of a process of investment in new equipment.

In speaking of the expectations and intentions which compose a Hayekian equilibrium as 'single tracked' I mean that their perfect mutual compatibility, which is the essence of the conception, has meaning only if the course of affairs in time-to-come, which any particular individual envisages, specifies for any randomly-chosen moment no more than one point in the space (of no matter how many dimensions) required for the description of that course. Such a conception has, perhaps, its greatest usefulness in compelling us to ask, in view of its evident utter unattainability, what in fact the process of history must be like. Individuals will not necessarily surrender the freedom of imagination, of enterprise, of attempted exploitation of the void of time-to-come, in order to try to reconcile their ambitions with those of all other individuals. The seething cauldron of history mocks such a notion. Even at a lesser level of generalness, the difficulties multiply. Different individuals will plan their respective courses of action in differently-defined, differently conceived spaces. A dimension which appears in one such space will be absent from others. Two men cannot arrange to walk side-by-side when each is studying a map of a different country. We have to ask also up to what horizon the plans will be carried, and whether and why it should or can be the same for all. Hayek by no means presses things thus to extremes, but his classic article was one of the very few which called in question, in those days or since, the *accessibility* of equilibrium, either as an intellectual or a practical solution. Re-contract and tâtonnements are merely gestures. Equilibrium is analytic, telling us how things would be if we ever got there.

I think the idea that a great work of the intellect can be created by starting with 'an open mind' must be misleading. The impulse must come from some question which has seized the thinker's curiosity and from some suggestion which has leapt from his long meditation on it, a spark from some chance conjunction of impressions. There must be some inspirational idea, some line to be followed, before a man can gather the moral and nervous force which such a task requires. He must be seized by a faith. The decision to pursue a particular suggestion, whether that the earth goes round the sun or that capital is time, must irresistibly *impose itself* in virtue of incisive beauty or immensity of potential revelation. The notion that problems of capital are problems of the necessity for time to elapse between effort and result in production is, at its first impact, arresting in its suggestion of simplicity and power. The advancement and secure founding of knowledge demanded imperiously that this conception should be examined by a powerful mind with dedicated zeal and stringent thoroughness. To have done this once and for all is Hayek's very great achievement.

'Economics and Knowledge'[14]

The word *equilibrium* pervades economic theory. It names in turn the members of a plurality of ideas plainly distinct from each other. Yet this ascendancy arises from a deep common source. Equilibrium is the expression of a fundamental adoption of method, an assumption about the nature of the human individual and his essential predicament. Equilibrium is, in fact, the name of a view of the Scheme of Things. In that Scheme, the user of this term supposes, human conduct and thus history itself are the manifestation and upshot of the successful employment of reason. Equilibrium characterises human affairs when, and because, the participants have responded wisely to their circumstances. Those circumstances evidently include, for each person, the existence and activity of other persons. Equilibrium thus means the wise response of individuals to each other. In one of the most brilliant and perceptive of all his works, the essay called 'Economics and Knowledge', Hayek set out the profound, subtle and intricate questions which flow from the making of the equilibrium assumption.

In 'Economics and Knowledge' Hayek takes what is often called the subjectivist standpoint, the view that for the human being the business of life is *thought*. For the individual in deciding his course, what he thinks is the case, *is* the case. The data, the description of his circumstances, the account of the universe with whose immediate posture and basic laws he has to reckon, is the account which he has himself extracted from his own experience and judgement. This experience, the things and events that have come under his notice, the modes of thought which instinct or education have implanted in him, the intuition which Nature gave him, are to some degree peculiar to each individual. Yet we are bound to assume that they have a basic likeness amongst different people. To be human is to have some insight into human nature and human responses. If it be true that equilibrium, the *best* for each individual that he can attain in face of the competition of all the other individuals, is a goal sometimes actually approached by society, what in detail is the process by which the different individual conceptions are reconciled with each other? That is to say, how do the data assumed by the different individuals come to be, so far as they need to be, the *same*.

A student of human affairs not already enmeshed in received economic theory might at first be inclined to question the basic premise. Do we try to guide our conduct by applying reason to a carefully built-up picture of the world's principles and its momentary state? Or is equilibrium no more than an intellectual obsession? Despite history's record of ferocity and evil, which seems so vividly to bear out Macbeth's assessment of life, there is a vast contrary evidence: the all-encompassing web of markets and diplomacy, the fabric of laws and contracts, the international basis of calendars and navigation. If humanity tries, however erratically, to organise itself, it tries for equilibrium. But there is still a danger in this word for the theoretician. He must not take equilibrium to be an account of the world's process. What would 'equilibrium' mean, if we had to use this term to describe a game of football? It could only mean that the final whistle had already blown.

'Economics and Knowledge' declares its Hayekian birth. All the caution, subtlety and rigour which a training in the law elicits from a first-rate mind is here brought to bear on problems of meaning. Sometimes in the course of it a new vista of theory is glimpsed, only to be left unexplored in favour of the clearing-up of an immediate semantic riddle. However, the vital and novel central theme rightly claims ascendancy. 'The only part [of economic theory] which is concerned with causes and effects, and leads to propositions capable of falsification,[15] consists of propositions about the acquisition of knowledge'. This carries us a long way, and places us on that ground where Hayek's meaning for equilibrium can be built. From that ground a far horizon will draw some readers' eyes to the notion, not just of the gathering of information but of the origination of new possibilities. But this is not the business of Hayek's essay and he does not turn that way.

Equilibrium, Hayek says, refers to relations amongst actions. Actions of an individual are in equilibrium so far as they can be understood as part of one plan; that is to say, 'only if all these actions have been decided on at one and the same moment and in consideration of the same set of circumstances'. By this last phrase we must understand, of course, the same body of subjective knowledge, the same set of circumstances supposed by the individual to be the case. There follows in the text, however, an enigmatic statement: 'Since the actions of one person must necessarily take place successively in time, it is obvious that the passage of time is essential to give the concept of equilibrium any meaning'. I think the distinction is needed here between the notion of time-to-come, which is plainly essential to the existence of any plan, and the notion of the actual lapse of time, that is, the enactment of an historical sequence of events. How can a thing *be,* save in a single (I would say, solitary) moment? This moment, however, can transform itself, as every moment does, into a successor. And provided the individual's relevant knowledge is unchanged by that transformation, the new equilibrium can be identical with its predecessor. (But can even a moment pass without change of knowledge?) So much for equilibrium as the state of a single mind at a single moment. But we are still at the threshold of the real problem. In what sense and by what steps can there be an approach to equilibrium amongst the actions of many persons?

If at some moment the body of subjective knowledge, the conception of the nature and the posture of things, including, so far as needed, the ideas in the minds of others, entertained by one member of a society, differs from that of another member; if, let us say, such differences prevail generally amongst the members of the society; then evidently the bodies of knowledge respectively entertained by some of them must change if there is to come about a unity of outlook amongst all the members. Change does involve more than a single moment, it involves, in some sense, a comparison of moments. Thus the lapse of historic time, which Hayek invoked as we noted earlier, is called for when we consider the *approach* to equilibrium. The perceptions and judgements, which cause some members of the society to change their subjective knowledge or beliefs, will 'take time'. Hayek insists many times that equilibrium is only of interest to us, and only serves for providing refutable propositions (in contrast with the tautologies of abstract and self-sufficient logic) when we consider how the unity of knowledge amongst the members of a society could *come about*. The unity itself is a state, and characterises a 'single moment'. The approach to this unity is a process, and occupies historic time. He renounces the task of describing the process of approach. That is an empirical task (perhaps, we might add, an endless one). His real concern, in 'Economics and Knowledge' is to define the state of equilibrium when it embraces a number of individuals: 'For a society, then, we *can* speak of a state of equilibrium at a point of time–but it means only that the different plans which the individuals composing it have made for action in time are mutually compatible'. With this definition of the goal, the form of the question concerning the pursuit of it is also determined: How can the (subjective) knowledge of each individual, such as bears on his plan, become the same as the knowledge on which each other individual bases a plan of his own?

To have attained these questions and definitions, to have made knowledge, its subjective nature, its governance of individual action and the enigma of its formation, the central strand in the economic theoretician's skein of themes, shows Hayek as one of the great innovators. He himself in his book refers to other pioneers: to Ludwig von Mises, Frank Knight, Maynard Keynes and Gunnar Myrdal. His own achievement is to have brought all such suggestions to a focus and a verbal encapsulation.

There are still some points of semantics and internal logic to be cleared. In the course of its attempted execution a plan will encounter, besides the actions of other individuals, the events in the non-human universe. If these have been wrongly assessed, the plan will prove not to be realisable. Must we then deny it the standing of a component of an equilibrium? To do so would conflict with the principle that equilibrium characterises plans as such, existents at a single point of the calendar. At such a moment, no judgement is possible, and no judgement is meaningful, which refers to realised events of later moments. To do so would involve a contradiction in terms. A related question is the possible meaning of a *change* in the course of events in the non-human world. The question can best be answered by first asking what is its relevance. The non-human world can disrupt a plan. When will it do so? Evidently when its behaviour proves different from what the maker of the plan assumed. Change in the non-human world must be defined as a course of events different from what was expected. If the plans which are thus disrupted composed an equilibrium, what was expected, and is proved false, was the universal expectation of all the makers of the plans. Instead, the expectation could prove justified. Evidently, expectations and plans can envisage an evolution, a succession of states of the world differing from each other. Equilibrium, it follows, does not imply stationariness. 'Equilibrium analysis' Hayek says, 'becomes in principle applicable to a progressive society and to inter-temporal price-relationships'. Ought we not still to add 'in expectation'?

Let us finally ask whether the theme of the essay as a whole, that the concept of the equilibrium of a society is definable, and claims a central importance in economic theorising because there is a natural tendency for the subjective knowledge and opinions of different individuals to converge, can be accepted as an ascendant principle of general application? The kind of objection that suggests itself can be illustrated by the concept of a *speculative market*. All goods whose effectiveness in serving human needs can be conveyed through calendar time; all goods, that is, which are either durable or preservable, or are capable of embodiment in the successive stages of a productive process and emerging, in effect, at the end of it, are *necessarily* objects of speculation. But a speculative market is only brought into balance and temporary rest by the presence in it of camps holding *opposite* opinions about the impending movement of price.

Scientism and the study of society

Political economy stands in a peculiarly fruitful relation to intellects of a particular kind. The pursuit of this discipline calls for a mind whose natural motion is that of strict and critically exacting logic, yet which has powers and sensitivities of another sort from the algebraist's ingenious insight and surprising conjuration of truths. For political economy deals indeed in abstractions, but does so in the service of the study of mankind and its affairs. The political economist must not be colour-blind in the face of history's tides of colour and variegated light. He must be interested above all in what can flow from the thoughts of the human individual. If those thoughts themselves are, in their taking place, the very act of origination of history, *ex nihilo* so far as that origination is a mundane business, then the study of human affairs must seek in the individual mind the roots of its insight and its explanations. The nature of history, in that case, is the overt manifestation of the nature of human thought in the richest meaning of the word *thought,* the meaning which embraces perception, reason, emotion, imagination and decision. The political economist, seeking the essential nature and the ultimate sources of the engenderment of history, the transient being of 'the news', must be ready to acknowledge in his field a limitless potential for novelty and the unprecedented. The universe is open. The political economist needs the Renaissance mind.

Such a specification of total competence is, of course, beyond human compass. Dante, Michaelangelo and Newton have not been rolled into one. But some men have shown that they could have turned in any one of many directions and carried that one path into new ground. Some claim of this sort can be made for Hayek.

The nature and source of history is one of the oldest of humanity's unappeasable enigmas. Some have believed the appearance of movement to be illusory. The Parmenidean stillness or Sir Karl Popper's orally expressed view that time is an illusion, would presumably change the form of the problem. Could we then meaningfully ask for a source or origin? Short of so radical a solution there is determinism. In some sense, in the determinist view, things happen, but only in the way they were necessitated from the beginning to happen. Why bother, then, with the fact that they seem to us to happen? Or in contrast with all this we can assume that humans have some responsibility for their own history. Among those who believe that the course of things is bound to follow one unique predestined path, which they can somehow describe, there is still a division between those who exhort us to strive to bring about that inevitable result, and those who enjoin us to prevent it. Does not each of these ironies reveal some instinct of belief in our freedom?

Such questions, the unsolvable riddles of existence, must hang in every scholar's consciousness with more or less insistence. But the practical scholarly arts, the writing of history, the making of theory in the moral sciences, perforce must let them ride. Hayek has answered the question of determinism or non-determinism only by implication. But no reader of *The Counter-Revolution of Science*[16] can doubt where he stands in his practice. History is made by human beings in their spontaneous exercise of human faculties.

Hayek as economist has not allowed these dilemmas to impede him. As a social philosopher he lightly brushes them in the course of an argument about the proper method of economic theory. This argument, though it occupied a whole book and invoked an immense erudition, is really concerned with one question only: Can economics be pursued in the manner of a natural science? His unequivocal *no* rests on the answer to another question: What kind of thing can we observe and study as a natural, self-delimiting whole, an essential and organic unity, a genuine thing-in-itself? He answers: In the affairs of men, only man himself satisfies this condition. Man is a product of nature. The social products of men's activity, the institutions, customs, constitutions, codes of law and morality, the forms of culture in a wide sense, and also, and especially, the episodes which compose history, are the largely undesigned and uncovenanted results of the efforts, enterprises and experiments made by individuals in a groping pursuit of private ends. These results cannot be understood by a direct inspection of their forms and processes, for their coherence is not something expressly designed by man or nature. It is in a sense accidental. These self-evolving phenomena can be understood only by considering the ends from whose pursuit they unforeseeably emerge, and the human needs and desires, the instinctive or intuitive responses and thought-processes of individuals which are their sources. These human characteristics are known to us direct. Each of us seeing them in himself infers them in others. By contrast with the entities which the natural scientist discerns or conceives as the solutions, mathematical or other, of natures enigmas, the social artefacts are shaped by too variable a conflux of forces to have a necessary being of their own. Most especially of all it is to the episodes of history that Hayek ascribes this character and to them that he denies an inherent necessity which would make possible a *theory of history*. There is no necessary sequence in which definable stages, phases, systems or styles of events must in the nature of things follow each other, for this is not the nature of things.

The question of the nature of history is of course a profound and encompassing one. It gathers into itself the whole human or the whole cosmic riddle. It is the question of determinism, no less. Historical determinism takes forms differing widely in their degrees of clarity, consistency and incisiveness. Some of them seek to leave room for human initiative and scope for effective political action other than mere obedience to the pre-ordained development. Strict determinism would have none of that. But economists and other social theorists do not look in the face of the question what role and what meaning, in strict determinism, would be left for a notion of *choice*. Hayek leaves open the door for choice in some interesting sense, without offering a suggestion as to its nature.

Hayek on freedom

A great part of Hayek's immense intellectual effort has been moved and directed by the single idea of *freedom*. As an economist he has argued with untiring passion for free competitive enterprise as against the total direction of all economic activity by a central authority. An economist as such will rest his case for freedom on its superior economic efficiency. Hayek is immeasurably more than an economist and in his massive later works, *The Constitution of Liberty* and *Law, Legislation and Liberty* he has examined the indispensable foundations of freedom itself in its essence. Compared with the ultimate nature and meaning of freedom for the free and for the unfree, economic efficiency is perhaps a lamp of minor brilliance. Even the notion of economic efficiency is itself elusive and hard to define. But more arresting than that question is the argument, surely invincible at the first impact, that authoritarian central control of business is a huge and all-encompassing waste of the original powers of the human mind. Every instance of an individual's having a practical improvement of his own invention which he is *not allowed* to put into practice is the destruction of possibilities, the closing of some vista which might lead beyond any horizon. Even this is a lesser aspect of a far greater whole. To be free is breath itself. But would life be a keen invigorating air if it did not release the poet's splendour of words and the painter's tide of colour, and encourage the mathematician's web of gossamer entailment and even the business man's enterprise and ambition? Hayek as economist has perhaps been eclipsed by Hayek the apostle of freedom. On any reckoning he must be accorded by friend or foe his unquestioned place amongst the giants.

NOTES

1. *Prices and Production* (London: Routledge & Kegan Paul, 1931).
2. K. Popper and J. Eccles, *The Self and Its Brain* (Berlin: Springer, 1977).
3. *The Constitution of Liberty* (London: Routledge & Kegan Paul, 1960).
4. *Law, Legislation and Liberty* (London: Routledge & Kegan Paul, 1973–6).
5. *Prices and Production*.
6. *Profits, Interest and Investment* (London: Routledge & Kegan Paul, 1939).
7. *Geldzins und Güterpreise* (Vienna: Fischer, 1898).
8. *Lectures on Political Economy* (London: Routledge & Kegan Paul, 1934).
9. 'Economics and Knowledge', *Economica*, n.s., IV (1937) 33–54, repr. as ch. 2 of *Individualism and Economic Order* (London: Routledge & Kegan Paul, 1949).
10. *The Pure Theory of Capital* (London: Routledge & Kegan Paul, 1941).
11. *The General Theory of Employment, Interest, and Money* (London: Macmillan, 1936).
12. *Beiträge zur Geldtheorie* (Vienna: Fischer, 1933). Myrdal's essay was called 'Der Gleichgewichts Begriff als Hilfmittel in der Geldtheoretischen Analyse'.
13. 'Economics and Knowledge' (see note 9 above).
14. Chapter 2 of *Individualism and Economic Order*.
15. Hayek adopts this theme and expression of Sir Karl Popper's in a footnote, in place of 'verification' in the text.
16. *The Counter-Revolution of Science* (Glencoe, Ill.: Free Press, 1952).

Index